Preserving the Press

Preserving the Press

How Daily Newspapers
Mobilized to Keep
Their Readers

Leo Bogart

COLUMBIA UNIVERSITY PRESS
NEW YORK

Columbia University Press

New York   Oxford

Copyright © 1991 Columbia University Press

Printed in the United States of America

c 10 9 8 7 6 5 4 3 2 1

p 10 9 8 7 6 5 4 3 2 1

CIP data appear at the back of book

For Otto, Joe, Bob, and Marie

Contents

Preface

"You can't bend a trend." This was a favorite aphorism of William Fielding Ogburn, who had chaired President Herbert Hoover's Committee on Recent Social Trends during the Great Depression, and was one of my professors of sociology at the University of Chicago after the end of World War II.[1] I was often reminded of Ogburn's admonition during the six years (1977–1983) of the Newspaper Readership Project, of which this book is an account. The Readership Project was indeed an attempt to bend the downward trend in daily newspaper circulation and readership in the United States, a trend that reflected great and complex changes in the way Americans spend their time and get their information. In this effort, the newspaper business was trying to determine its own fate, an endeavor that human institutions rarely manage to accomplish.

The Newspaper Readership Project was a small episode in the story of an industry that has long attracted the interest of historians and biographers because of its important place in American society. The Project provided a channel for intense discussion, by publishers, editors, and other newspaper people, of fundamental questions regarding the functions of the press. This discussion sometimes produced heated debate between those who saw newspapers as a unique voice of free democratic expression and those who regarded them essentially as a business that had to please its customers.

Newspapers were profoundly affected by the advent of radio

and later of television, as well as by the great changes in American society that occurred at the same time. The impact of television was not felt immediately, however. In a book called *The Age of Television*, published in 1956, I investigated the evidence of TV's effects upon the other mass media. In its few years of existence, television already had reduced moviegoing and radio-listening hours and was producing major changes in the types of magazines that were being read, as well as in magazines' advertising income. Newspapers appeared, however, to be uniquely unaffected by TV. They had remained the preeminent medium of advertising, with a stable one-third share of the total. Their audiences and circulation were as strong as ever. That was my conviction in 1960 when I came to the Bureau of Advertising of the American Newspaper Publishers Association as vice president of marketing planning and research.

I came to the Bureau from Revlon, Inc., where, as director of market research, I had been preoccupied with the mysterious, passionate proclivities of women for lipstick shades that differed only imperceptibly from each other. I ruminated on the bizarre oscillations of brand shares in the market for roll-on deodorants. Before that, I had worked at advertising research for the McCann-Erickson agency on accounts that ranged from Chrysler to Coca-Cola. And before that, I had done public opinion research for the Standard Oil Company (New Jersey), which later renamed itself Exxon so that it could become a national marketer. In going to work for the newspaper business, I felt I was coming as close as I could to fulfilling the class prophecy in my high school yearbook, which portrayed me as the irascible publisher of *The Moronographic* ("The Paper for People Who Can't Think").

This book must be read as a personal memoir rather than as a history. Histories are best written by those who can examine the events they chronicle with detachment. Future historians of journalism may want to know how the twentieth-century press sought to adapt to a changed communications environment, but I have not tried to fit the sequence of events into an overarching framework of theory. I prefer to consider this tale as a case history that describes how ideas get translated into actions, how organized programs emerge from conversation, and how human beings work, sometimes harmoniously, sometimes at cross-purposes, to adjust their established schemes of thought and behavior to a challenge they face in common.

The Readership Project can be understood only by knowing something about the American newspaper industry. Quite a few books have been written in recent years about individual newspapers and newspaper groups, and about leading newspaper personalities who have earned places in contemporary history. I shall avoid this well-trodden ground. Rather, I shall be describing how newspaper organizations and people interact with each other. The story of the Readership Project illuminates this process.

The Project was an attempt by the principal organized forces within the American newspaper business to stem a decline in readership that threatened advertising revenues and therefore the survival of the business. The period since the ending of World War II was punctuated by the disappearance of great dailies in what had been lively, competitive newspaper markets. Each newspaper hung on its own statistical track record and saw its fortunes as somehow independent of those great abstract trends that represented the industry at large. Circulation figures, which represented sales of subscriptions and of single copies, had to be seen in relation to the growing population of potential readers, so that when they held level, they really represented a drop in a paper's ability to penetrate its home market. Circulation sales, which could be rather precisely measured, merely reflected changes in the strength of established reading habits and in the hold that newspapers retained on the public's loyalties.

The loss of readers took place so gradually that one of the Readership Project's major tasks was to alert newspaper managements to the reality and seriousness of the decline. This required a strong communications effort to sensitize newspapers to the problem and to urge them to do something about it, individually and in concert.

In its six years, the Project developed a significant body of information that illuminated the changes taking place. It used its research findings to move newspapers to confront the social realities, psychological factors, and competitive forces that had changed the world in which they operated. It produced a substantial number of presentations, manuals, and programs that newspapers could use or emulate in their own efforts to strengthen their readership. It launched programs to upgrade the distribution function through better training of personnel and by applying advanced technology. Later chapters describe all these activities in detail, and the appendix provides a complete list of the individual projects.

A program of this kind and scope was not produced at the touch of a button. The Readership Project involved the participation of hundreds of people at the national level and of thousands in individual newspaper locations. A consensus had to be formed about the tasks to be undertaken. Achieving this was not easy. The newspaper business was large, heterogeneous, and structurally complex, beset by competitive rivalries among papers and professional groups. Moreover, it was notoriously a refuge for cantankerous individualists who looked with suspicion upon industry-wide activities. An operating plan had to be devised and agreed upon, millions of dollars had to be raised to implement it, and a system of planning and oversight had to be set up. And then, on top of it all, the work had to be done. This book is the story of how all this happened.

The first chapter sets the stage and introduces some of the players. Chapter 2 tells how the industry's leaders became aware that readership was a problem. Chapter 3 describes the planning and organization of our action program and the jockeying for power that accompanied it. Chapter 4 explains how research on readers crystallized the philosophical dispute over newspapers' social functions and expressed the antagonism that editors felt toward the marketers who threatened to usurp their authority. Chapter 5 discusses the relationship between research and its implementation, between knowledge and action. Massive changes were taking place in newspapers' distribution methods. Chapter 6 describes the Project's efforts to professionalize the people and modernize the machines and systems involved in this side of the business. Promotional activities, described in Chapter 7, represented some of the Project's most visible and controversial actions and illustrate the difficulties of maintaining support in a multipartite enterprise. Chapter 8 reviews the problems of translating the national program into local terms. It shows how and why the Project, originally planned as a three-year crash program, went on for another three years before it was terminated and offers an appraisal of its accomplishments and failures.

This is a tale told with many meanders, in part because a great many different things were going on at the same time during the six years I am writing about and in part because as we go along, the reader will want to join me in reflecting upon their meaning. The principal findings that emerged from the Project's research program have been reported in my book *Press and Public: Who Reads What When Where and Why in American Newspapers.*[2] I do not duplicate that report in these pages, though I summarize some of the individual studies as part of my story.

A great many people were involved in the Readership Project, in one way or another. Every one of them might have written a book different from the one you are about to begin.

A Glossary of Abbreviations

AAAA	American Association of Advertising Agencies
AANR	American Association of Newspaper Representatives (later renamed Newspaper Advertising Sales Association [NASA])
AAPOR	American Association for Public Opinion Research
ABC	Audit Bureau of Circulations
ADI	Area of Dominant Influence (Arbitron television ratings term)
ADS	Advertising Dimension Standards
AEJMC	Association for Education in Journalism and Mass Communication
ANA	Association of National Advertisers
ANCAM	Association of Newspaper Classified Advertising Managers
ANPA	American Newspaper Publishers Association
APME	Associated Press Managing Editors
ARF	Advertising Research Foundation
A&S	Audits and Surveys, Inc.
ASNE	American Society of Newspaper Editors
BCG	Boston Consulting Group
CDNPA	Canadian Daily Newspaper Publishers Association
DMA	Defined Market Area (Nielsen television ratings term)

E&P	Editor and Publisher
ICMA	International Circulation Managers Association
INAME	International Newspaper Advertising and Marketing Executives (formerly International Newspaper Advertising Executives [INAE], and before that, Newspaper Advertising Executives Association [NAEA])
INFE	International Newspaper Financial Executives (formerly Institute of Newspaper Controllers and Financial Officers [INCFO])
INPA	International Newspaper Promotion Association (formerly National Newspaper Promotion Association [NNPA] and later, International Newspaper Marketing Association [INMA])
NAB	Newspaper Advertising Bureau (formerly, Bureau of Advertising of the ANPA, Inc.)
NABSCAN	Nationally Advertised Brands Scanning Service
NIC	Newsprint Information Committee
NIE	Newspaper in Education
NNA	National Newspaper Association
NPRA	Newspaper Personnel Relations Association
NRC	Newspaper Research Council
NRMA	National Retail Merchants Association
NRP	Newspaper Readership Project
SMRB	Simmons Market Research Bureau
SNPA	Southern Newspaper Publishers Association

Acknowledgments

Marie Thornton, who worked with me for many years at the Newspaper Advertising Bureau, brought dedication, good judgment, and an intelligent mastery of detail to every aspect of the Readership Project. She was also my amanuensis for the first draft of this memoir. Ann Brady and Yannis Takos helped me verify facts about the changing newspaper business.

W. Phillips Davison, Arnold Ismach, and John McMillan provided invaluable and constructive criticism and comment on the manuscript. I am grateful to the Gannett Center for Media Studies at Columbia University for providing an ideally supportive setting for completing this book. The Center's Director, Everette C. Dennis, offered encouragement and helpful suggestions. Penny Panoulias word-processed my hieroglyphics with extraordinary accuracy and speed, and Lisa DeLisle patiently assisted me in my own word-processing attempts. My wife, Agnes Bogart, gave me time off to do this whole thing and deserves special thanks.

Preserving the Press

CHAPTER 1

The Newspaper Business: Behind the Scenes and Up Front

The Newspaper Readership Project was the joint creation of the two major organizations in the newspaper business, the American Newspaper Publishers Association (ANPA) and the Newspaper Advertising Bureau (NAB), and this book chronicles the vicissitudes of their collaboration. Interdependent though they were, they differed markedly in mission and method. We can understand the Readership Project's accomplishments and failings only if we know something about these institutions and the varied and remarkable constituency of newspaper publishers that they both represented.

Are Newspapers Necessary?

The Project raised considerable funds, produced a substantial output of words in printed and audiovisual forms, and aroused a great deal of attention. All of this activity was based on the assumption that it could affect the behavior of the millions of Americans whose newspaper reading habits had undergone a slow but steady change.

Was this a reasonable assumption? Is it possible to preserve an industry that is technically obsolete or a form of cultural expression that has no longer retained its usefulness? At the heart of most discussions of the future of the press has been the vision of the ailing dinosaur, flourishing for millennia in a propitious environment but unable to adjust to the vast climatic and ecological transformations that occurred around it. The image of this ponderous, powerful, weak-brained, and doomed creature haunted newspaper managements. At an editors' convention, Barry Bingham, Jr., the irreverent, waxed-mustachioed publisher of the *Louisville Courier-Journal*, once described newspapers as "the last dinosaur in the swamp," much to the discomfiture of his advertising sales staff.

Yet, somehow, the metaphor did not quite fit. Newspapers lost readers and some of their share of advertising. Great newspapers went under after protracted death agonies. Yet American dailies continued to attract vast audiences of more than a hundred million readers a day, and to sell great quantities of goods and services for their advertisers. They employed nearly half a million people and were the nation's seventh biggest manufacturing industry. The strength of the press and its ability to resist advertiser influence have always been derived from the variety of its advertising sources. Newspapers remained the country's largest advertising medium, drawing advertising investments that went from less than $6 billion in 1970 to $32 billion in 1990. Some privately owned chains like Thomson and Donrey were reported to skim profits equivalent to 50 percent of their gross revenues from their monopoly papers in smaller and middle-sized markets. These may have been extraordinary cases, but newspaper profits averaged twice those of a typical corporation, and the stocks of publicly held newspaper companies were a perennial favorite of Wall Street. In the face of the electronic revolution in communications, newspapers introduced a dazzling array of technological innovations in their own production systems. These lowered their labor costs, increased their operating flexibility, speeded up their production schedules, and transformed their appearance.

Most important, newspapers continued to serve a function that remained unique, even in an era of expanded media choices. No medium, not even the more ubiquitous and time-eating medium of television, touched people in so many different aspects of their lives. Newspapers embodied and articulated the spirit of community in thousands of American cities and towns, raising issues for public discussion, and providing leadership and direction on myriad subjects of local, regional, and national significance. Although their political role in national presidential elections was widely considered to have been usurped by television, newspapers exerted a powerful influence on the public's perception of local controversies and candidates. Because they covered so much wider an array of subjects than any other mass medium, newspapers gave members of the public an opportunity to define their individual identity at the same time that it gave them a sense of civic identity. Newspaper reading was a highly selective process that well served the interests of advertisers who wanted to attract the attention of likely prospects for whatever they were trying to sell.

In spite of all these strengths, the Readership Project brought to the surface a great many anxious questions about the continuing viability of the daily press. With the emergence of new electronic communications technology—teletext and videotex—more and more casual talk was heard in media circles about the obsolescence of print. The disappearance of well-established metropolitan dailies reinforced the uneasiness that many newspaper people felt about the prospects for the industry to which their careers had been dedicated.

Organizations and the Management of Social Change

Diverse and discordant, American newspapers defied generalization and seemed loath to confront their common problems collectively. In this respect, their situation exemplified more general issues of organizational behavior.

Individuals, by an exercise of will, can shape their own destinies, to some degree. But human organizations are harder to manage because of the uncertain qualities and conflicting motives of the people who comprise them and the implacable pressure of external forces over which they can exercise no control. Whole societies are the most difficult to mobilize in a changed direction. Where this has been achieved, as in fascist and communist dictatorships, it has been through the power of the state to coerce, a power that lesser institutions rarely enjoy.

To change the ways of organizations, individuals must act in concert. This is hard enough to accomplish when they are members of a single, cohesive, entity like a business firm. It is much more difficult when the institution is loosely defined, like a voluntary association, or when it is defined primarily by common activities and interests, as in the case of an industry functioning in a competitive economy. Such an industry, like the newspaper business, is made up of many hundreds or thousands of individual enterprises, each with its own leadership and operating style, its own characteristic goals, values, and interests. In many instances, these enterprises are in embittered conflict with each other. Still, the people who run them, and in most cases the people who staff them, have something important in common.

Since the beginnings of civilized society, the development of occupational specialties has led to a sense of kinship among those engaged in the same craft or trade. The consciousness of a shared identity, overriding individual competitive instincts, found its expression in the medieval guilds and survives in today's professional associations. But since the start of the industrial revolution, modern industry has been characterized by its ability to combine and coordinate diverse skills. These often lack any functional similarity to others used in the same enterprise but may be identical to those employed in totally different forms of business. A draftsman, a machinist, an accountant, a designer, a sweeper may as easily be employed by General Foods as by General Motors, yet each is acutely aware of what larger business he is in.*

The degree of identification may differ widely, both among crafts and among individuals. In the mid-1960s, the linotypists in New York City appeared indifferent to the survival of the newspapers their strikes shut down,[1] because their union seniority entitled them to employment priority in the job printing trade. But, even among them, there must have been some residual sense of belonging to the newspaper business, a nostalgia for what they had helped destroy. Such a sense of belonging, with all the emotional attachments it represents, is inevitably more acute in those occupations whose skills are less easily transferable into other industries.

Trade associations are made up of the people who own or manage businesses, whose interests are hardly identical with those of the masses of employees. But while trade associations and labor

---

*Note: The masculine pronoun is used throughout this book in its traditional generic sense. However, it must be noted that the executive ranks of the newspaper business were overwhelmingly male.

unions bargain and periodically square off in combat, their members generally have a mutual interest in the prosperity of the business itself, on which both profits and jobs depend.

Industries may in fact be said to acquire an identity through their associations, which represent points of reference for their own work forces, for government agencies, and for the public at large. New industries become differentiated as their members break away from existing associations and establish their own networks and rituals in the form of meetings, exhibitions, publications, and promotions. In the newspaper business, the art of association had evolved to a very high degree.

The ANPA

The American Newspaper Publishers Association was one of a host of organizations through which individual industries sought to advance their common interests in the face of growing government regulations in the post-Civil War era. The spread of the railroad network and the invention of the telephone facilitated the growth of gigantic national corporations—the "trusts." They also made it possible for individuals engaged in similar local enterprises in widely scattered cities to come together and to talk about matters of mutual interest on the easy basis of personal acquaintance.

Like similar associations in other industries, the ANPA provided a forum for exchanging useful information about operations, technology, and personnel. It also represented a political force that could speak with a single voice to the general public, before the courts, and in response to the growing encroachments of government. As in other industries, newspaper managements confronted the growing power of organized trade unions and of the suppliers of equipment and raw materials (in this case, newsprint and ink). Newspaper publishers held one distinctive interest in common over and above the particular vested interests whose counterparts could be found in every other industry. That concern was the freedom of the press.

Under the American Constitution and its First Amendment guarantee of free expression, the press enjoys a special and privileged status. Freedom of the press has been under continual challenge and reinterpretation since the earliest days of the Republic from every branch of government. Since its founding, the ANPA has provided a mechanism through which publishers and editors could maintain and assert the rights of a free press as embodied in the association's motto. But it was solid business reasons, not ideological motives, that brought the organization into being.

In the era when the ANPA was established, newspapers were unchallenged as the principal means through which news, information, and opinion were expressed and disseminated. They were also, by far, the biggest medium of advertising.

The ANPA was founded in Rochester, New York, on February 16, 1887, at the initiative of William H. Brearley of the *Detroit Evening News* in a meeting with forty-five other daily newspaper publishers present, nineteen of them from nearby New York cities and towns.[2] In his history of the Association,[3] Edwin Emery points out that one of the first items on the agenda was the subject of the commissions paid to advertising agents, which spread over a wide range. "Brearley's main concern was that the advertising agents who had come to the convention should not learn the details of the discussions regarding them." The new association was "concerned with all business problems of daily newspapers," but Brearley commented, "This afternoon it looked as though no one wanted to discuss anything but advertising." The question of "What are the qualifications of an advertising agency?" was answered by one publisher: "Cheek is the main thing."

As Emery describes it, the ANPA "seldom discussed or took action on questions of an editorial or a news character, unless they also involved business considerations."[4]

After attending an ANPA convention many years later, the columnist Heywood Broun said, "They did not talk of journalism but of the industry. If a man from Mars had happened in, I think he might have spent an hour and still remained puzzled as to whether he had happened in upon a convention of bankers, cotton mill owners, or the makers of bathroom supplies."[5] But this would be an inaccurate comment today, when a high proportion of convention content is devoted to public affairs and to discussion of journalistic coverage and credibility.

From the start, ANPA's bulletins included items about tariffs on wood pulp, libel suits, wage scales for printers, second-class postage rates, and the return of copies by news dealers. But the greatest emphasis was on advertiser credit ratings, warnings about advertisers and agents, and new business tips.[6]

An ANPA bulletin of February 24, 1899, warned, "All of these bills are against the interests of the proprietary article manufacturers who are large advertising patrons of newspapers, and if passed would ruin their business. Members of the Association should aid through influence with their local senators and assemblymen in killing off these measures." But such concerns disappeared a few years later.

As the ANPA moved toward the century mark of its existence, its functions had broadened to meet the intricate requirements of a great industry. It functioned through numerous committees drawn, not just from the ranks of its Board, but from all quarters in the newspaper business. These committees dealt with such subjects as new technology, government affairs, telecommunications, waste disposal, newsprint, production, libel insurance, and other arcane subjects. Typically, they met twice a year, and their somewhat diffuse agendas were crowded with reports of activity from participating organizations.

The ANPA's Legal Department dealt with the innumerable court cases and legislative or regulatory issues with which the newspaper business was faced. It negotiated with the Pentagon over its news blackout during the invasion of Grenada. It submitted briefs to the Postal Board of Governors arguing against third-class postal rates that presented newspapers with growing competition in the form of shared direct mail advertising. It dealt with the growing public and legislative concern over the disposal of waste newspapers. In collaboration with several newspaper professional associations, ANPA ran a program of management training seminars and workshops. Its Labor Relations Department kept an eye on wage rates, working conditions, and labor union activities.

There was a Technical Services Department (formerly the ANPA Research Institute), staffed by engineers who monitored technological developments, sought technical standardization, and encouraged manufacturers to produce useful new types of equipment. This group ran a huge technical conference each summer that attracted some 14,000 production and management people from around the world to see the latest in advanced computer systems, presses, plate-making machinery, and other equipment.(This gathering was later renamed the ANPA Technical Exposition and Conference or ANPA/TEC.) The huge industrial show was accompanied by a program dealing with technical developments related to newspaper production and matters of broader industry interest.

Readership and circulation fell within the province of the ANPA, to the degree that these subjects received any attention from publishers at all. Through its Foundation, the ANPA (since 1952) sponsored a "Newspaper in Education" program to encourage the use of the newspaper in the classroom.[7] In 1986, it began a new program to encourage higher levels of literacy.

The ANPA moved its headquarters to Reston, Virginia, early in 1972, reportedly to escape high New York City rents and to be in proximity to the Federal government. Perhaps the decision to move may also have had something to do with the small town publishers' persistent view of New York as Sodom and Gomorrah. The same suspicions may have underlain ANPA's 1975 decision to move its annual convention from New York's Waldorf Astoria Hotel, where it had traditionally been held each spring since 1889, in favor of cities with more inviting cultural attractions, like Honolulu, New Orleans, and Miami Beach.

The move to Reston had been superintended by ANPA's general manager, Stanford Smith, a decisive personality who had clashed with a number of his directors and chairmen. Upon his departure, he assumed active rank as a brigadier general in the Pentagon. He was replaced at ANPA by Jerry Friedheim, a former assistant secretary of Defense in the Nixon administration who handled the Pentagon's relations with the media during the Vietnam war. He managed this unenviable assignment with finesse and minimal offense to all parties. As a spokesman for newspapers (until he resigned in 1991), Friedheim held his counsel well, avoided commitments in public, and had an exquisite sense of the limits within which a functionary could operate when surrounded by powerful figures with strong wills and strongly differing opinions.

The ANPA communicated with its members by churning out a prodigious number of reports and newsletters. Eventually it consolidated its bulletins into a handsome and expensively produced monthly publication called *presstime*, designed to report in depth on the broad trends and issues of the business.[8]

The Newspaper Associations

Soon after the ANPA's move to Reston, its building came to serve as home for a number of other newspaper organizations.[9] Rivalries over professional boundary lines were rife throughout the newspaper business. Each specialized group had its own professional association. Apart from the Newspaper Advertising Executives Association (NAEA, then INAE, and eventually relabeled the International Newspaper Advertising & Marketing Executives —INAME—to reflect its members' expanded ambitions), there were the Association of Newspaper Classified Advertising Managers (ANCAM), the International Circulation Managers Association (ICMA), the International Newspaper Promotion Association (INPA, which subsequently became the International Newspaper Marketing Association—INMA), and the Newspaper Research Council (NRC). There were the Newspaper Personnel Relations Association (NPRA), the International Newspaper Controllers and Financial Officers (INCFO, later renamed the International Newspaper Financial Executives—INFE).[10]

There were a number of editorial groups. The American Society of Newspaper Editors (ASNE) was made up of the principal or senior editors of papers and considered itself a very exclusive club indeed. The Associated Press Managing Editors (APME) represented most of the second echelon, though a number of top editors also belonged. Unlike the ASNE, whose annual meetings were held in Washington and featured addresses on cosmic issues by cabinet members, the president, and visiting heads of state, the APME convention moved around the country, and its programs were filled with intense discussions of newspapers' workaday problems. There were also the Society of Editorial Writers and the Society of Newspaper Designers.

All these organizations operated on slender resources. For instance, the paid staff of the International Circulation Managers Association in the mid-1970s consisted of a director and a secretary, whose main functions were to produce a monthly newsletter, organize the annual conference, and handle routine business affairs. The International Newspaper Promotion Association was staffed in a similarly skeletal fashion. Its members' responsibilities related to the promotion of circulation and readership, as well as to advertising and general public relations.

In addition to all the national organizations, there were state and regional press associations that in most cases covered both dailies and weeklies. They served the particular interests of smaller publishers and their top managements. Noticeably absent from the association scene were organized groups representing the crafts involved in the mechanical production of newspapers. All of these were, of course, the terrain of trade unions, but only a fifth of the newspaper workforce, blue collar and white collar, was actually unionized. The Newspaper Guild, which had begun as a labor union of journalists, had long since become a catchall covering employees in nonmechanical jobs. Sigma Delta Chi[11] (the Society of Professional Journalists) and occasional ad hoc groups like the Reporters' Committee for Freedom of the Press were concerned with professional issues in journalistic practice. The newspaper unions were, however, concerned almost exclusively with traditional bread-and-butter issues: compensation and work rules and conditions. In the mechanical crafts they had traditionally operated to restrict entry to their guilds, and their attitude toward new technology was essentially one of Luddite obstruction.

The newspaper associations expressed their members' strivings for professional status. Like all organizations, each had its own dynamic of self-preservation and expansion, which went beyond the individual goals of its constituents.

The rank and file did not participate in the professional associations of newspaper executives. When a publisher permitted an executive to join an association, this tacitly carried with it the privilege of attending its meetings. Modeled after those of the ANPA itself, newspaper conventions generally began on the last evening of a weekend and continued through the morning of the following Wednesday. Speeches, presentations, and panels of speakers alternated with social events and with small group discussion sessions on specialized subjects. Generally an afternoon or two was allowed for recreation or a group excursion.

As at any trade and professional convention, the formal instruction provided by the program was not the principal attraction. These meetings were an occasion to renew old acquaintances, to negotiate job changes, and to pick up gossip and tricks of the trade. Spouses (99 percent of them wives) were generally in attendance, with a special "ladies' program" of interminable coffee hours and shopping expeditions.

In the railroad era, the major newspaper conventions were held annually at fixed locations. Each springtime was greeted by the ANPA in New York and by the ASNE in Washington. The Newspaper Advertising Executives Association met each January in Chicago; it managed, however, to hold a second convention each July. The coming of air travel made it possible to shift locations to different places across the country.

In addition to the national meetings, almost every association on the business side had regional subdivisions or affiliates—sometimes reaching down to the state level. These divisional meetings drew participants from many smaller newspapers whose publishers chose not to pay for longer trips. They were held at a different time of year than the national conventions and repeated the opportunity to meet old friends and to affirm a shared occupational identity, which was hard to keep up among specialists working in one-newspaper towns.

Some publishers resented the many hours their executives spent away from the shop attending meetings. One even argued that there should be one gigantic newspaper convention held in one place once a year that everyone would attend. It was not quite clear who would be minding the store if this were ever to happen.

As in many other businesses and professions, the conventions were often the highlight of the year for the membership. Association office was highly coveted, and association-related activity was a significant expression of individual achievement.

In most national newspaper organizations, an individual was chosen by a nominating committee for the lowest position on the ladder of office (the second vice presidency, for example). The nomination was reviewed by the executive committee and the Board before it was submitted to the membership (as part of the full slate) for a pro forma vote. There was much jesting about "the democratic process at work," but no strong sentiment for a change in the procedure. The only genuine electoral contests (and these were keen and rivalrous) were among publishers for membership on the Board of the Associated Press, and among editors for directorships of the ASNE. (Real races were run for the newspaper directorships on the Board of the Audit Bureau of Circulations (ABC), but these were effectively ended when the NAB Board decided to endorse a slate of candidates in 1984.)

In the professional associations, an officer proceeded from the first position to progressively more exalted rank, usually culminating, after the presidency, in the chairmanship of the nominating committee. Since opposition candidacies for office were never introduced, the whole process ensured the smooth continuity of a compatible elite. Newly fledged officers had apprenticeships of several years, which allowed their bosses to become accustomed to their periodic absence on association business. Newspaper publishers, experienced at serving on boards and committees, moved effortlessly into the chairmanships at the Bureau and ANPA. The transition in lesser associations was not always as smooth.

The permanent staff of any membership organization must win the confidence of elected officers who serve their brief terms and go on their way just as they are beginning to learn the ropes. These officers invariably differ in philosophy and in operating style, and staff executives must quickly learn their proclivities, strengths, and frailties. The staff has to make every elected officer a hero, providing agendas and proposals, and drafting letters, articles, speeches and presentation scripts. The *quid pro quo* is usually an officer's understanding of the staff's own motives and interests and an unhesitating stance of public support.

Individuals were driven to take office in newspaper organizations, as in any other type of voluntary association, from a variety of motives. They may have shared the common desire for achievement and glory. They may have gotten the biggest charge from their personal attachments to their professional associates, with all the sociability and fun involved in these human contacts. They may have wanted to expand their horizons by travel beyond the narrow precincts of their day-to-day business. They may have looked on their organizational participation as a learning experience. Serving in national office, moreover, might represent opportunities for career advancement, offering high visibility and good contacts for future job openings.

A person becoming president of a major newspaper organization, like the American Society of Newspaper Editors or the International Newspaper Advertising and Marketing Executives, had to be prepared to give up a substantial amount of time during the presidential year to travel around the country. Innumerable meetings were on the schedule, not only for committees of the national association, but also for related regional groups. At these meetings, the international president was customarily the keynoter or at least a principal speaker.

Publishers rarely refused to allow one of their senior executives to accept organizational office. Opposition would hurt the morale of one of their own key managers, and the word would get around that they were themselves unwilling to cooperate in the industry's collective interests and did not share its compulsion for self-improvement. In a number of instances, publishers were known to bide their time until the individual in question had completed his term of office, before moving him into a cubbyhole with a face-saving title or making him walk the plank altogether.

The Bureau and Newspaper Advertising

The realm of the Bureau was generally well demarcated from that of the ANPA. Although it had been set up in 1913 as the Bureau of Advertising of the ANPA, it had a separate corporate identity, funding base, and organizational structure. Links to the ANPA remained intimate, but the two organizations evolved rather different operating methods that reflected their distinctive functions and the way they were staffed and governed. For many years, both were headquartered in New York City, in adjacent twin buildings for a part of that time.

The Newspaper Advertising Bureau (renamed in 1973) was, in terms of budget, the biggest voluntary association in the newspaper business. Although the staff of the ANPA was the same size as that of the Bureau (both had approximately 140 employees in 1990), the personnel and styles of the two organizations were quite different. The ANPA operated much like many of the hundreds of other national trade associations that have their headquarters in the Washington area. The Bureau prided itself on being a sales organization and rejected the appellation of "trade association" when it was applied.

At the time of ANPA's founding, the United States had 1,311 daily newspapers; by the time the Bureau was set up, the total had risen to 2,200. In 1913, the daily press reigned supreme as the principal advertising medium, with nearly three times as much revenue as magazines. Specialized business publications, outdoor billboards, and transportation car cards had begun to attract substantial amounts of advertising. Miscellaneous forms of promotion were also widely in use, ranging from advertisements on matchboxes to display signs at the point of sale. Advertising had grown with the American economy; by 1913 it was already a billion dollar industry. Newspapers had profited mightily from this growth; for years they had passed on progressively more of their operating costs to the advertiser and fewer to the reader. A metropolitan daily sold for two cents.

The earliest newspapers had treated commercial information as news and charged the advertiser nothing to publish it, but publishers (or "printers" as they proudly called themselves) quickly learned that these messages carried even more value for the merchant than for the reader. Since colonial times, the American press had sought advertisements as a source of revenue. By the middle of the nineteenth century they accounted for more than half of all newspaper income. By 1913, they represented nearly two thirds.

The growth of a consumer economy had created a self-evident need for a centralized source of service and standardized information about newspapers. Even the most fundamental facts about the number of paid copies that a newspaper sold each day could not be assembled on any consistent basis. Advertisers had to make their own evaluations of each publisher's integrity and the honesty of his claim.

Advertising agencies had been set up in the nineteenth century to broker space to advertisers located outside a newspaper's own community. The early advertising agents charged a commission to the newspapers and other periodicals in which they placed ads. They acted as representatives of the publication, not of the advertisers.

By the beginning of the twentieth century, there was a split in functions. Some representatives settled into the traditional role of selling space in a particular set of newspapers to multimarket or national advertisers. Other advertising agents reoriented themselves and took the advertiser as the client, although they continued to collect a commission from the advertising medium. These agents prepared ad copy, art, and layouts for ads; they tried to make objective assessments of individual media and to draw up advertising schedules based on the client's interests and sales objectives. They were predecessors of today's advertising agencies, which provide advertisers with a wide array of services, including such specialized functions as consumer research, sales promotion, public relations, television program production, merchandising support, marketing counsel, and new product development. All these activities supplement their basic job of producing and placing advertisements in the great variety of media available today.

The rise of advertising agencies reflected the growing importance of national—as opposed to purely local—advertising. A particular newspaper, through its own sales staff, could deal with retailers and other local display advertisers on the spot. Similarly, it could accept classified ads over the counter at its office or take them down over the telephone. But it was another matter for the newspaper's national advertising sales department to cover manufacturers located in remote cities who advertised in many markets at once.

The newspaper's national sales representatives thus took on considerable importance. They maintained offices in key advertising centers like New York, Chicago, and Detroit. The principals of representative firms were gentlemen of means, polish, and presence, adept at entertaining advertisers and agency executives, as well as the publishers they represented. Because representative firms vied with each other to attract the allegiance of publishers, their offices always had to be ready at a moment's notice to supply hotel reservations, tickets to the theater or the ballgame, and generous dining hospitality.

The sales efforts of the representatives were essentially directed to the enhancement of their client newspapers' market share. Their first job was to get their markets on an advertiser's buy list and, in competitive markets, to make sure that their newspapers were higher on the list than the other papers in town. In this hard-hitting, rivalrous selling climate, representatives found little occasion or reason to espouse the generic merits of newspapers when they talked to their customers. This condition more or less persisted, but the number of independently owned representative firms dwindled remarkably as a result of the decline of competition among metropolitan dailies. (Where there were dozens of these firms in 1913, only three substantial ones still existed in

1990.) With the growing number of newspapers under chain ownership, company-owned sales organizations were established by such major groups as Gannett, Newhouse, Hearst, Times Mirror, and Knight-Ridder. (In 1990, the last two combined with Million Market Newspapers, a cooperative formed by a number of large independent dailies, to form a giant new sales company.) The corporate operating style of these organizations was less expansive than that of the traditional old-style "reps."

The generic merits of newspaper advertising were precisely what the Bureau of Advertising was set up to sell—with a budget of $50,000 and a staff of three. Its domain was defined strictly as that of national advertising. The dues paid by its members were based on the amount of national advertising they carried. (The highest bracket, for such big papers as *The New York Times* and the *Chicago Tribune,* carried a dues assessment of $500; by 1990 it had risen to $165,000.)

Selling Newspaper Advertising

Like an advertising agency, the Bureau was split between staff and line functions. The National Sales Department was made up of individuals known internally as "salesmen" and to the outer world as "account executives." They were responsible for individual advertising agencies and companies, with the assignments usually made along industry lines. There were regional sales offices in Chicago, Detroit, San Francisco, and Los Angeles, with individuals covering different sales territories.[12] The Creative Department produced a variety of publications for the use of members, as well as presentations on cards, slides, and occasionally on film.[13] A Retail Training Department ran workshops, clinics, and seminars for newspaper retail sales people and for small local advertisers, teaching the rudiments of advertising budgeting, scheduling, copy, and layout. The Research Department analyzed statistics on the medium, followed advertising trends, measured audience characteristics, analyzed the current status of competing media, and produced a considerable volume of market research.

The Marketing Department (which we set up shortly after my arrival) served as an intermediary, translating research into strategy for sales presentations. These were prepared by the Creative

Department and shown to customers by the Sales Department. A Business Office and Public Relations unit completed the staff assignments.

The heart of the Bureau's sales program was "target account selling" focused on individual companies who were selected as plausible prospects for increased use of newspaper space. The targets were usually leaders in their industries. A balance always had to be struck between our desire to go after large advertisers who hardly used newspapers at all and our need to demonstrate the success of our efforts—which meant going after some accounts that were already committed to newspapers. We developed these presentations after preliminary contacts with the client and its agency, which was usually suspicious of any attempt to question its good media judgment (which had usually put the client into television and thus made it a target for us in the first place).

The entire program rested on an ambitious series of consumer surveys. The idea was to learn something about the client's business that would allow us to formulate marketing objectives that could be met through newspaper advertising. We made specific proposals, compared the reach and cost efficiency of our recommended newspaper schedule with what we reckoned to be the results of the current advertising campaign, and prepared sample ads to suggest how the research results could be applied in creative practice. In the initial years of this effort, before the charm wore off, we were able to use the good offices of newspaper publishers to make contact with the principal executives of leading companies.

In addition to these targeted productions, we also produced a variety of generic presentations about the medium and showed them to advertising audiences that ranged in size from 1 to 10,000. The Bureau's own direct sales activities acquired a multiple effect through the versions of our presentations that we sold to our members for use in their own markets. We ground out a variety of reports and publications for the use of local newspaper sales people.

Corporate conglomeration and agency mergers brought an ever smaller number of organizations to account for a larger and larger proportion of the total advertising business. It was increasingly difficult for an individual newspaper's sales staff to contact directly the people who made the decisions that determined whether or not that paper would be on an advertising schedule. By 1958, television had become the dominant medium in national advertising. It took up to 90 percent of the expenditures of packaged goods companies producing low-interest products that closely resembled their competitors. These advertisers were convinced that customers could be induced to buy their brand not by rational argument but by creating the right kind of "image" and that this could best be done by summoning the power of television's sight, sound, and motion.

As newspapers' share of manufacturers' ad budgets fell, their advertising represented a decreasing portion of newspapers' total. Smaller daily newspapers received hardly any national advertising at all. Newspaper advertising schedules tended to be concentrated into a handful of major papers in bigger markets. These papers had large audiences and rates that were more efficient by the crucial criterion of "cost-per-thousand," by which advertisers evaluate media efficiency. (This simply means the cost of putting an advertisement in front of a given number of households or individuals—either in general, or of a certain desirable kind. In calculating this, advertisers can define their own terms, including the size of the ad unit they want to use.)

Newspapers were getting only a small part of all national advertising; their hold was also slipping over retail advertising, traditionally their principal support. Mass retailers ventured into broadcasting to sell promotional events rather than specific merchandise items. More and more of them turned to direct mail, first selectively to reach charge account customers and later to address the general public at rates that were highly competitive with those for newspaper advertising inserts.

The Bureau's original mandate was to represent the newspaper business to national advertisers. However, the growth of mass retailing steadily eroded the difference between national and local advertising. Chains operating in many markets accounted for an increasing proportion of all retail volume. Advertising management was increasingly being centralized, even in categories of business that traditionally had been thought of as local. Decisions were made at headquarters by bureaucrats who sometimes were unfamiliar with the individual markets or their media. A growing percentage of newspaper revenues came from advertisers headquartered in distant cities, devising their plans on a broad national or regional scale.

Circulation and readership represented the principal attractions that newspapers offered their advertisers. Traditionally, an advertiser running ads in the local press of a community did so with the conviction that the message would be put in front of everyone. Not every reader of the paper would pay attention to what the individual advertiser had to say, but most advertisers understood instinctively that people tended to see or pay attention to the items in the paper that interested them and to the ads for products or services for which they were prospective customers. This commonsense assumption was supported by a considerable volume of research that the Bureau produced.[14]

Newspapers needed the same kind of sophisticated representation with Sears and Safeway, K-Mart and Kroger's that they expected the Bureau to give them with General Motors and General Mills. So the Bureau's functions were expanded in the retail area, and its dues base was changed to reflect this. Later, in the early 1970s, a Classified Advertising Department was added to the Bureau's functions. Advertising agencies specializing in recruitment ads accounted for a large part of all employment classified ads, and franchise operations like Century 21 and Better Homes & Gardens represented a growing proportion of the newspapers' real estate advertising. These, too, required promotion and representation on a national level.

In 1960, when I joined the Bureau, we were fond of saying that newspapers carried more advertising than television, radio, and magazines combined. Thirty years later, newspapers still retained an edge over television, but it was uncertain how long they could continue as number one. This decline certainly heightened the Bureau's importance as the unique sales voice of the entire newspaper business. But it also raised publishers' expectations, unrealistically, as to what the Bureau could accomplish to buck the trend. In 1990, the Bureau had a $17 million annual budget in a business that collectively spent more than $3 billion to sell, service, and promote itself to advertisers. Yet the Bureau represented the only sales pressure on behalf of the medium, while all the remaining effort went to advance the competitive interests of individual papers.

The recurrence of major meetings on an annual timetable provided a rhythm to the Bureau's work schedule. There were the winter and summer meetings of the ad directors, the ANPA convention in the spring, the fall Board meeting, a winter meeting of the Board and the country's leading retailers, and spring and fall meetings with the management of the automobile manufacturers. These events put cyclical pressures on the Creative Department, restricted vacation timetables for most executives, and affected the production schedules of all the presentations, publications, and reports that represented our most essential output. The big meetings absorbed what everyone agreed was an inordinate proportion of our energies, yet it was considered essential to communicate effectively (even brilliantly, if possible) with our members; the conventions provided our only contact with many of them.

Preparations for the meetings inevitably took the form of a frantic last-minute rush, in spite of periodic resolutions to do things differently from here on in. But the meetings themselves provided bright punctuation points on the calendar, involving travel and conviviality. The January convention of the ad directors put the greatest demands on the stamina of the staff, since it was preceded by three days of committee meetings and required participation in discussion sessions, as well as on the main program.

The convention was described by the *Chicago Sun-Times*'s Charles Fegert as "Like being in jail for a week with all you can drink." Indeed, hospitality suites were always open almost around the clock, and many of the delegates hardly ever left the hotel. (In the railroad era, the convention was held for decades in the frigid and wind-battered Edgewater Beach Hotel on Chicago's lake front, where the temperature stayed at 20 degrees below zero through one memorable meeting.) Whatever the limitations of the program (which featured inspirational speakers who provided the secrets of salesmanship with evangelical fervor; advertisers who berated newspapers for their high rates, inflexible demeanor, and other shortcomings; and case histories of newspapers who had met competition "head on"), conventions were stimulating occasions, a change of pace, a time to find out the hot topics of concern and discussion at the grass roots.

The Wider World of Advertising

Voluntary associations were also a prominent feature of the wider advertising world of which the newspaper business was a part. The sense of having a common occupation and a mutuality of interest was fostered in advertising clubs around the country which held weekly or monthly luncheon or dinner meetings featuring cheery cocktail gatherings and "outside speakers." These grass roots organizations found their expression at the national level in the American Advertising Federation, which devoted much of its energy to warding off the tentacular encroachments of government. Advertising clubs had no strength, however, in the principal centers of power, New York and Chicago, where the membership was heavily weighted toward matchbook printers, outdoor advertising salesmen, and the principals of one-man agencies. The New York and Chicago ad clubs were largely ignored by the executives of the major media headquartered in those cities and by the big agencies that handled about two thirds of the whole national advertising business. In Los Angeles and Detroit, however, the advertising clubs were prestigious and potent. (Both cities were highly decentralized and opportunities for professional contact away from the freeways were perhaps more precious.)

As ambassadors to the decisionmakers of advertising, the Bureau maintained a highly visible presence at the principal advertising conventions, "getting close" (as the sales expression went) to important clients. The annual meetings of the American Association of Advertising Agencies (AAAA) and the Association of National Advertisers (ANA) both attracted large contingents of media executives cultivating customer connections on the golf course and in the cocktail lounge. As a result of such contacts, individuals occasionally leaped over the barrier and went from an agency to a client organization or vice versa. Movements from advertiser companies or agencies into the media were more common than shifts in the opposite direction. The top executives of the Bureau were in this tradition.[15]

Lipscomb and Kauffman

Charles T. Lipscomb, Jr., the first chief executive of the Bureau to take on the title of president (the previous heads had been "directors") described himself and his sales vice president and successor, Jack Kauffman, as "peddlers." Both men had begun their careers as salesmen for packaged goods companies, but they represented two different generations of sales management.

Lipscomb was a jovial, ruddy-faced giant who walked with a bandy-legged gait that he had acquired playing football for the University of North Carolina. Working first for the Coca-Cola Company and then for the wholesale druggists McKesson & Robbins, he had lived the life of an old-fashioned sales drummer of the railroad era, spending his evenings rocking on the wooden porches of small hotels in Southern towns. When I first met him in the early 1950s, he had risen to be president of the Pepsodent Division of Lever Brothers, a client of the McCann-Erickson advertising agency, where I had recently gone to work. On a walk over to the brand new glass Lever House on Park Avenue, the management supervisor on the account took pains to warn me that "when Mr. Lipscomb talks, we all listen." An army of minions had been assembled to hear the client's imperial pronouncements. And listen we did, for what seemed like a solid hour, at the great mahogany table in the corporate board room.

From the toothpaste and mouthwash business, Lipscomb moved on to become president of a shaving products manufacturer, the J. B. Williams Company, which he eventually sold on behalf of the owners. He was brought to the Bureau in 1957 by a special committee of the board, which had grown increasingly dissatisfied with the Bureau's previous director, Harold "Rusty" Barnes. Barnes was comfortable with the administration of his small organization but trembled before his bosses. He would lock himself up in his hotel room during the revelries that accompanied Board of Directors' meetings.

There was considerable consternation in some quarters when Lipscomb was appointed to head the Bureau. Didn't newspapers have within their own ranks an advertising salesman good enough for this choice sinecure? How could any outsider possibly understand the technical intricacies and the arcane competitive politics of the industry? Lipscomb compounded these anxieties when he summarily fired a high proportion of the sales staff and replaced them with executives whose experience, like his own, was as a buyer or customer rather than as a seller of advertising.

Jack Kauffman had enjoyed a rapid ascent during the years of World War II at Procter & Gamble and had eventually moved on to become sales vice president for the Toilet Goods Division of Colgate Palmolive. During the year and a half that I spent as head of market research at Revlon—known as "the firing line of marketing"—Kauffman appeared briefly on the scene. He was brought in at the unheard of salary of $100,000 a year by Charles Revson, the legendary tyrant who ruled the company. As marketing vice president, Kauffman was put in charge of an unruly, bright, and temperamental group of brand product managers. He faced hostile sniping from well-established cabals in sales and operations. His number may have been up when he took a weekend off to go to the Kentucky Derby. Revson disdained such frivolities, insisting that his key executives learn consumer tastes firsthand by spending their Saturdays behind the cosmetics counters of department stores.

Several months after he left Revlon, Kauffman called me to report that in his new job as sales vice president of the Bureau he was now traveling "first class" and with "the nicest people." (Presumably the executive corps at Revlon did not warrant this label.) My eventual appointment as the Bureau's vice president of marketing planning and research came only after I was interviewed by the chairman and vice chairman of the Bureau's Plans Committee, the advertising directors of the *Chicago Tribune* and *The New York Times*. As Lipscomb later told me, the usual anxieties about hiring someone from the outside were compounded in my case by concern over the possible contamination I had suffered from close association with television, about which, as already mentioned, I had written a book. However, someone looked at the book and decided that it was "objective."

While the staff of the ANPA was subservient to its directors, the Bureau's management believed that publishers' whims were unpredictable and dangerous and that the safest policy was to keep them at arm's length. This came naturally to Jack Kauffman, who publicly told publishers, "You ask us to jump, and we'll say, 'how high?' " but who spoke of them far less reverentially in private.

As a personal salesman, Kauffman's touch was deft, and his instincts unfailing. On one memorable 8:00 A.M. call that he and I made at the Wiedemann brewery in Cincinnati, we were ushered into a meeting room that was no more than a glass-partitioned cubicle adjacent to the plant cafeteria. The president offered hospitality. "Would you like some coffee?" Then as an afterthought, "Or a beer?" I took coffee, Kauffman a beer. When it arrived, he took a hearty sip, set it down and exclaimed, enraptured, "Say! This is *delicious!*"

In the Lipscomb era, the two principals would occasionally retire behind closed executive doors for a genial gin rummy game, which was described to the staff under the euphemism of "studying the business." Lunches were always at Christ Cella's, a pricey steak house across the street that some of us called "the company cafeteria." Kauffman enjoyed passing folded obscene messages to his subordinates at business meetings and grinned at their outrage.

As president and chief executive, between 1967 (the year I became executive vice president and general manager) and 1982, Kauffman was notably successful in recruiting talent from client organizations to staff specialized jobs at the Bureau. His extraordinary assemblage of key executives operated with great autonomy and reported to him directly rather than through an intervening hierarchy. He was fond of telling the directors, "We've got fewer people, and we're paying them better." Morale, he always added, was "at an all-time high."

Under Kauffman, independent organizations whose activities in some way overlapped the Bureau's were skillfully maneuvered out of existence and their functions and some of their personnel absorbed. This happened to Newspaper One, a sales cooperative of major market newspapers. It happened also to the Newspaper Preprint Corporation, which originally had been set up by an engraving company to promote and coordinate the handling of preprinted, roll-fed inserts. (These were an expensive though attractive form of advertising that eventually lost customers as freestanding inserts gained popularity.) Kauffman understood very well that the Bureau provided the industry with a unifying force that could only be weakened if separate sales organizations were allowed to divert resources and attention.

Publishers' Expanding Interests

The media marketplace had evolved into quite a different world than that of 1913, when the Bureau was founded. First radio and then television carved out substantial shares of a growing advertising market. In the 1920s, publishers were among the first people to secure licenses for radio stations. In the 1940s and 1950s, many moved on to acquire television franchises. In the 1960s and 1970s, a number of them set up or bought cable systems. But among most of those who were both publishers and broadcasters, there prevailed a sense that their newspapers came first. In sheer volume of revenues, newspapers usually constituted the largest element in their business. Newspapers, rather than their radio or TV properties, provided their main source of prestige and political power.

The same individuals served at different times on the Boards of the Bureau and of the Radio and Television Advertising Bureaus (comparable organizations that were set up on the model of the newspaper organization). But this conflict of interest did not, except in rare cases, inhibit competitive enthusiasm. (Occasionally a publisher took offense at the Bureau's aggressive sales efforts. Charles Thieriot, publisher of the *San Francisco Chronicle* and also owner of a very profitable TV station, objected to presentations that picked away relentlessly at the shortcomings of television and resigned from the Bureau after serving on the Board.) Most publishers felt that their corporate interests were best served when every media sales organization in which they had an interest exerted maximum competitive pressure.

What was in the corporate interest of a particular media company that owned newspapers was not always identical with what was in the collective interest of the newspaper business. Publishers seated with their peers at a Bureau Board meeting were always under pressure to play the role of industry statesmen, sometimes in conflict with their roles as corporate managers.

For example, the matter of admitting nondaily publications to Bureau membership periodically became a matter of Board discussion. The ANPA had admitted nondaily newspapers to its membership in 1975, though only a few hundred of the country's estimated 8,000 weeklies joined. Community weeklies whose subscribers paid for them obviously had almost everything in common with daily papers, except the frequency of publication. But such newspapers were losing circulation even more than dailies, faced with growing competition from weeklies with free distribution. These "shoppers" ranged from well-printed four-color publications with high quality local news content to shoddy advertising "free sheets" laced with only a sprinkling of boilerplate recipes and gardening hints. The growth of the shoppers was fostered by chain retail advertisers who wanted saturation coverage of the specific localities from which their customers were drawn and who were dismayed by dailies' loss of market penetration.

The line between paid and free weeklies was hard to draw. Most shoppers carried a spurious subscription price on their mastheads, and many of them actually tried to convert some of their readers to paid subscriptions. At the same time, paid weeklies often gave part of their circulation away in an effort to recruit new subscribers and to provide larger numbers to the advertisers.

An argument could be made that the Bureau's main concern was the generic sale of print. Publishers of weekly papers periodically applied for membership. Many daily newspaper companies published weeklies and shoppers of their own. Yet when the point of decision came, although the corporate interests of many directors would seem to support a broadening of the Bureau's franchise to include weeklies, the Board always voted to remain exclusively a daily newspaper organization. The trouble and expense of serving an additional constituency of small nondailies would not have been covered by the additional income they represented. More significantly, newspaper advertising directors, in particular, feared that if weeklies were let into the Bureau, the shoppers—whom they saw as aggressive competitors—would slip in too.

Publishers—Hereditary and Professional

The ranks of newspaper publishers included some memorable personalities. There was Britt Brown of the *Wichita Eagle-Beacon,* whose view of humanity was expressed in the shrunken head of an Amazonian Indian, hung on the wall behind his desk. (When I made his acquaintance he had just gotten out of jail, where he languished in defiance of a court's alimony award.) Brown was, however, not unique in his fascination with taxidermy. Times Mirror's Otis Chandler kept in his office suite the stuffed carcasses of a grizzly and a polar bear, each rearing ferociously to a 10-foot height.

There was Darrow ("Duke") Tully of the *Phoenix Republic* and *Arizona Gazette*, trim, vigorous and outspoken at Board meetings. A lieutenant colonel in the Air Force Reserve, he wore his uniform back home on all possible occasions, complete with a chestful of medals won as a flying ace of the Korean and Vietnam wars—or so he said until his own newspapers exposed him as a phony and banished him. (He ultimately resurfaced as the publisher of a small paper in California).

At one time, the publishers who were Bureau directors endowed each other, only half jokingly, with titles of nobility. This was sometimes done in doggerel verse at Board meetings. Palmer Hoyt, the redoubtable "Duke of Denver" (where he was publisher and editor of the *Post*), delighted in conferring duchies and principalities upon his colleagues. He referred to Hale Steinman, publisher of the Lancaster, Pennsylvania papers, as the "Earl of Lancaster." (Steinman already was titled, since he never relinquished the use of his wartime rank of Colonel.)

Though all the publishers were conscious of their power within their own ducal domains, they varied considerably in the degree to which they publicly displayed their self-importance. Among these aristocrats there were levels of rank and different circles of intimacy. Partly, these groupings reflected their wealth and lineage, partly their ages, partly their past connections in the various associations and organizations of the newspaper business. (These connections in turn were linked to money, ancestry, and age.) Widely varying in their degrees of cultivation and sophistication, the publishers tended to congregate into social clusters that reflected a commonality of background, outlook, or intelligence.

They saw each other throughout the year at meetings of the Inland Daily Press Association, the Southern Newspaper Publishers Association, the Fédération Internationale des Editeurs de Journaux (FIEJ), the Inter-American Press Association, and a host of other occasions for business-related travel to agreeable sites.

They discussed politics rarely in terms of principles or theory, but rather as gossip they had picked up through their news departments about political personalities. For some, the most joyous occasions were the all-male gatherings at the semi-annual meetings the Bureau organized with the managements of the automotive companies in Detroit. Gin rummy and poker games went on far into the night. An occasional inebriated miscreant misbehaved at the black-tie dinners in Ford's corporate executive dining room. William Randolph Hearst, Jr. one evening provided unscheduled reminiscences of "Dad" and of escapades of his gilded youth in the company of the host, Henry Ford II. Amon Carter, Jr., the publisher of the *Fort Worth Star-Telegram*, on another occasion brought forth a notebook labeled "Texas Scratch Pad" on its embossed leather cover. A quarter of an inch thick, each of its pages was made up of four uncut $100 bills.

One publisher (the *Philadelphia Bulletin*'s Robert Taylor) was somewhat skeptical of the business value of contacts made at client dinners like the annual one the Bureau held for the Board of the Retail Merchants Association. "I usually draw two old, retired fellows who are loaded," he complained. Raleigh's publisher, Frank Daniels, Jr., was quick with an answer: "They keep asking for you."

The companies represented by the forty or fifty (the numbers varied depending on how many ex-chairmen and "graduate directors" were in attendance) directors of the Bureau accounted for a good two thirds of daily newspaper circulation, and the dozen members of the Executive Committee represented the elite of this elite.

Cooped up together for three or four days in an intimate social space at the fall Board meeting, it was difficult for the publishers to manifest their business antagonisms. At a time when the *Washington Star* was battling fiercely for survival, and stooping to savage the *Post*'s Katharine Graham in its gossip column, she and the *Star*'s owner, the Texas financier Joe Albritton, flew amicably off to the East together on a private plane from a remote meeting site in the Rockies.

In the 1960s, golf was the official sport at the fall meetings of the Bureau Board, and those few publishers who didn't play were definitely out at the social fringes. Some new directors were known to take golfing lessons to prepare themselves for the chores of office. By the 1970s, tennis moved up as a strong rival activity. The sporting triumphs of the day were a major subject of conversation at the cocktail parties that preceded dinner each night. But the real work of the newspaper business was also done within the intimate circles of discussion on these social occasions. Someone with an idea or a problem gathered a few congenial associates around him. Gradually the discussion would be extended to draw in those key individuals in the room who were close to the center of influence. At some point in the conversation it might be proposed that some specific action was indicated. And so the matter would be brought up before the Executive Committee and eventually find its way before the whole Board.

The Publishers at Dinner

"Friendship is what makes ANPA work and what makes newspapers work," Richard Johnson, the shrewd publisher of the *Houston Chronicle* (and chairman of ANPA, 1984–86), once told a convention audience. "No other medium has this attribute."

The Bureau of Advertising Dinner was, for many years, the social highlight of each ANPA Convention at the Waldorf. The directors, resplendent in white ties and tails, marched to the dais the Tuesday evening of Convention Week to the sound of "Pomp and Circumstance." After rousing performances of "Dixie" (accompanied by rebel yells from well-lubricated but unreconstructed members of the audience) and "The Battle Hymn of the Republic" by the West Point Glee Club or its Annapolis counterpart, the assembled newspaper executives and hangers-on were treated to an address by the President of the United States, the British Prime Minister, the Prime Minister of Canada, or perhaps an occasional Vice President or Secretary of State. Sometimes the spotlight was on nonpolitical luminaries, like Captain Eddie Rickenbacker, who, when summoned to say a few words, babbled on and on in alcoholic incoherence until he had to be pulled away from the microphone by main force. Aviation and space fascinated the Bureau's dinner program committees ever since the days of Amelia Earhart; they also honored the father of the Nazis' murderous V-2 rocket, Wernher von Braun, and the astronaut Alan Shepard, who was presented with a magnificent life-sized Boehm porcelain eagle, which slipped from his hands and was smashed on the floor in front of several thousand horrified guests.

Seating arrangements for these dinners were a matter of the most sensitive diplomacy. Publishers seated behind pillars or at tables with less than a full stage view sometimes resigned angrily from the Bureau in protest over their mistreatment. Although the hotel's charges became excessive for some of the membership to accept cheerfully, the dinners inevitably lost money. The Bureau's management and staff were delighted when the ANPA, in 1973, expressed a desire to take over this annual function. The usual speech by a leading world figure was replaced by a dinner dance augmented by a comedy act. Even the dinner dance finally gave way to the membership's desire for another free evening out on the town.

The management of such social events was only an incidental function for either the ANPA or the Bureau, but it was a far from trivial matter. For the staff of any membership organization, the task of maintaining the loyal support of constituents must always take primacy over all others, and social events are the most fundamental sources of that loyal support.

CHAPTER 2

Perceiving the Problem

No winged messenger arrived suddenly on the newspaper scene to announce that readership was now a problem. Recognition of its seriousness came as a series of minor insights rather than as a sudden revelation. The evolution of a plan of action took even longer.

Newspaper managements became aware that they faced a changed situation in the mid-1970s, as they saw their competitors and contemporaries failing and their own circulation numbers going down. From my vantage point, the story began with a subtle shift in the habits of readership as these were measured through the Bureau's research. To clarify this, I must explain how this research evolved in the first place.

Measuring Audiences

It started with the fierce rivalry of advertising media in the heyday of radio. Listening to radio and (later) watching TV were intangible and freely diffused experiences, while newspapers and magazines were sold to their readers, and the proceeds were highly tangible evidence of their popularity.

As part of the same burst of energy in the newspaper business that saw the creation of the Bureau of Advertising in 1913, the Audit Bureau of Circulations was formed two years later. Its purpose was to bring order into the chaotic sales reporting of all kinds of publications.

The ABC was ruled by a Board that represented advertisers, agencies, and newspaper and magazine publishers. Although newspapers paid most of the cost, it was the advertisers and agencies who dominated the Board and who determined policies and practices. The ABC carefully defined what was paid circulation and what was not; it conducted field audits to verify publishers' claims and statements independently. Thus it succeeded in making circulation measurements the solid foundation on which advertisers could calculate what they were getting in return for their investment and compare the figures reported for individual periodicals.

The advent of broadcasting changed the rules of the game. Broadcasting had no equivalent for circulation (although broadcasters have applied the term to measurements—like the number of households who tune in to a particular station at least once a month—that have no analogy whatsoever to print circulation). In the concept of "audience," broadcasting brought a new dimension to the measurement and comparison of media. Radio adopted the term to describe the number of people listening to any part of a given program or at a particular moment. The resulting numbers were inevitably much higher than the circulation figures for periodicals, since there might be a number of listeners to a radio set, just as there are generally several readers for every copy of a publication that someone has bought. The great mass magazines, particularly picture magazines like *Life* and *Look*, were commonly passed along from one family to another, and they generated many readers per copy. They could get credit for all these readers by adopting audience measurement techniques themselves. This made their statistics competitive with the large numbers produced by radio and later by television.

Audience research became the cornerstone of the whole American mass media system. Networks vie with each other for dominance in the ratings, even though their lead may totally lack statistical significance. Programs are cut off the air when their ratings drop. The fortunes of publications rise or fall along with their audience levels, which often show capricious and unaccountable variations from one survey period to the next.

The magazine audience surveys begun in the mid-1930s are still continuing. Advertising planners conventionally compare the total number of people who read an average issue of a publication with the number who watch or listen to a broadcast program or to a schedule of programs on which an advertiser's announcements are to appear.

A given issue of a publication will have more readers the less often that publication appears; the longer the interval between issues, the greater the opportunity to accumulate readers. A publication that is read by a high percentage of the public, like a typical newspaper in its own market, is less likely to be passed along to people who have not paid for it than a publication that is bought by only a minority of the public. As a result, the number of readers per copy is generally far less for a newspaper than for a magazine. Newspapers were therefore more resistant than magazines to accepting audience as a criterion of their size.

The meaning of audience measurements is in fact inherently different for newspapers than for other mass media. Magazines appeal to distinctive and limited publics, even when they achieve very wide readership. Broadcast programs, even when they are extremely popular, can garner only a minority of the viewers at one time, across the country or in an individual market. But newspapers have historically identified themselves with the fortunes of their local communities and with rare exceptions have sought to attract the broadest possible readership. Their political influence has depended on the universality of the newspaper reading habit; this has also been their basic selling point to advertisers.

The percentage of a market that any given newspaper covers inevitably reflects the degree of local competition that it faces. Even a newspaper with millions of readers like *The New York Times* was read on a given day in 1990 by only 23 percent of the adult public in the New York metropolitan area, and the *Los Angeles Times*, a paper of even larger size—and the only surviving metropolitan daily in the nation's second city—was read by 34 percent of the adults in metropolitan Los Angeles. By contrast, small town newspapers with concentrated circulations and little or no competition can generate a very high level of household coverage or "market penetration" (the ratio of circulation to the number of occupied dwelling units).

Newspapers provided a means by which an advertiser could reach masses of the public on a single day on a scale that no other medium could match. They blanketed their communities. Great magazines and the radio networks could also reach huge audiences, but no single issue of a magazine or any broadcast of a radio program could reach more than a fraction of the entire public. To compensate for this limitation, broadcast advertisers bought schedules in which messages were repeated and mass audience size was accumulated over time.

The advertising business had developed an insatiable demand for audience data. While magazines commissioned their own individual studies for many years, the agencies preferred to get all their data from a single source. This meant that interviews became much longer and the responses much less reliable. But media planners were eager for numbers to play with and tended to be more concerned with the acceptability of those numbers than with their accuracy. A number of organizations came into being to supply the needs of the magazine industry for syndicated audience research that appeared on a regular schedule and could be related to consumer buying habits. Several of these services also incorporated newspaper and television measurements.

The Daily Newspaper and Its Reading Public

By the time I joined the Bureau, audience had become a universal criterion in evaluating advertising media, and it was perfectly clear that newspapers would have to fall into step. One of my first projects was to launch a nationwide study of the newspaper audience, through the research firm of Audits & Surveys, Inc., which was widely respected for its statistical expertise.

This study was funded by the Newsprint Information Committee (NIC), a group of Canadian newsprint companies who had banded together in the late 1950s under the aegis of Hill & Knowlton, the public relations firm. Eventually the newsprint company managements were persuaded that they could sell more newsprint by stimulating the growth of newspaper advertising, but their original aim was simply to mend relationships with their principal customers, American newspaper publishers. They first approached the Bureau in 1959 to investigate what projects of mutual interest they might sponsor. By coincidence, a suitable proposal was ready to hand. It came from Raymond Bauer, a specialist in Soviet political communication who had transformed himself into the senior professor of advertising at the Harvard Business School. He was proposing an experimental study on the effects of repetition in newspaper advertising.[1] The results would presumably persuade national advertisers, who were becoming steadily more dependent on television, that they should use newspapers in sustained campaigns rather than for occasional promotional advertisements. At Lipscomb's urging, the NIC agreed to fund the project.

The field work was just beginning when I arrived in my new job. Analysis of this intricately designed study proceeded at a glacial pace. It was hampered by a continuing series of programming errors and malfunctions on the computer, which was brand new in its application to survey research. The delays threatened to destroy the whole NIC relationship. I insisted on getting tabulations by the tried and true mechanical method of the IBM countersorter. The results suggested that an advertiser would do better to run different ads than to show the same old ad over and over again. We put together an interim report and presented our conclusions (along with a very expensive steak luncheon at New York's Plaza Hotel) at a successful seminar that brought the Harvard team together with several dozen leading advertising researchers.

Meanwhile, as the newsprint executives grumbled impatiently for a final report from Harvard, I persuaded them to ante up funds for the national audience study that I felt had highest priority. I titled it "The Daily Newspaper and Its Reading Public."

Its principal innovation was the definition of a reader as someone who volunteered the information that he had last read a particular paper "yesterday." To ensure the study's acceptability to advertisers, we brought our research plan for review before the Technical Committee of the Advertising Research Foundation (ARF). Having formerly served on this Committee, I respected its work and felt that its seal of approval was essential.

Like the Audit Bureau of Circulations, the ARF represented the interests of media, advertisers, and agencies. (Research companies were admitted as regular members in 1967.) It was created in 1936, when the measurement of audiences had become a substantial enterprise, both for radio programs and for print. Competitive business pressures, the personal rivalries of researchers, and differing judgments about research methods all combined to create a need for agreement on technically acceptable standards and on procedures through which the standards might be applied in specific studies. Over the past half-century, the ARF has ventured into other areas of advertising research, such as copy testing and the measurement of effectiveness, but its principal preoccupation has continued to be the elusive subject of audience measurement.

The Mystery of the Shrinking Newspaper Audience

Our audience survey, released in 1961, found that 80 percent of adult Americans read a paper on a typical weekday. With these impressive data in hand, the Bureau made the near-universality of readership the basic theme of every sales presentation delivered to advertisers. A series of charts demonstrated the point that newspaper reading showed only minor variations by region and city size and even by age, income, and education, although the high audience figures were even higher at the upper income and educational levels.

Not all our information came from the reader survey. Another chart in the presentation showed the parallel upward growth of newspaper circulation and the population. In the years following World War II, newspaper circulation, daily and Sunday, enjoyed continuing growth as the population grew and as the national standard of living improved. The total population was, however, a poor index against which to measure newspapers, because the postwar baby boom had caused disproportionate growth in the juvenile age groups. Therefore, at the point when the two growth curves seemed to be moving farther apart, we changed our charts to show newspaper circulation keeping pace with the "active" adult population 21 to 64. (The voting age had not yet been lowered to 18. When it was, in 1971, we changed our definition of adults accordingly.) Because readership was somewhat lower among the increasing numbers of older people, including them would have altered the apparently steady balance of circulation and adult population growth.

In the course of charting these statistics year by year during the 1960s, we found that the growth of newspaper circulation had slowed down, while the number of households had continued to grow. As a result, newspapers' penetration levels had dropped. I was afraid that advertisers might perceive this as a loss of dynamism, a weakening of newspapers' hold over their readers. Partly the change could be explained, of course, by the fact that the average family was getting smaller. A household with fewer adults was less likely to be reading several papers a day and thus adding to the circulation totals.

But circulation was not the only yardstick. The critical measure —at least for national advertisers—was not the number of copies sold but the number of people reading—the audience. By that criterion, newspapers throughout the 1960s seemed to be doing as well as ever before.

The methods we had developed in our initial Audits & Surveys study eventually became accepted as standard throughout the newspaper business, as we shall see later. In 1967, the Simmons Market Research Bureau, which annually measured the audiences for magazines and television, began to ask about newspaper reading as well. They found levels of daily readership very close to those of our 1961 study.

Audits & Surveys repeated their first survey for us in 1963, and the results were similar to those of 1961. In 1971, we engaged them to repeat their research a third time. The initial findings seemed to suggest a weekday audience level some three percentage points below the SMRB figure of 78 percent, which had just been released. Was this a statistical aberration or a meaningful difference? My immediate assumption was that it was a fluke. My years as a practitioner had made me acutely aware of the human imponderables that made survey research something less than a precise science. The SMRB study used a very large sample, approximately 15,000 interviews. But it questioned people about a great variety of subjects, of which daily newspapers were only one. The Audits & Surveys study, with a sample of about 2,000, concentrated directly on newspaper readership and used a somewhat more rigorous measurement technique. In both these surveys, as is common in today's research, extensive statistical weighting procedures were used to bring the sample into line with what the Census described as the true characteristics of the population.

In an earlier era, George Gallup, Elmo Roper, and other pollsters seeking representative samples had used "quota" methods, by which interviewers were sent out with instructions to speak to specific numbers of men and women of designated ages and of particular social classes. The failure of the 1948 election polls to predict Harry Truman's victory caused a sudden surge in the use of "probability" sampling in market and opinion research. With probability sampling techniques, the individual household is pre-designated by a random selection method, as is the individual respondent. Nothing is left to the interviewer's judgment.

That at least is the way things work in theory. In practice, the interviews actually obtained rarely represent the perfect cross-section planned by the supervising statisticians. The difficulties sustained in the field work of the 1990 Census demonstrated the problems that interviewers encounter in getting cooperation from all sectors of the public. Some people are just easier to reach and more cooperative than others. The statisticians' solution is to compensate for the inadequacies of the fieldwork by adjusting the results so that harder-to-get respondents are represented in their proper proportion. This may be done through questions that allow the hard-to-get individuals to be identified, or it can be done simply by multiplying the answers from people whose characteristics identify them as underrepresented types.

"Sample balancing" by age, sex, income, or geography is much more easily managed in the computer era than it was in the past. Its aim is to restore the original probability sampling design; in practice this means that some respondents are given far more weight (even 100 times more!) than others. As a result, the percentages reported in poll results are generally not the percentages of responses from actual interviews but rather weighted percentages adjusted to compensate for the original variations in the completion rate.

The difference between the Audits & Surveys and Simmons results was a shade beyond the conventionally acceptable statistical tolerance that arises from the laws of chance. After some reflection and discussion with my colleagues, we came up with what we thought was the explanation. The A & S interviewers had carried in their kits copies of all newspapers whose circulations represented at least 5 percent of the number of households in each county where they worked. Thus, the study did not include readers of distant newspapers. For example, it had not counted exclusive readers of the *Wall Street Journal* (which then had a circulation of well over 1,000,000) or of the national edition of *The New York Times.*

The project was being supervised for Audits & Surveys by its executive vice-president, Lester Frankel, soon to be president of the American Statistical Association. Frankel was a brilliant, mild-mannered man with a staccato style of speech and a perpetual but genuine smile. He readily (though, in retrospect, somewhat uncomfortably) came to the conclusion that the deficiency we had uncovered might have deflated the results by as much as a percentage point and a half. This adjustment of the already adjusted findings raised the readership level from 75 percent to 76.5 percent. We could easily round the number off to 77 percent in our promotional applications of the research. This reduced the discrepancy between our survey and SMRB's 78 percent to a single percentage point—a relevantly innocuous difference.

The entire survey, like its predecessors, underwent review by the ARF Technical Committee, so all the adjustments had to be laboriously explained and argued. The advertiser and agency media research specialists who served on the Technical Committee were convinced of their validity, with the guidance of the ARF's technical director, Ingrid Kildegaard, a statistician of deceptively stern mien and unassailable integrity.

The Bureau's resulting sales presentation was called, "A Million Miles of Newspapers." (The title was based on our estimate of the aggregate length or width—I forget which—of all the newspaper pages in the hands of Americans each day.) The theme, as with "The Daily Newspaper and Its Reading Public," the slide show on the 1961 survey, was that newspaper reading was a universal and deeply engrained habit. Newspapers were read on any day by "nearly four out of five" people. (We had previously said proudly that it was "four out of five.") Yet while I went about the country enthusiastically putting on this presentation at breakfasts, luncheons, and cocktail parties for advertisers, I was uneasily conscious that the percentage was really closer to three out of four than to four out of five.

Newspapers and the Decline of Cities

An early warning signal had been sent out even before the circulation and readership figures began to turn down. The number of American daily newspapers was steadily dropping. Papers merged; papers failed. The abortive *New York World-Journal-Tribune* went under on April 24, 1966, a day when I was putting on a stock presentation on newspapers' "nearly universal readership" before a convention of the International Advertising Association. I added a requiem peroration for the departed newspaper, the victim of archaic labor practices. That it was, but I couldn't bring myself to add Charlie Lipscomb's blithe rationalization when newspapers went under: "This makes the business more profitable and stronger. It's going on in every kind of business today—weeding out the ones that can't make it."

The Newspaper Preservation Act was passed by Congress in 1970, in an effort to stave off further newspaper failures. It exempted competing papers from the antitrust laws, when at least one of them could prove that it was in danger of going under, and allowed them to set up joint operating agreements and agency arrangements. This meant that they could retain separate editorial products but combine their production and business operations to cut costs.

The problems were concentrated among afternoon papers, which were taking consistent circulation losses in most parts of the country, even though historically they had been dominant in some large markets. A variety of explanations were offered for this. Most obvious was competition from the early evening television news, which was extended over longer and longer time periods. Some observers thought that the long-term switch from a manufacturing to a service economy had shifted work schedules in the direction of nine to five and away from the factory worker's seven to four, thus leaving people less time for an evening paper. The great increase in the number of women at work added to the domestic burdens on men. With everyone busier, there was less time to read two papers a day, and the morning paper was the one most likely to be kept.

In big cities, afternoon papers always concentrated their circulation close in, while the morning papers could be distributed overnight to a broader territory. In my opinion, the major cause of the difficulties of afternoon papers was the change in the cities, which during the 1960s had been losing population to the suburbs and which were being transformed racially and in their social class composition.

Racial change in the cities was a subject to which I was personally sensitized. In 1951, I had directed a large-scale field study of troops in Korea and the United States, which prompted orders that finally desegregated the U.S. Army.[2] Three years later this was followed by the Brown decision of the U.S. Supreme Court, which desegregated the schools. The resulting rapid changes in urban school systems were blamed (perhaps not altogether incorrectly, as the evidence now indicates) for the steady flow of white families into segregated suburbs.

With the flight of the middle classes, black and white, American urban centers underwent massive changes that were absent in Canadian and European cities. Downtowns became deserted at the end of the workday, with hotels and theaters closed, storefronts boarded up, parking lots and weed-filled fields replacing abandoned buildings. Newspapers' prime advertising customers, the retailers, were deeply affected by these changes. A new breed of chain retailers based their growth on systematic study of real estate trends and concentrated on the development of new suburban shopping strips and malls. Traditional department stores were stuck with expensive property or long-term leases in deteriorating downtown locations.

I sketched the connections between newspapers' advertising health, the state of downtown urban retailing and the changing racial composition of the cities in a 1964 memorandum to Lipscomb. To get the publishers' attention, naturally, there had to be a direct sales angle. A "high-level two-day seminar on the marketing implications of downtown urban decay . . . would provide an opportunity for intimate social contact in the evening between the publishers and major retailers."

> The problems of urban decay have been of perennial interest to newspapers editorially, but they are also of vital importance to newspapers in their competitive fight against neighborhood weeklies, shoppers, mail circulars, and the electronic media. Yesterday I sat at lunch with newspaper people from Philadelphia and Cleveland who exchanged examples of how their established old-line

downtown department stores were folding and having their business taken away by suburban discounters who do relatively little advertising in newspapers. . . . The program would include both prepared papers and a considerable amount of open discussion.[3]

In addition to leading publishers and department store principals, the participants in the proposed seminar would include representatives of "the specialized academic disciplines which are concerned with various aspects of urbanism, ranging from architectural design to juvenile delinquency" and a handful of municipal, state and federal officials.

This proposal received a mixed reaction from the Bureau's directors, to whom Lipscomb referred it. Gene Robb, publisher of Hearst's Albany newspapers (and later chairman of ANPA in 1964–66), called it "an eminently desirable project" and added, "I especially like the idea of identifying local newspaper leadership with a constructive program of civic improvement."[4] In contrast, the publisher of the *Buffalo Evening News*, James Righter, was unenthusiastic: "Frankly I would not want to attend a conference with several of our top retailers. It is dangerous enough on the golf course for four hours with one of them!"[5]

In the absence of strong publisher support, my proposal was shelved, but not my concern. As the civil rights movement gathered force in the South, the problems of Northern cities became even more visible. Three years later, I revived the idea with a presentation to the Board, charting the trends that made the subject urgent. Again I proposed a conference, this time scaled down to about forty participants "from the very highest levels."[6] A key sequence of questions for discussion was: "Is downtown worth saving? Realistically, can it be saved? What steps, if any, can be taken to save it?" I now felt it was important to be candid about the real purpose.

> Although my original proposal suggested a meeting which would be largely aimed at getting publishers and their big retail customers together, I now think that this promotional purpose would be secondary to the real objective of the conference. We have in the last dozen years seen too many deaths of big downtown stores and big-city newspapers to assume that the problem of urban survival is something that ought to be talked about merely for advertising sales promotion purposes.[7]

The reaction at the Board meeting was unenthusiastic at best. An unreconstructed small-city publisher from the deep South said gleefully, "It's just fine with us that all the niggers are leaving the South and coming up to live with you guys in the North. We like that real fine!" Ed Wheeler, general manager of the *Detroit News*, commented with greater dignity, "We've looked into this problem, and we've decided there's nothing that can be done about it." (This was one year before the great Detroit riots.) The general manager of the *Los Angeles Times*, a tough former meat-packing executive named Robert Nelson, said, "We don't have this problem in Los Angeles." (This was two years before Watts.) But the Board chairman, Gordon Strong, publisher of the *Canton Repository*, had the final word after Lipscomb nervously explained that the presentation was the product of my sociological training: "What we need is less sociology and more selling!"

Several directors took the trouble to amplify their comments in letters sent after the meeting. Wheeler wrote that my proposal "is a few years too late," and "I don't believe it is a proper function of the Bureau."[8] Nelson said that

> there is no question but what the metropolitan areas are faced with growing deterioration, but—I do not think there is a thing the Bureau of Advertising can do to stem the tide. Most of the large retail establishments appear to be taking the attitude of moving the mountain to Mohammed so to speak—planning new locations where population shifts are expected to take place. Metropolitan newspapers are going to have to be similarly flexible and far-sighted. . . . What I am really saying, Leo, is that although the urban problems are very real they can also afford great opportunities for the far-sighted merchants —and publishers.[9]

I told Lipscomb that the Board's response to my idea left me

> disappointed and at moments distressed . . . I don't believe it is possible to discuss so serious a subject in so brief a time with all the resulting temptation to be frivolous, but apart from that I don't feel that I effectively registered that the number one reason why newspapers should sponsor such a conference is to assume leadership in coping with a problem that nobody wants to touch. The decay at the heart of our big cities . . . has already hit hard at the downtown department and specialty shops which provide the metropolitan newspapers' economic base. This decay also threatens the reader-

ship and the very function of metropolitan dailies as the editorial voices of communities that are real to the people who inhabit them.

The discussion, I said, revealed to me that "(1) there is a great lack of interest on the part of some smaller papers in the problems the big cities face; (2) among some of the Directors from big cities there is a tendency to think of every city's problems as unique; and (3) there is a feeling of hopelessness as to whether these problems can be solved. I am in strong disagreement with all three of these premises." But I added, "I don't believe the Bureau should take on any project which arouses strongly controversial reactions from our Board."[10]

Although the sense of urgency and of common cause may have been absent among newspaper publishers in 1967, the rejection of my conference proposal reflected an underlying assumption that might have been expressed no differently at a later time when the adverse consequences of urban change were better recognized. This assumption was that the Bureau should stick to its primary task, the sale of advertising, and leave to other, wiser, or at least more appropriately designated organizations the task of coping with the underlying conditions that made the sale of advertising possible. This point of view, which still prevails, holds that institutions can always go out and find the talent required to pursue their missions, but that they should not modify their missions to fit the agendas of the individuals who staff them. This is a reasonable position, but the character of institutions is inseparable from that of their personnel; institutions survive by modifying their objectives as managements perceive the need to do so.

Preaching to the Business

It was nine years before I returned to the theme of racial change in the cities, in an address to the ANPA. In the meantime, however, I began to intersperse references to the trends in circulation and readership among the usual charts on advertising revenue trends in my presentations to the Bureau's Board of Directors.

There was a logical reason for this. Newspapers' share of advertising was going down minutely but steadily year after year, from 30.8 percent of the grand total in 1960 to 29.5 percent in 1975.[11]

This decline was not surprising, since they had started out with a very high share of the advertising market and had no place to go except down as other media came along.

Newspapers were also becoming progressively less economical by the yardstick of cost-per-thousand. Partly this reflected the escalation of their advertising rates, as they faced mounting costs of newsprint, energy, and labor and keener appetites for profit. Even if rates stayed the same, cost-per-thousand would go up when a paper delivered fewer readers in its market. It appeared crystal clear that the continued prosperity of newspaper advertising depended upon a restoration of readership to its former levels. Advertisers' confidence would be shaken when they became aware that the public's reliance on newspapers had diminished. The political and civic influence of the press was bound to suffer as impressions of its failing vitality spread. On a personal note, my sentimental attachments to newspapers went back to my childhood, and I felt bad to see them losing ground. Probably most important, I wanted to feel myself part of a successful enterprise; its weakness somehow reflected on me.

My presentations to the Board of Directors incorporated the growing evidence from audience surveys that showed a particularly sharp drop in newspaper readership in large cities and among young people. They tracked the fall in the regularity or frequency of reading and in the proportion of people who read more than one paper a day. To maintain the attention of the Directors, the presentations used cartoons to enliven the tedious progression of statistical tables.

Charts showed the changing nature of the workforce and of the American household as well as the movement of people from cities to suburbs. More and more young people were pulling up stakes; they found it increasingly difficult to identify with the community in which they lived and whose affairs the local paper reported. Our surveys showed sharp changes in their values and reading interests.

The decline of the cities had intensified the problems of newspaper distribution. It was harder to recruit carriers. Collecting money from delinquent subscribers became more difficult. There were fewer newsstands and candy stores where newspapers were sold. Vending racks were pilfered and vandalized.

My warnings of the dangers of further declines in newspaper

reading were not just directed to the publishers on the Bureau Board. With some trepidation—since I was spending most of my time preaching the doctrine of newspaper strength to advertisers —I began to take them public. I sounded the same theme in convention addresses to editors, circulation managers and promotion executives and discovered that I was echoing some of their own concerns. At the same time, I began to venture beyond the limits of reporting bad news in order to suggest some remedial measures. In July 1974, I told the ICMA annual conference:

> Many of you feel that the real problem of building circulation is one of assuring delivery and improving service. I agree that this is vital. But my own analysis of the trends in readership leads me to the conclusion that our problem is not merely one of getting the paper to the reader, but of making him feel that when he has it he has something of value. Value to me means that there is something in it that he doesn't get from the television news. Value means that it is worth the increased cost he has to pay for it. Value means that although he has more demands on his time, the newspaper still represents an essential guide for his daily life.

I went on to list a series of issues the industry faced, in being editorially responsive "to the changed outlook of the people who will be running this country ten and twenty years from now," in attracting minority readers, in responding to the new role of women, and in keeping up with an increasingly sophisticated public. I called for intensive study of "case histories of success and failure," for a heavier investment in Newspaper in Education programs, for more promotion and for "more high-level attention from newspaper managements" for the circulation function. This was hardly a plan of action, but it was a step in the direction of producing one.

The Television Information Office/Roper Surveys

Editors and publishers were being confronted with yet another imposing and growing body of dismaying statistics. They came from a series of studies made for the Television Information Office by The Roper Organization, a research company with whose principals I had a long personal association. They showed television overtaking and widening its lead over newspapers as the public's primary source of news. The studies had been initiated in 1959, at a time when the television industry was under attack in the wake of a scandal over rigged quiz shows and Congressional investigations of its violent programming. The initial survey dealt largely with matters that related to television's problems with the government and the public. The question comparing TV and newspapers as sources of news was added almost as an afterthought.

Over the years, as the question was repeated and other questions comparing the media were added, the trend of opinion in television's favor became more pronounced. The research became a competitive sales tool that was heavily used by television advertising salesmen as proof of newspapers' waning effectiveness. Curiously, the findings were given wide publicity by the press itself. They were frequently cited by the officials of a series of federal administrations and became part of the conventional wisdom in Washington. In the process, the original figures were often transformed and reinterpreted in a way that overstated newspapers' losses. For example, Roper found in 1986 that 66 percent of the public claimed that television was their main source of news about what was going on in the world, while 36 percent percent named newspapers and 14 percent, radio. (Fourteen percent volunteered more than one source.) Soon afterward, these findings were misinterpreted in an advertisement placed by the International Paper Company to promote newspaper reading. Over the signature of television newscaster Walter Cronkite, it announced that "65 percent of the public now get 100 percent of their news from television." This statement appeared destined to become a source for innumerable future citations.

In my role as public defender of newspapers I dutifully critiqued the Roper studies when they first appeared, in a memorandum prepared for release to the trade press. But my reservations about the validity of the question wording could not negate the fact that those same questions had been asked year after year by a reputable research organization and showed an unmistakable shift in response. I therefore warned editors and publishers, "The trend is real." The Roper studies thus reinforced the declining circulation and readership figures, and the failure of metropolitan dailies, to create a growing concern about the future of newspapers.

Batten

When I first began to intrude the topic of readership into my reports to the Bureau Board on the state of the advertising market, I was somewhat apprehensive about how the message would be received. No one likes to hear bad news. As salesmen of newspaper advertising, our task at the Bureau was to be optimistic and positive. My grave diagnosis hardly accorded with this stance. Frank Batten, our chairman (1972–74), assured me that publishers were grownups and could take bad medicine. Professionally, moreover, they wanted to know the facts.

Batten himself typified the kind of publisher who had dominated the Bureau Board when I first joined the organization but who was fast becoming a minority. His newspapers in Norfolk, Virginia, were the flagship of what became Landmark Communications, a media conglomerate that encompassed daily papers in seven other cities,[12] plus weeklies, television and radio stations, cable systems, and the cable Weather Channel network.

A courtly, earnest, trim Virginia gentleman of the old school, Batten eventually was elected by his peers to the chairmanship of the Associated Press, an honor awarded to his personal distinction rather than to his political prowess. He represented the third generation of his family to be publishers of the Norfolk newspapers. Like others of his breed, he had been born not only to wealth, but to power—in the city and in the state. It was this sense of the political power that went with the title that made publishers more attached to their newspapers than to their broadcasting or other properties that were often the source of much greater profit.

Batten's privately owned Landmark Communications stood somewhat midway in the process by which the nineteenth century independent newspaper, established by entrepreneurial initiative, was being transformed into a communications empire. The nation's three greatest newspapers, *The New York Times*, the *Washington Post*, and the *Los Angeles Times*, had all branched forth into broadcasting, had acquired magazines and other newspapers, and had entered into other types of publishing. All were the property of family dynasties reincarnated as publicly owned corporations but with corporate structures devised with different classes of stock to ensure control by the original family.

From Family Business to Public Corporation

Not every newspaper-publishing family has been able to maintain harmony and an unbroken tradition from one generation to the next. The recent history of the American press abounds with instances of dissension and sometimes of bitter acrimony between siblings (Morris Communications, with newspapers in the deep South; Field Newspapers in Chicago; Horwitz Newspapers, based in Ohio, and the Bingham Newspapers in Louisville) or cousins (Cowles Media in Minneapolis and Cowles Newspapers in Des Moines).

Continuity of ownership was maintained even in several notable cases where fathers and sons were estranged.[13] These family battles often took on the character of high drama and were sometimes the subject of sensational articles in the press (especially in the newspapers that were themselves the spoils of the struggle). While there was no lack of gossip about such matters when publishers met, at the height of the action the protagonists themselves were commonly addressed as though everything were perfectly normal. As public personalities, most were skilled at feigning nonchalance.

In many cases, the proliferation of interests among a growing number of heirs prompted a family decision to sell out and take the cash. Zest and aptitude for a publishing career are not transmitted in the genes. Inheritance taxes sometimes forced extended families to liquidate properties whose multiple owners had other interests. These pressures to sell coincided with an incredible escalation in the market value of newspapers and television stations. Surviving dailies became all the more valuable as their competitors dropped by the wayside.

The growth of the chains and giant media companies followed inexorably. A comparatively small number of these companies competed aggressively for the newspapers that became available in single-ownership markets at the same time that huge money-losing second papers in big cities scrambled to find new owners.

The fantastic prices (up to $4,650 a unit of circulation) that Gannett, Times Mirror, and others were willing to pay in part reflected the bullish temper of the stock market, since most of these companies were publicly owned and in a number of cases concluded their deals in exchange for stock certificates rather than cash. In a business world where to stand still was to lose ground, expansion and acquisition were the essential rules of the game. Such activities required capital and propelled companies into public ownership.

In the cases of the Chicago Tribune (the Tribune Company) and the Gannett chain, the original family interests were fractionated, so that these companies went public with an already diversified ownership and a professional management firmly in control. John (Jack) and James (Jim) Knight had no heirs to whom they wished to entrust their newspapers, but the Ridders had an abundance of them. When the two groups merged as a public company, Ridders stayed on as publishers in Long Beach and San Jose and for a while in St. Paul and at the *Journal of Commerce*. (In 1990, Anthony Ridder, a grandson of the founding patriarch, headed the company's newspaper division.)

The growth of the publicly held newspaper chains meant that independent publishers and representatives of family dynasties occupied fewer seats on the Bureau's Board of Directors. A growing proportion of directors were self-made professional managers who had worked their way to the top on their own abilities.

In 1990, a third of the daily circulation of the American press was accounted for by publicly held companies. It is as difficult to generalize about their management styles as about those that prevail under private ownership. The best of the traditional independent publishers exemplified all the classic virtues of a hereditary aristocracy; others revealed ineptitude or eccentricity. Joe Knowland, the last of his clan to be publisher of the *Oakland Tribune*, was an actor who enjoyed appearing in his plant in disguise and under various aliases, speaking in exotic accents to confound members of his staff.

Under the reign of George Hearst, Jr., a grandson of the fabulous William Randolph Hearst, circulation of the *Los Angeles Herald Examiner* plummetted from 731,000 to 347,000 after a disastrous strike and labor boycott. Having turned his plant into a fortress protected by armed guards, he retreated into a penthouse office that could be reached only by a catwalk over a roof. There he once confided to me, "Do you want to see my marketing plan? Here's my marketing plan." It turned out to be a copy of that morning's *Los Angeles Times* marked to show off the ads that were not being carried by his own paper. He explained, "I ask my salesmen, 'Why didn't we get this one? Why didn't we get that one?' " On another occasion, when we assembled a half dozen of the leading retailers in Los Angeles for a sales presentation, Hearst had to be introduced to most of them for the first time, although they were his principal customers. They moved in different social circles.

Among the major newspaper organizations, four consistently stayed under private ownership, but of these only the Newhouse empire was truly run as a family business, with members of the clan ensconced at the power centers from an early age. A Hearst, a Scripps, and a Cox (by descent) were chairmen of their respective companies,[14] and family members popped up in various positions, even as publishers. But for the most part these companies were run by able executives who had made their way up through the ranks.

Alvah Chapman, then chairman of Knight-Ridder, once told the business managers of Scripps-Howard Newspapers (before their company went public) that the only difference between the way he ran his company and the way they ran theirs was that he spent an enormous amount of time answering questions from security analysts. That may have been true in Chapman's case. A Citadel graduate and a World War II flying ace, he was the very model of military rectitude, with a mind so disciplined and methodical that one could virtually hear it tick. (He could flip rapidly through a bookful of financial information and point to a discrepancy between the numbers on page 43, column 5, row 6 and those on page 27, column 2, row 4.) His route to the corner office was by way of the comptroller's department, but perhaps because he was the son of a newspaper publisher he had a deep sensitivity to the prime importance of the newspaper's editorial quality and integrity. This concern was shared by the heads of three other publicly owned newspaper organizations that remained under the control of their founding families: The New York Times Company's Arthur Ochs ("Punch") Sulzberger, the Washington Post

Company's Katharine (Kay) Graham, and Times-Mirror's Otis Chandler—all the products of a patrician upbringing in which the dignity of the publisher's office was taught to succeeding generations as pervasively and unobtrusively as in the education of a future King of England.

The Pressure for Profit

The head of any publicly owned newspaper company automatically faced a conflict between an inculcated sense of responsibility to the community or the reading public and a responsibility to the stockholders. The independent newspaper publisher was often no less eager to maximize profit, but generally he was not in need of ready money. To preserve the institution he could afford to think long range. Besides, an improvement in quality might provide the publisher with deeper, nonfinancial satisfactions: an awareness of accomplishment, the admiration of associates and of the public.

An investment in the product could take a long time to pay off, but it would eventually be justified. The most commonly cited illustration of this principle was the decision by *The New York Times*'s Arthur Hays Sulzberger to turn down advertising during wartime paper rationing in order to maximize the amount of news coverage. The *New York Herald Tribune* took all the advertising it could, lost ground to the *Times,* and finally went under after years of struggle.

During the years of the bull market on Wall Street, corporate managements were impelled to maximize current earnings as a way of boosting the price of the stock. Stockholders might be less motivated by the need for dividends than by the desire for long-term appreciation. The price of stock not only was the accepted index of management's success, but also could represent a large part of its compensation. Growth targets were set and achieved in a variety of ways: by acquiring additional properties, expanding sales, cutting costs, and raising prices. In a period of general inflation, price increases occurred almost automatically among all advertising media, at a rate that generally exceeded the changes in the consumer price index or the rates at which advertisers were marking up their own products.

Precisely because of newspapers' unique suitability for certain kinds of advertising, their customers found it hard to find alternatives. As local competition among dailies dwindled, newspapers acquired an even tighter hold. Not surprisingly, therefore, between 1965 and 1975, newspaper advertising rates went up 67 percent while consumer prices overall increased 74 percent. Between 1975 and 1990, newspaper rates were up 253 percent, consumer prices, 141 percent.

To some degree, of course, these increases reflected such factors as the cost of newsprint (up 94 percent between 1965 and 1975 and another 163 percent between 1975 and 1990). These costs were somewhat offset by the labor-saving technical innovations in typesetting that newspapers introduced during the same period. In practice, rate increases were in many cases being set by the publisher's profit objectives. Each year's budget was prepared with the previous year's as a base. "Excess fat" was trimmed with much anguish and travail, unavoidable additions were factored in, and revenue estimates were made based on the business outlook and on current rates for advertising and circulation. The shortfall between expected net income and the targeted objective was then met by rate increases, with the advertising and circulation departments haggling over the details of how the burden would be shared.

Since public companies reported their earnings quarterly, their management focus tended to be on the here and now of the "bottom line." Publishers who worked for publicly owned companies felt the fire at their fannies at every moment. One, faced with a serious local business recession, told his group management, "I'm not going to be able to meet my profit goal this quarter." He was told, "That's not one of your options." Even in privately held companies, management bonuses were often based on quarterly earnings performance, so the short-run mentality prevailed there as well.

Perhaps, as has been charged, this narrow perspective was fostered by the prevailing orientation of the graduate business schools. The doctrine of management by objective defines and reduces tasks to measurable minutiae, to the point where the broader vision of the enterprise fades from view. But whatever the reasons, a concentration on the immediate rewards inevitably entails an attrition in the willingness to plan and invest for the long term, when the outcome of planning and the return on investment are not clearly apparent. In the technical realm, for example, newspapers were willing to invest millions of dollars in new presses that could produce a more attractive and colorful product and boost their advertising revenues. They invested millions in computers and mailroom equipment, because the cost savings could be precisely calculated. But no such precision was possible in reckoning the return from investments in editorial quality, in manpower, in promotion, in services, in systems. It is precisely in these areas that great newspapers are different from undistinguished ones.

If I hoped to get publishers to shift their perspective from short-term profit to long-term survival, one recurring question was what a reasonable long-term planning horizon should be. In a business that produced a daily product, long term might mean the day after tomorrow.

This was well illustrated by the effort to establish a system for satellite transmission of advertising, first proposed to us by the Associated Press when it was switching its news service to this method to escape mounting telephone line charges. The idea was to send advertisements over the air from a central location to all the papers on an advertiser's schedule, eliminating the cumbersome, time-consuming and expensive practice of sending out production materials by mail or express services.

With much enthusiastic support from the Bureau, the matter was taken up in 1980 by the ANPA Telecommunications Committee. For a feasibility study, they turned to a management consulting firm, the Boston Consulting Group (BCG). In traditional form, BCG sent in a team of recently minted MBAs who interviewed a number of us at the Bureau along with agency and client executives, read our memoranda on the subject, and produced an impressively bound report complete with flow charts. Their conclusion was that a satellite ad transmission system could not be "cost-justified" over a ten-year period.

When the report was orally presented to the Committee, I asked the head of the consulting team whether he thought such a system would be in place by the year 2010. "No question it will be," he said. I asked whether planning for it should start in 2009, and if earlier, when. The reply was waffled. Of course my real concern was that the field, with its potential control over billions of dollars of advertising revenues, would be taken over by others whose interests might not be congenial with those of newspapers. (A company called Ad/Sat was established by the British media tycoon Robert Maxwell for the purpose in 1985 and proceeded to lose a fair amount of money, as projected.)

Of course every investment decision involves this kind of ambiguity about timing. In the case of newspapers the question was especially murky because the advertising payout would come from what the business did collectively through the investment decisions of all the diverse and uncoordinated managements of individual papers.

The Fear of Collaboration

It may seem perfectly normal for executives of different newspapers to get together just as executives of other businesses do, but newspaper executives were especially wary of the antitrust laws. Rate wars and circulation wars have recurred throughout the entire history of the American press. Advertisers had a tendency to cluster in the most successful newspaper in a market, thus widening its lead and encouraging the creation of local press monopolies that were strongly contrary to the advertisers' own self-interest. Extreme and sometimes cutthroat competition might tend to make newspaper publishers wary of venturing into collaborative efforts. So, curiously, might the opposing fear of government intervention to prevent collusive trade practices.

In spite of the camaraderie that prevailed at newspaper industry meetings, there was a strong concern to avoid any appearance of collusion in restraint of trade. Orville Dryfoos, publisher of *The New York Times* from 1961 to 1963, walked out of a Bureau Board of Directors meeting when the subject of advertising rates came up in the discussion. From time to time, other publishers threatened to do so, on the advice of counsel. This traditional inhibition against common effort presented a serious hindrance to the solution of newspapers' common problems.

Advertising Dimension Standards

One such problem was the difficulty that advertisers faced with the mechanics of placing ads in papers with different physical dimensions. Newspaper publishers prided themselves on being loners. They cherished their autonomy. This tradition of independence had well served the cause of editorial integrity, but it had not always worked to the business advantage of the press. Because each paper always wanted its own distinctive typographic look, there was great diversity in those elements of their appearance that affected advertisers. Newspapers had always acquired presses and composing equipment from different manufacturers and laid out their papers in different ways. Individuality in type faces, layout, and general design was as much a source of pride as the editorial features that made each paper unique.

Such individuality of formats became more noticeable as newspaper technology underwent tremendous changes in the 1960s and 1970s. Type was set and pages were made up on the computer. Letterpress printing, as initiated by Gutenberg and Caxton, was giving way to the offset process, which promised better reproduction quality, especially for color. While there had long been a difference between broadsheet and tabloid papers, now there were both broadsheets and tabloids of startlingly different dimensions.

After the oil crisis of 1973, the cost of paper went up, since energy is a significant component in its manufacture. There were periods when newsprint was in short supply, making publishers more eager than ever to conserve it. Specialists at the ANPA reckoned that widening the page and increasing the number of columns made for more economical use of paper. Fewer pages could be used to publish the same number of words; waste space in the form of margins and gutters would be kept to a minimum. However, the opposite philosophy eventually prevailed, with papers reducing the width of the page and thus the number of columns. Some papers, like *The New York Times*, left the traditional eight-column format for six wider columns, while others, like the *Chicago Tribune*, increased the number of columns from eight to nine. It was relatively simple for publishers to order newsprint in different size rolls than formerly in order to shrink or expand page width. They were unlikely to do anything about the length of the page, because this depended on the diameter of the cylinder used in the presses.

The proliferation in the variety of publishing formats created genuine problems for any advertising agency that wanted to place the same ad in many newspapers. Ads could be forced into a space that was too small by cropping them, or they could be "floated" in a space that was too big, with white space above and below. They could be reshaped to fit any desired dimensions through the use of an anamorphic lens, but this distorted the illustrations. It was an expensive matter to prepare ads to fit papers of different sizes to make sure that the proper mechanical requirements were being met and to see that the right reproduction proofs were sent to each paper on the advertiser's list. The added cost of preparing a newspaper campaign discouraged advertising business and worked against newspapers' financial interests.

The problem was a perennial topic of discussion in the mid-1970s at the semiannual joint meetings of the INAME and the American Association of Advertising Agencies' Newspaper Committee. The agency specialists who made up the Newspaper Production Committee of the AAAA had come up with proposals for standardization that were not acceptable to all the technicians on the newspaper side.

With growing clamor for action on an industry-wide scale, a joint committee of the Bureau and ANPA Boards was set up to find a solution; its chairman was Otto Silha, the publisher of the *Minneapolis Star* and *Tribune*. It was unusual for the two boards to collaborate in this fashion, but the subject overlapped the Bureau's advertising jurisdiction and the ANPA's production capabilities. A technical solution proposed by the ANPA Research Institute[15] was eventually adopted by the committee. The proposal became the Advertising Dimension Standards—a term selected because it made the useful acronym "ADS." The scheme set up a limited number of standard ad formats that could be accepted by six-, eight-, or nine-column newspapers and by tabloids. Each ad of a given size could now be prepared in only two or three versions instead of in many formats and with a risk of distortion.

The effort broke ground in that it asked newspapers to change their ways in the common interest. As an interested party, the Bureau had shifted its role from that of merely selling what the papers chose to sell; it was now actively engaged in getting them to do something that the advertisers wanted. My own primary concern was to get the necessary clearances and agreements and then to communicate what had to be done both to the newspapers and to the advertisers and agencies. The real test was whether newspapers would be willing to do what we asked them. Although they still had the option of using their own individual ad units as well as those of the ADS system, the conversion involved a substantial expenditure of effort. Remarkably, most publishers fell into line, albeit with some hesitation.

The ADS was, however, short-lived. At the time it was created, most of the big papers were still using the hot metal process of stereotyping lead half-cylinders from cardboard mats formed by pressure against a metal page of type and engravings. Since mats shrank, the printed page was not exactly the same size as the original made-up page. More and more papers switched to a new process in which plastic plates were prepared photographically from pasted-up pages with type set on the computer. This meant that different newspaper sizes and formats continued to multiply and that the ADS standards fast became obsolete. A few years later (in 1984), the ANPA and the Bureau[16] moved to create Standard Advertising Units that would fit every newspaper and finally lead to a standard sized newspaper page. This made newspapers more like magazines in consistency of format and provided advertisers with uniform dimensions.

The willingness of newspapers to work together to standardize advertising units laid the groundwork for further cooperation in other areas. The painfully extended discussions required to achieve consensus among strong-willed individualists were a prelude to those we were to encounter in the Readership Project.

My work on the ADS project forged a close working relationship with Silha. Our discussions of ad standardization generally ended in talk of a more critical subject, the decline in readership.

Silha

The industry had to act, but there was no mechanism in place through which action could be channeled. The need for such an agency was clearly perceived by Silha, who became vice chairman of the Bureau in 1975. Two years earlier he had alerted me to his hunch that the readership declines we were noting might be more than a statistical aberration.

Year by year, the circulation of the evening *Star* kept going down, though at one time it had been the dominant paper in Minneapolis. Silha asked his staff to compile the circulation figures for every large metropolitan newspaper, based on the semiannual flash reports issued by the ABC. He showed me these figures in great confidence, almost surreptitiously, although they were actually all about to be published and placed in the public domain. They showed an unmistakable pattern of losses for the big city afternoon dailies. The details were masked when total national circulation trends were compared from one year to the next. The pattern had not as yet shown up in audience surveys.

Silha's boss, John Cowles, Jr., was in the third generation of his family to own and run newspapers in Minneapolis. In the mid-1970s, his venerable father was still an imposing presence at management meetings within the paper, though he had long since stopped going to national conventions and meetings. John, Jr. was somewhat withdrawn and shy, but he was urbane, highly intelligent, literate, and charming. Exhibiting an impulse not uncommon in those born to great wealth, he was eager to show what he could do on his own and took steps to expand his company into a communications empire. Silha, his confederate in this enterprise, began his newspaper career as a campus reporter at the University of Minnesota and moved on into the newspaper's promotion department. As promotion manager, he was elected president of the Newspaper Promotion Association, which put him on the national scene. He moved up to become general manager and then publisher. At one point Silha and Cowles exchanged titles as president and chairman, respectively, of Cowles Media.

Like a number of other newspaper managements, these men were looking beyond their hometown to wider horizons. The considerable earnings of the Cowles newspapers and their broadcasting stations were plowed into the acquisition of interests in other enterprises. The first was *Harper's* magazine, in which John, Jr. took a particular interest. There he became embroiled in a highly publicized conflict with the editor, Willy Morris. The company also acquired half ownership of the book publisher Harper & Row and interests in a number of small market research and sales promotion businesses (none of which proved successful). In 1979 Cowles Media bought a number of cable systems and the *Buffalo Courier-Express*, which had to be folded after three years in defiance of the prevailing trend in favor of morning papers. Not long after the Buffalo debacle, Cowles was deposed by his board of directors, a majority of whom were family members.

While all this was going on, great editorial experimentation was under way at the ailing *Minneapolis Star* with heavy reliance on readership research. A new, mathematically oriented research director, William Miller, sold the editors on the idea that every article in the paper could be evaluated in terms of its yield in readers-per-inch, as measured by surveys. Formulas developed on this basis could be used to reduce the amount of space "wasted" on articles that aroused low levels of interest. (By contrast, my own research indicated that items with low general readership were sometimes of passionate interest to a minority, and the newspaper's overall attraction was the sum of its appeal to many small constituencies.) Stephen Isaacs, the former director of the *Los Angeles Times-Washington Post* News Service, was later brought in as editor of the *Star*. He transformed it into a kind of daily magazine, drastically changing its makeup and apparently alienating faithful old readers in the effort to attract new ones. (In 1982, Minneapolis became a one-newspaper town.)

Silha was a perpetual enthusiast, an indefatigable organizer and mobilizer and caller-to-action. When I introduced him to the INAE convention in Los Angeles (where he was awarded an honorary life membership), I cited his favorite aphorism, that these were "perilous times."

> This Renaissance man can rattle off the vital statistics on every player and team in big and not so big time baseball and football. But though he has an eye for minutiae, his vision is long range. His motto is "Nothing is simple," but his forte is to reduce complex problems to simple and therefore manageable terms. He has a million ideas, many of them pretty good, a thousand enthusiasms, and a lot of laughs.[17]

For many years Silha had devoted much of his limitless energy to the larger cause of the newspaper business, which he loved with a passion. He saw the decline in readership and circulation not merely as something that affected his own newspapers; it was a cancer that could destroy the whole business, and something had to be done about it on a grand scale.

The changes in reading habits were no longer a secret that could be kept inside the closet of the newspaper world. With a note of urgency, the pollster George Gallup wrote to one of Silha's associates:[18]

> I will regard it as a great personal favor if you will look over the enclosed confidential document and give us the benefit of your thinking about how newspapers should deal with the problem presented in the report. The report itself notes that a sharp decrease in the number of adults who read newspapers has been recorded. This is the first time since 1957 that an important change in newspaper readership has been found. The situation is serious enough in our opinion to warrant an aggressive and continuing program to combat the downward trend.

The proportion telling the Gallup Poll that they read a newspaper "yesterday" had dropped from 68 percent in 1973 to 63 percent in 1976.

By this time, Silha was already in high gear. He periodically reminded his fellow directors of the Bureau that all my analyses of the readership problem were being done "off the corner of the desk." He invited me to a meeting of Cowles executives[19] at which the industry's problems were discussed with uncommon candor, and followed this with a letter to the *Boston Globe*'s John Taylor and Knight-Ridder's Derrick Daniels:[20]

> Where do we go from here? I guess I come back to Leo's general concept that we have most of the research in hand and what we need now is action. I think we should try to get 10 to 15 newspaper organizations to agree on $100,000 a year for three years. Perhaps $50,000–$60,000 of that would be spent on local readership research, mainly directed to before and after readings on changes in editorial style or features or emphasis or whatever. The remainder would be allocated to national research to aid the signal calling, perhaps with Leo as the focal point.

Smith

When Silha assumed the chairmanship of the Bureau in 1977, his opposite number as chairman and president of the ANPA was a temperamentally most dissimilar man. As a young Army officer in World War II, Joe D. Smith, Jr. had married Jane Jerraud, whose family owned the Alexandria, Louisiana, *Daily Town Talk*, a newspaper of about 40,000 circulation. Like Silha, who was active in Minneapolis civic affairs and had been a regent at the University of Minnesota, Smith was a formidable political force in Louisiana and was a regent of the state university. He had resisted suggestions that he run for the U.S. Senate, of which he no doubt would have been a significant adornment. He was certainly gifted both with keen judgment and with that robust and mellifluous style of address for which Southern senators have long been noted. Possessed of great tact and sensitivity to others' feelings, Smith had the diplomatic graces and political skills required to lead an organization of independent-minded spirits like the American Newspaper Publishers Association.

The chairman of the ANPA automatically sat on the Bureau Board and on its executive committee. Occasionally he was one of those unusual individuals who had managed to devote time to both organizations and had won acceptance as a confrere. But often he came to the Bureau Board without extensive experience and exposure to marketing and advertising, perhaps not even at his own paper. The Bureau's directors received, however, an extensive indoctrination in these subjects at Board meetings, and a Bureau chairman, who had usually served several terms as a director, was generally familiar with them.

The subject of circulation, which had become of such urgent importance to the survival of newspaper advertising was, according to the already described traditional division of labor between ANPA and the Bureau, a direct concern of the publishers association.

Applying the Marketing Concept

Kauffman had persuaded the Board of Directors to change the organization's name from the Bureau of Advertising of the ANPA to the Newspaper Advertising Bureau in 1973, but he resisted my suggestion that the Newspaper Marketing Bureau would be a more appropriate term to describe our activities. At that time I argued that

> you can't divorce the planning, shaping and promotion of the product itself from the job of getting it distributed and sold. . . . Our job

has always been to sell the product as it is and not to suggest any changes. But with the reduction of newspaper competition, I think a lot of people in the business are ready to reexamine that premise.[21]

Marketing was a term that was increasingly being heard in the newspaper industry. In the years of the Readership Project it became a rallying cry for the advocates of radical change in newspapers' editorial formulas. For many journalists, it was an infuriating catchword that symbolized the pretensions of the business office for dominance over their own professional prerogatives.

Marketing is, indeed, a somewhat vaguely defined term that refers to the whole chain of activities through which products and services are designed to match consumer needs and then consumers are persuaded that their needs are actually being met. In packaged goods companies, such departments as advertising, merchandising, sales promotion, sales, market research, planning, and product development have for some years generally been encompassed under a single marketing division. In the newspaper business, this development came much later, in the 1970s; it was, in fact, accelerated, as we shall see, by the Newspaper Readership Project. On most newspapers, advertising, circulation, and promotion (which generally included research) were separate fiefdoms with clearly demarcated boundary lines. Their chiefs vied with each other for the attention of management.

The move to bring these departments together under marketing direction generally initiated with the advertising department, whose director was therefore likely to be first in line for the coveted title of marketing vice president. This created an understandable suspicion on the part of circulation managers and of the majority of promotion managers who were not already reporting to the advertising director. In a number of instances, promotion managers had already renamed themselves marketing directors, to indicate that they not only ran the research function but also used research to develop their plans.

The Long Range Plans Committee

Among the groups that ventilated concerns about readership was the Bureau's Long Range Plans Committee. This had been headed for many years by Vance Stickell, the marketing vice president of the *Los Angeles Times*. Stickell's deceptively mild manner, bronzed good looks, and impeccably tailored, pastel-shaded Southern California wardrobe disguised both considerable ability and keen ambition, which later brought him the national chairmanships of both the American Advertising Federation and The Advertising Council and—after his death in 1988—posthumous election to the Advertising Hall of Fame.

Like other appointees to the Bureau's various committees, Stickell's predecessor, Frank Gatewood of the *Washington Post,* had served for only two or three years. But sensing Stickell's importance, Kauffman left his term of office open-ended. This permitted him and his elegant wife to attend all the Board of Directors' meetings and to enjoy an egalitarian social relationship with publishers, something that every ad director craved and that few ever achieved.

Unlike the Bureau's Plans Committee, a large and heterogeneous cross-section of advertising directors that acted as a twice-a-year sounding board, the Long Range Plans Committee was a group of about ten advertising executives who commanded respect because of the size of the papers they represented or because of their personal stature in the regard of their colleagues. The committee served as a device by which Bureau management was able to alert the directors to the need for major action, usually involving some expansion of activities and budgets, without the necessity of making such petitions directly. It was not Lipscomb, as president, who urged the Bureau Board to move the organization from an almost exclusive concern with national advertising to a major emphasis on retail sales; it was the Long Range Plans Committee that made that recommendation. Similar expansions into classified advertising, cooperative advertising, and insert advertising received the blessings of the same committee. The partnership of Kauffman and Stickell worked so smoothly that the members of the committee may well have imagined that they had originated the proposals themselves in the course of their deliberations. In the same spirit, we turned to them to ask for action in the area of readership.

On March 2, 1976, I sent Stickell my "thoughts on the circulation penetration problem," saying that "the decline in both circulation and coverage is now well known to our competitors and highly visible to major advertisers, especially retailers," and that "sensitizing publishers and editors to the seriousness of the situation we currently face is only the first step toward investing the effort, ingenuity, time, and budgets required both at the level of the individual paper and through an industry-wide program." This, I suggested, should include:

a. Experimentation and research on the editorial product.
b. In-depth study of the causes and cure of our weakness among young people and minority groups.
c. Operations and systems research to improve methods of subscription and single copy sales, delivery, reader service —and collection.
d. Better tools and training procedures to upgrade circulation personnel.
e. Strengthening the newspaper-in-the classroom program.
f. A continuing promotional campaign to attract more readers.

The subject, I concluded, was "vital to the task of holding, and increasing, our advertising share."

Stickell rose to the occasion. On behalf of the Long Range Plans Committee, he strongly recommended that the Bureau Board give the readership problem high priority.

CHAPTER 3

Organizing the Project

A person aware of a problem can decide very quickly to do something about it. An institution may take more time to deliberate but operates by the same instincts. The newspaper business, as we have seen, was an aggregation of many separate and rivalrous elements, and the evolution and execution of an action program could not be achieved so easily.

Setting the Stage

The subject of falling circulation and readership was already surfacing in publishers' social conversations, reaching a crescendo by the spring of 1976. At the ANPA convention, I spoke on "The Readership Challenge" and sought to "distinguish between our continuing concerns and the short-run decline in circulation which has suddenly made readership a fashionable agenda item at newspaper conventions." The short-run problem could be attributed to the joint effects of large price increases and the current business recession. The more serious long-range problem was one of big-city readership, much of which had been lost when papers failed or merged.

> By now, we all know that when a paper goes, much of its readership simply evaporates, so unique is its place in the life of its

readers. Does that mean that the majority of you who are publishers of smaller and middle-sized papers can sit back and enjoy life while the big guys take their lumps? No way . . . Major advertisers . . . make up their schedules only after they have arrived at a basic decision on the merits of using newspapers. . . . Little papers are the first to be lopped off the list when newspaper advertising budgets are trimmed. So this is everybody's problem.[1]

I pointed out that "newspapers are perceived by their readers in very individual terms, and not as part of some big abstraction called 'the medium.' " The most helpful research would be "specific to your own individual features and character." Repeating my message to the Long Range Plans Committee, I proposed industry-wide research on the reasons for success and failure, the economics of the business, the mechanics of circulation and distribution, and the reading habits of the young. "But the need for research is, to my mind, secondary to the need for action." After listing a dozen actions for publishers to take, I urged, "Spend what it takes to solve the readership problem. You'll invest over $100 million to upgrade your production facilities this year. Should you be investing less to make what you produce more exciting, more necessary, more valuable to the readers?"

If newspapers agreed that something had to be done, whose responsibility should it be to do it? Douglas Armstrong, president of the Lancaster, Pennsylvania, newspapers, wrote Silha:[2]

Frankly, I feel NAB should apply its considerable talent to the readership-circulation segment of our business. Advertising is our lifeblood but readership is our life line. It pays 30 percent of our bills—plus or minus. But it's slipping. Why? NAB is a high-powered, highly talented organization doing an exceptionally fine job. The organization is there, the management and direction is firm and positive. Why not add a wing to mother the readership-circulation portion of our business? Hire the best circulation brains (as was done for advertising) and turn them loose on the industry's No. 1 problem. . . . NAB has been a superlative sales arm for advertising. But where are we on circulation-readership? Consider it Marketing. NAB already serves the area effectively from which we derive 70 percent of our dollars. Let's zero in on the other 30 percent through the NAB which has demonstrated its drive, talent and creative expertise.

But circulation, as we have seen, had always been considered ANPA's affair. A genteel jockeying over turf was about to begin. The initiative for action came from the Bureau, with relentless prodding from Silha. With prior approval from the Bureau's Executive Committee, he met in Las Vegas with ANPA's officers— Chairman Smith, Vice Chairman Allen H. Neuharth (the supercharged chairman of the Gannett Company) and Treasurer Leonard Small (owner of a string of middle-sized midwestern dailies) to discuss a possible "summit meeting" of the heads of the industry's principal associations. As ANPA's President Friedheim put it, "there was agreement that such a meeting was worth a try."[3] Friedheim appeared to believe that solutions to the readership problem had to be sought in additional research. He suggested that the industry confabulation be linked to the next meeting of the ANPA's News Research Committee, which was essentially dedicated to a review of research ideas. I felt that the meeting should be devoted to "specific actions" and "the mechanics and financing of a program to accomplish these actions," rather than to research.

If we extrapolate our circulation decline of the last two years, we could lose one fifth of the circulation we now have by 1985, with disastrous results for our advertising base and for the economics of the business. If we can restore the reading habit to the level of 1970 and ride the trend of growing population and education, we can increase our circulation by as much as one fourth over its present level and become even more attractive to advertisers than we are now. Our business ought to be willing to make an investment commensurate with what is at stake. Most of that investment will have to be made on individual newspapers working to improve their own products in their own communities. But an important part of the job has to be done on an industry-wide basis, and it should include extensive programs of training, promotion, and communication, as well as research.

My feeling is that we need several days of very concentrated discussion among a group that is small enough so that its members can interact without the need for formalities. Over the last year, I have been in a good many meetings of newspaper people who have talked about the subject of circulation decline; the discussion always gets most interesting when it is time to adjourn. To get things started, I would propose this agenda:

1. Very quick status report on circulation and readership trends; statement of the problem.

2. Distribution systems; opportunities and limitations in new technology; organizational and compensation questions; adult carriers; competing with the Postal Service.

3. The editorial product; limits of experimentation; editorial excellence and readership results.

4. Reaching the young adult reader. Sales, distribution, and promotion techniques.

5. Minority readership and staffing programs.

6. Fostering the reading habit among the very young. Reading ability and the school curriculum. "A print equivalent for Sesame Street."[4]

These points did indeed become the basis of the subsequent agenda for our "summit" meeting, which was not linked to that of the ANPA research group. I suggested to Silha[5] that there were four possible options for the meeting to consider, "unless it decides either to sweep the readership problem under the rug or to remand it for further procrastination and study." They were to give the assignment to the Bureau, to a new division within the ANPA, to a new separately funded organization that might buy the Bureau's services, or to "an ad hoc Action Committee" that would coordinate and "initiate projects within the framework of the individual organizations." This last option, I argued, was the next best thing to saying, "Why don't we all just think about it and get back together again in six months or a year.

"This whole thing needs money. The million dollars is for starters. There ought to be a long-term commitment, just as there is to the RI [ANPA's technical Research Institute]."

Addressing the ICMA convention a few days later, Silha quoted an unnamed publisher who had suggested that the Bureau was the most qualified organization for a "jet-assisted attack" on the circulation problem. He warned the circulation managers that "despite all its outward appearances of prosperity and good health, the newspaper business has been, and is, undergoing severe stresses."[6] Referring to the "content-marketing-circulation (CMC) project," he said that

the content of newspapers will have to undergo serious reappraisal in the months and years just ahead to measure whether that content is satisfying and serving readers. . . . We're going to have to demonstrate, promote and sell the usefulness of the daily newspaper.

He suggested that newspapers might join magazine and book publishers in setting up a "National Print Institute to study an apparent decline in reading as a means of communicating."

Following Silha's speech, the *Los Angeles Times'* Nelson wrote him that

> although I believe NAB can play an important role in this area, they really have very little experience or expertise in circulation. Selling, of course, is selling, which is really their forte, and I'm sure they could help develop more sophisticated and professional circulation sales approaches. But that really isn't our major problem. Most circulation departments can generate as many orders as a publisher is willing or able to pay for. The problem, as you know, is holding these subscribers.

At a later session of the same ICMA convention that Silha had already addressed, I insisted that,

> Our job at the Newspaper Advertising Bureau has been and always will be to promote newspaper advertising . . . but can this assignment any longer be logically separated from the larger job of newspaper marketing, in which circulation now has high priority? . . . We at the Bureau are not asking to extend our assignment. We do know our product must be marketed to readers before we can market it to advertisers. We will only get into this area if you ask us to, and we could only do the job with your full cooperation, counsel, and help. . . . Falling circulation has been described as an editors' problem and I agree that is what it is. . . . But I would also insist that it is a management problem, a pricing problem, a sales problem and a distribution problem. . . . Research on the customers to define their needs is the essence of the marketing approach. To act on that research information requires a combination of skills that cut across departmental lines.

As more newspapers took the marketing approach, two consequences were inevitable. "One is a further professionalization of circulation management. The second is a reexamination of the whole circulation system as it now exists." Professionalization

> requires the development of specialized knowledge. We still have a long way to go to build up what might be called a body of scholarly

research on newspaper readership and circulation. There is a very substantial amount of survey data that tell us who the non-readers are and what answers they give when they are asked why they don't read the paper. We know a good deal about the other media to which readers and non-readers are exposed. We have far less systematic knowledge about the economics and logistics of circulation. About the cost of getting a paper to different types of readers through different distribution methods and in different types of urban and suburban environments. About the cost of selling an order and the cost of keeping it going. About the cost of stopping and starting. About the cost of delivering and servicing.

An unidentified officer of ICMA told *Editor & Publisher* that the organization had taken no official position on my proposals and that I "was just another speaker. . . . Just because the speech was well received doesn't mean we took whatever he said as being gospel." He said it was "foolish to think that any particular group could come in and solve the circulation problem" and added that he personally "feels the ICMA is making progress on its own to remedy slumping circulation." According to *E & P*, I said that "the Bureau was not 'making a pitch' to get involved in the circulation area" but added, however, that "someone has to do it, and we certainly have the skills to fulfill some of their needs. . . . We will do whatever the board authorizes . . . it certainly is important enough that action on it will not be put off in favor of a lengthy study."

An Action Program

In preparation for the meeting of association heads, I drafted a plan[7] for "A Marketing Program To Build Newspaper Circulation." This was to be done through (1) research, (2) training, (3) promotion, and (4) communication.

I argued that, while "circulation growth will come about as a result of independent and specific actions taken by individual newspapers," there also had to be "a pooling of effort for the common benefit," with "active and intimate collaboration among: general management, editorial, circulation, promotion, personnel, production, and advertising."

Under the heading of research, I proposed a confidential "clearing house and repository of readership studies" made for individual papers, so that they could be reanalyzed and generalizations drawn and disseminated. "To facilitate comparability, common questions and analytical approaches would be developed." A newspaper industry in-house staff facility would "analyze circulation and readership trends; identify case histories of success and failure; determine the effects of price changes; examine the effects of variations in editorial quality; conduct systems analysis on distribution methods, and collect basic data on newspaper economics."[8] There was an extensive plan for original research, which I describe in the next chapter.

An industry-wide program was needed to upgrade the skills of circulators and their staffs. I proposed "five basic slide and cassette presentations (along with appropriate supplementary printed materials) aimed at (1) district managers, (2) telephone subscription sales personnel, (3) door-to-door crew members, (4) juvenile carriers, and (5) educators involved in the Newspaper in Education program." In addition I suggested five series of workshops and training seminars: a basic management workshop for circulation executives and central office staffs; a seminar on problems of minority staff recruitment and training; a workshop for district managers; a workshop on the editorial applications of readership research; and an expanded series of workshops to support the Newspaper in Education program.

In the area of promotion I proposed that ANPA's existing Newspaper in Education program be strengthened by research, by promotion to educators, and by showing newspapers how to do a better job with it. Four advertising campaigns would be developed annually for newspapers to run as house ads. "The first four would be aimed at young unmarried readers, young married apartment house dwellers, blacks, and working women."

> These campaigns would aim (1) to promote subscription sales to the increasing number of single-copy readers who no longer buy the paper each day and (2) to encourage more intensive readership among casual readers in families that already have a subscription. The merits of different copy appeals for these campaigns will be determined through pre-tests.

A clearing house would collect examples of newspaper promotions, and a procedure would be set up to give them independent critical reviews. A continuing publicity and public relations campaign would be launched "to improve the credibility, authority, and importance of newspapers in the public's opinion" and to enhance their visibility. Special efforts would be targeted at blacks and the Spanish-speaking population. A new film would be produced each year on the social needs served by newspapers. The plan also called for a communications mechanism to exchange reports of experience and activities. To supplement the membership bulletins already produced by the associations, we would set up a monthly newsletter, publish special reports, and provide a clearing house for presentations and speeches.

A second paper was titled, "How To Implement the Marketing Program." It suggested that the proposed new activities be closely coordinated with some already going on.[9]

> The program should be funded and staffed as a continuing activity rather than as a special project. It is essential to have the full participation of all the newspaper groups with a strong interest in the subject. The best talents of the newspaper business should be mobilized to provide guidance and counsel and to help set priorities, but a program of this scope must be run professionally.

Who would run this operation and how? I offered the same four options I had earlier listed in my letter to Silha and added a fifth: "Expand the scope of the ANPA Foundation by giving it this responsibility."

I went on to describe the Bureau's qualifications in the areas of research, training, and promotion and submitted a one-year budget that totaled $330,000 in these three areas. The option of turning the whole assignment over to the Bureau was never a serious possibility, since it left no management role for the ANPA, whose leadership considered the matter to be of vital interest, solidly within its job description, perhaps even central to its mission. The two organizations served the same masters, but each was internally driven to hold or expand its terrain.

The "Summit" Meeting

The "summit" meeting, called jointly by Silha and Smith, was held[10] at Airlie House, an elegant red brick mansion turned into a conference center, located in the hunt country of Virginia a few miles from Washington. Present were the heads of all the major newspaper associations and of the Associated Press and United Press International. Despite the gravity of the subject, it was a cheerful and sociable occasion.

In the course of an evening and a day of meetings, the group of sixteen organizations approved a plan for a special fund-raising campaign to support a three-year crash program. Activities were to be conducted under four headings, but not quite the way I had proposed. They were: (l) promotion, public relations, and Newspaper in Education programs; (2) research; (3) circulation training, and (4) circulation systems and equipment.

Although the possibility of setting up a permanent organization was considered, earlier discussions by the Bureau's Executive Committee had made it clear that the principals of the newspaper business had no use for an additional permanent drain on their generosity and attention. There was no need or desire for a new and separate organization that would create its own bureaucratic superstructure, its own self-perpetuating governance system, and its own inevitable rivalries with existing organizations.

The plan called for close cooperation between the Bureau and the ANPA. Most of the work was to be done as far as possible by the existing staffs of the two organizations, with additional new temporary hires for the duration of the program. In the aftermath of the Airlie House meeting, Smith wrote Silha[11] that

> ANPA will be able to fund its portion of this effort from regular income sources by adjustments to our program priorities. Thus the stage would be left clear for any special appeal that NAB feels it might require for its assigned responsibilities. Although this plan may not be as dramatic as some we might mount, I believe that therein it has great merit. We do not overemphasize our problem; we attempt to involve those groups and individuals who are best qualified to study the causes and provide the solutions; we reduce the danger of overoptimistic expectations for easy answers to a variety of complex, individual situations.

Smith attached a memorandum prepared by ANPA's staff. It said that "since readership and circulation improvement is an individual newspaper undertaking, the campaign's primary objective is to develop and make available 'tools' " for that purpose.

The final division of labor was defined in the first Report to Contributors:[12]

> NAB is responsible for (1) promotion, (2) the development of materials to be used in the training program, (3) research to be conducted by its own professional staff and through commercial research organizations. ANPA will (1) expand its work in the area of training, in cooperation with API, ICMA, and NPRA. (2) Its News Research Center will continue to report on and support university-based research studies. (3) The ANPA Foundation will step up its Newspaper in Education program. (4) The Research Institute will work on new equipment and circulation systems. ANPA and NAB will collaborate on a program of communications to the newspaper business.

After listing the committees and explaining their scope and initial assignments, we added a cautionary note:

> The Newspaper Readership Project was initiated to provide a catalyst for the individual efforts being made by newspapers to build readership and circulation. The real success of the Project will not be measured by the programs undertaken by ANPA and NAB, but rather by the parallel efforts of individual newspaper organizations at the local level.

ANPA was reallocating existing resources but the Bureau needed extra money. I prepared a program and budget to cover its assignments.[13] This assumed that contributions would amount to $400,000 annually, beginning June 1, 1977 (the start of the Bureau's fiscal year).

The proposal was to hire a professional staff of three in promotion and four in research. "Although the Bureau will have to add manpower to cover its assignments, we do not expect to create any special new divisions within our research or promotion departments, but rather to integrate Project tasks between existing and new staff members." We promised two circulation promotion campaigns a year, each consisting of six newspaper ads and six radio commercial scripts, and each aimed at a specific target. In addition, there would be two films, suitable for showing to theatrical audiences, and a public relations program. I also suggested that "the Airlie House group could be converted into a Project Review Board that would meet twice a year for the duration of the

Readership Project to go over plans and to offer suggestions."
This was the genesis of the Newspaper Readership Council.

The Word Gets Out

As we were laying our plans, word of the industry's difficulties
was reaching advertisers and the general public. A long article in
the *Los Angeles Times,* by press analyst David Shaw, was headed
"Newspapers Challenged as Never Before; Their Future Depends
on Meeting Changing Needs of Readers."[14] It opened with a
question, "Are you now holding an endangered species in your
hands?"

At meetings of publishers and advertising executives, we used
to advantage a recent comment by an executive at Montgomery
Ward:

> The time is long overdue for the newspaper industry to take dy-
> namic action toward reversing the trend toward shrinking market
> coverage. In our key markets, average metropolitan newspaper cov-
> erage has dropped from 95 percent to 78 percent in the past decade.
> Needless to say, the situation is worse in many individual markets.
> Even more than the problem of escalating rates, the reduction in
> newspaper coverage is the greatest reason behind our increasing
> use of competitive media.

The newspaper advertising fraternity showed their support for
the Project by inviting Silha to be the keynote speaker[15] at their
winter convention. It was held in Hollywood, Florida, at the Dip-
lomat Hotel, parts of which were occupied by Saudi princes and
their suspicious and suspicious-looking bodyguards. The ad directors alternately basked in the sunshine with their consorts and
exposed themselves to "motivational" spellbinders, buzz sessions
on coop and real estate classified, and a very wide selection of
cocktail parties.

Silha took the occasion to announce publicly the establishment
of the Project and of the Newspaper Readership Council. He said,
"All of us—advertising people, publishers, editors, controllers,
production people—tend to be concerned with our narrow piece
of the action." Unveiling a "strategy for the marketing of our total
product that will make our industry even stronger and healthier,"

Silha said there were three "elements of this strategy: (1) we've got to maximize our utility to our readers, (2) we've got to work as a team, (3) we've got to make things easier for our customers." He added, "We are not under any illusion that the long-term challenges we face in the area of readership are going to disappear in the next three years, but there is no intention of making this a permanent project."[16]

The "Volunteers"

By their very nature, voluntary associations operate by accommodation and compromise—that is to say, slowly. The newspaper associations we were trying to weld together for a common purpose could not be activated by a letter or a phone call, as in a business enterprise. Their deliberations were ponderous and infrequent. They took place on a fixed schedule determined by convention dates and meeting sites often set years in advance.

We understood at the outset that the success of the Readership Project would heavily depend on our ability to generate fruitful discussions among specialists of different types, from a broad cross-section of newspapers. Such discussions were essential to enrich the industry's thinking processes on the subject of readership and to broaden the technical knowledge of the responsible staff at the Bureau and ANPA. We also needed discussions to give all sectors of the business a sense of participation.

The project was to be led by a Steering Committee consisting of the chairmen and vice chairmen of the Bureau and ANPA and the presidents of the ASNE and the ICMA. The first meeting of the committee[17] discussed the preliminary results of the Bureau's latest research, current ANPA activities, and communications from lesser newspaper associations that felt neglected and wanted to be on the Readership Council.

The Council itself held its first meeting[18] the following week and heard reports from Smith and Silha on the fund-raising effort and on the proposed operating plan for the first fiscal year. The Bureau reported on its readership-related research and promotion work, ANPA on its News Research Center, its Research Institute, and its training programs. These included a marketing seminar for promising young newspaper executives, originally known informally as the "Sons of Publishers Conference."

Four committees were to develop and supervise programs for the substantive areas. The chairmanship of the Research Committee was assigned to the editors, that of the Promotion Committee to the promotion managers. Circulation Training went to the personnel managers, and Equipment and Systems to the circulation managers.

The four operating committees were all of manageable size. With the inevitable absentees, meetings ranged from four or five participants to an occasional twelve or fifteen. This meant that representatives of the various newspaper organizations were brought together in highly informal, problem-focused discussions in a way that had never happened before.

The ANPA had from time to time convened a committee of heads of newspaper organizations in a large formal meeting room in a Washington hotel. At these meetings, fifty or sixty people convened for brief reports and presentations on what the various organizations were doing. Valuable as this was, it did not provide much opportunity for close personal contacts or unbridled exchanges of views and insights. Such intense conversation did occur in the meetings of the intimate NRP committees.

Like other industry activities that entail periodic meetings of delegates or committee members from around the United States, the Readership Project required a considerable expenditure of voluntary effort by the participants in the form of time, energy, late night travel, and nights away from home. It also racked up substantial travel expenses for their managements. The newspaper industry is one of the largest employers in the United States, with a total payroll of approximately $10 billion in 1990. But the available talent pool was not unlimited. Inevitably, when task forces and committees were formed to deal with specific subjects of industry-wide concern, the same names came to the surface. These were individuals who by dint of their experience, energy, intelligence, diplomatic skills, or personal charm had developed a reputation or popularity beyond their own local community.

Since Alexis de Tocqueville, keen observers have noted as a distinctive characteristic of American culture the willingness of individuals to give generously of their time and energy in voluntary efforts. The Readership Project demonstrated that this occurs in commercial, as well as in noncommercial, realms. Voluntarism is elevated to a high degree in the newspaper business. The functions of a newspaper can easily be described in moral or civic terms: bringing truth to light, editorializing against irrationality and injustice, and providing communities with the cohesion that comes from commonly held information. Such activities endow newspaper work with a sense of mission that goes beyond its business objectives or the professional craftsmanship involved in its various specialties. Associations of coin-laundry operators and used car dealers undoubtedly evoke considerable good fellowship and devotion to the advancement of their respective arts. But it is hard to believe that these associations command the same degree of dedication that characterizes those in the newspaper field.

Unlike the members of most other guilds, newspaper executives, and many employees as well, are likely to consider their trade as an important element of a free society and to imagine that larger social values are enhanced by the success of their own enterprises. Newspaper mechanical employees probably do not regard their jobs any differently than they would if they were engaged in some other type of manufacturing business, and newsroom employees are surely afflicted by the cynicism that may be indispensable to the practice of journalism. Nonetheless, editors and, to some degree, other newspaper executives often regard what they do as a calling—even a noble one.

This helps explain why, in the Readership Project as in so many other industry-wide ventures, many of them were willing to worry about the problems of the business for reasons that went well beyond the immediate requirements and self-interest of their jobs. Besides, the discussions were enjoyable and intellectually stimulating. There was some opportunity for expense account travel, for a useful broadening of horizons, and for the establishment or renewal of professional contacts that cut across the local boundaries within which newspapers operate.

In setting up a newspaper committee on a national (or since Canada[19] is almost invariably included, international) basis, the organizers were required to pay attention to political considerations, as well as to personal qualifications. Inevitably they sought balance among geographic regions, between large and small newspapers, between chains and independents, and sometimes among members of different newspaper specialties or professions.

My original hope was to compose the four specialized committees of individuals who were outstanding in their respective fields. But the underlying concept of the Readership Council was to provide representation to the various associations, whose governing councils or executive committees designated their choices for committee membership. In most instances, they selected their presidents or president-elects. These were individuals of ability who had the confidence of their own professions and who could report back to their constituents at first hand. They were not always, however, the most qualified specialists in the particular subjects that came up for discussion.

Because the officers of the associations were replaced at different intervals, all the committees suffered from a certain amount of turnover, exacerbated as members missed meetings. Moreover, change in the upper echelons of the newspaper business was common enough to cause discontinuity. For example, Robert Clark, the distinguished and scholarly editor of the *Louisville Courier-Journal*, left his job while he was ascending the ASNE ladder. He became editor of the Jacksonville newspapers; when they were sold to Morris Communications, Clark left, then found a new job as the news vice president of Harte-Hanks Newspapers.

This kind of volatility affected the running of the Project. We were always in the position of playing catch-up, with a certain amount of time dedicated to bringing new or irregular attendees up to the information levels of the rest. Wheels were always being reinvented, and the same debates and arguments had to be held over and over again.

During the six years, each new chairman of both the Bureau and the ANPA, and each new set of officers of each of the other participating organizations, had to be indoctrinated and converted from their previous state of ignorance, apathy, indifference, or disapproval. In the cases of the Bureau and ANPA, their enthusiasm was mobilized by making them public spokesmen for the Project.

The officers of the ASNE and of ICMA generally saw the Project as an opportunity to accomplish jobs that were already on their agenda but for which their organizations had no funds. They came to committee meetings armed with proposals that had previously been discussed in their own executive committees or boards of directors and for which they were prepared to fight. But such projects were comparatively few. By far the bulk of the ideas taken up by the Readership Project originated with the Bureau.

How the Committees Worked

In anticipation of each new budget year, the committees met to review proposals, initiate new activities, and set priorities. For the Bureau's assignments, I assembled these projects into a proposed operating plan and budget for the consideration of the Steering Committee. In no case did its members switch a particular committee's priorities. They did, however, sometimes overrule my judgment on how the overall funds should be allocated among the four areas.

The discretionary funds to be divided up were actually only a portion of the total budget for each fiscal year. Both the Bureau's and ANPA's Project staff payrolls had to be met. It was agreed at the outset that certain projects would be handled on a continuing basis, without the need for an annual review. One was a monthly newsletter, The Editors' Exchange, which ASNE produced to pass along to editors good ideas that might be pertinent to building readership. On a different front, the ANPA Foundation was given the funds to hire a field worker to supplement its existing specialist in Newspaper in Education programs.

The ANPA assigned its newly hired Manager of Training Services, Robert Burke,[20] to be its staff coordinator for the Project. In his view,

Early experiences gained while the Council was in its embryo stage and was engaged in shaping its interests and giving guidance to the first projects, strongly suggest the need for central coordination of information for wide dissemination in the future concerning the activities of the Council and its committees. . . . Coordination can best be achieved by designating one agency as the central coordinating office for NRP communications.[21]

That agency was to be ANPA, and a dozen issues of a "Newspaper Readership Report" newsletter were prepared under his direction. Burke, a West Point graduate who had retired from the Army as a colonel, had been the Defense Department's chief public relations officer in Vietnam, where he came to Friedheim's attention. His military background seemed incongruous with his gentle, tactful style and his ready sense of humor. Throughout the six years of the Project he was a steadying balance, a source of useful and practical ideas, and a reliable chronicler and coordinator of our activities.

Minutes, Agendas, and Chairmanship

The project's pace was set by meeting after meeting, not only as we assembled newspaper people from around the country, but also in internal discussions within the Bureau. Staff members met to talk about the planning of proposals and projects, to review work plans and timetables, and to discuss the minutiae of presentation scripts and research questionnaires. Such meetings were informal and often called on the spur of the moment.

The meeting of an industry committee took careful preparation, not merely to set the agenda, but also to determine suitable dates —often through a series of letters or phone calls, to make sure that a meeting site was available when we needed it, to arrange for coffee, to select the menu for meals. Our progress depended on the conscientious execution of these unheroic, time-consuming administrative details.

Meeting agendas were checked with the committee chairman and sent out as part of the meeting announcement. As the Project proceeded, much of the agenda was devoted to progress reports on the activities under way, including informational reports on what the other committees were doing. Other time was always devoted to review of proposals for new projects.

An agenda does not always rigorously determine what gets discussed in a meeting, and its function must evidently be different in a small group than in a large one. The NRP committees were deliberately set up to be of manageable size, making discussion open and informal without the need for control or guidance by a chairman. In such a meeting, the agenda may be little more than a reminder to consider certain topics. At its most primitive level, an agenda is merely a laundry list of items that demand attention. At its best, it structures the efficient organization of energy and time by presenting issues for resolution in order of priority or in some logically connected sequence.

In formal business meetings like those of the Bureau Board or of the Readership Council, where votes had to be taken or actions approved, noncontroversial committee reports were normally scheduled at the beginning, to get the dull stuff out of the way. A skillful chairman manipulates and reorders the agenda as a meeting proceeds and moves to an uncontested consensus without the showdown of a formal vote. In the Readership Project committees, we did not always have experienced and facile chairmen. At any given meeting, with participants arriving on different timetables from various parts of the country, important matters sometimes had to be pushed away from the start in order to avoid excluding latecomers from the debate. And they often had to be moved up on the schedule before some of the participants drifted off to the airports.

The quality of leadership was extremely important in guiding the activities of our four working committees, in representing them to the Steering Committee, and generating interest and support for the Project within its constituent organizations. Some committee chairmen were activists who dedicated a substantial amount of time to the task. Others had no heart for it, skipped meetings, and generally appeared to consider their involvement as thankless, onerous, and futile.

At times it seemed that it took more paperwork to initiate projects than we ultimately generated in the form of presentation scripts or reports. Partly this stemmed from the staff's genuine interest in getting the widest possible array of suggestions from the specialists (like editors and circulation managers) whose needs we were trying to serve. But in even greater measure it reflected the political necessities of our enterprise—our need to keep everyone in the world apprised of what we were up to. We wanted no noses out of joint.

The ideas that come out of an open discussion are diffuse; they must be set down in writing, organized and evaluated in order to be put into use. When ideas are set forth on paper ahead of time, other ideas may be sparked less freely than in debate, but they are apt to be focused on the subject, and the discussion is likely to be less time consuming and more productive.

Ideas can be generated by a single individual who translates them into a written outline or plan for action: a research proposal, the scheme for a presentation or publication, the agenda for a conference, the specifications for a piece of equipment. Once on paper, these ideas generate reactions. There may be criticisms, or modifications of the original proposals. Or there may be new and different ideas altogether, which go off on a tangent from what has been prepared. In an open discussion, the process is shortcut. When ideas are advanced as part of a fluid discourse, reactions come faster, and the discursive tangents, while more spontaneous, may be less productive because they have not been thought through. To make such discussions fruitful, a good chairman controls and intervenes judiciously, circling back to the points that need further exploration, avoiding needless retracking of the same ground, and opening up new areas to be considered. Usually a good chairman has the additional task of evoking responses from the less outspoken participants in a meeting, but in the case of the Readership Project committees there were few shrinking violets.

The authorship of ideas that arise in a meeting is always hard to determine, since they undergo modification and embellishment. This becomes all the more true when the ideas must be executed into programs or products by individuals who may not have taken part in the original stages of the process. Often the same or similar ideas were advanced by different people at different times and in different contexts. This made the Readership Project, with its interminable series of meetings, memoranda, and approvals, the epitome of a collective effort.

Apart from the chairman, a committee's discussion can be useless without a diligent rapporteur. Brilliant conversation is worthless if it leaves no trace, and suggestions are pointless if they go unrecorded. Throughout the Project's six-year life, Burke's committee minutes managed to keep track of all the actionable ideas, as well as of the agreed-upon actions.

The topics that the committees considered were in turn talked about by committees in which the same individuals also participated within their own organizations. The constant turnover of membership, which made continuity of discussion such a difficult matter, also served the purpose of widening the circle of those who had an inkling of what we were up to and what was at stake. Thus the small groups that we summoned into existence, with their interminable, sometimes aimless palavers, set waves of conversation in motion that reverberated throughout the newspaper business.

Now, imperceptibly, something of lasting importance was happening. In the course of the Readership Project, the newspaper associations underwent some significant long-term changes in their relationships with each other and in their sense of participation in the industry. This alteration in outlook came about as their officers and leadership elites participated in the deliberations of the Project's working committees, where they necessarily confronted the industry's problems from a perspective that transcended their professional or occupational specialties. Gradually the process of indoctrination percolated down to the membership rank and file. Perhaps, even more important, there was a growing awareness that the industry itself was caught up in a process of significant transformation. This in turn created a greater willingness to try new ideas, a greater receptiveness to innovation. The medium itself was being reshaped.

Raising the Money

A program as ambitious as the Newspaper Readership Project could not be financed out of the operating budgets of either the Bureau or the ANPA. The assignment we faced seemed so enormous that it might have been possible to propose plausible and useful activities at almost any desired level of expense. As a practical matter, our plans had to start with a realistic assessment of what newspaper managements might be willing to pay voluntarily in support of a dubious enterprise from which they would share in any possible benefits, regardless of whether or not they contributed.

We began by setting a figure that we thought each of the largest papers would be willing to pay. This was a fraction of the dues they paid either to the Bureau or ANPA. Then we set other levels of suggested contributions for papers in smaller circulation brackets. I estimated what proportion of papers in each size group might be counted on to participate. The resulting total gave us a figure that could be used as a target for our project planning.

Silha wrote Smith,[22] "I think we should consider a three-year program that would cost $1.5 million—$500,000 per year. The worst thing we could do would be to undershoot and not be able to deliver on the promised program." He followed this with a "private and confidential" letter,[23] enclosing a draft of the marketing program that I had prepared. He commented, "Although the draft indicates that NAB would consider raising $400,000 a year for three years ($1,200,000), I still feel it would be more appropriate if you and I were to jointly sign the solicitation letters." Smith agreed, signaling his personal support—and ANPA's—for what was essentially a financial appeal for the Bureau.

Fund-raising[24] required individualized approaches to the newspaper groups, and letters following up with those who failed to contribute and thanking those who did:

> Every newspaper, large and small, has a stake in the revival and strengthening of the readership habit . . . Your paper may be one of those that have sustained involuntary circulation losses in recent years. In that case we don't have to convince you of the seriousness of the subject. Or your paper may be one of those that have cut back circulation voluntarily in the face of rising costs. You may even be one of the many whose circulation has held steady or has actually expanded with the growth of your market. In that case, we can only remind you that your advertising revenues depend to a large degree on your advertisers' belief that newspapers generally are the medium that covers their customers.[25]

Letters signed by Smith and Silha were addressed on a first-name basis to the publishers of all newspapers down through the 100,000 circulation level. Recognizing that sensibilities rose inversely to importance, "Publishers of all other papers will be addressed as 'Mr.' "[26] I reported to Silha that "we have gone through the roster of U.S. newspaper members of the Bureau and have identified the expected contribution from every newspaper."

The institutional relationship of the two chairmen was ripening into mutual respect and trust. Silha wrote to Smith,[27] "Your presence and participation help greatly in keeping our business united and 'charging.' Your enthusiastic comments on NRP were most encouraging."

Although the fund-raising letter went to the publisher of every member newspaper in the Bureau and the ANPA, the big contributors had to be approached personally. This was done by the co-chairmen wherever publishers congregated and could be button-holed.

The Project had been approved without dissent by the two Boards. Their Directors thus had a moral commitment to contribute, and almost all of them did. Since they themselves accounted for a high proportion of the expected contributions, the finances of the project were assured from the outset. Pledges were solicited for a three-year period, and in a few cases were paid in advance. In several cases, newspaper organizations wanted to make their contributions to the Project tax deductible by funneling them through their private foundations and earmarking them for educational purposes. (Ultimately, in the second three years, this required us to set up a special trust account at a considerable and in my view annoyingly unnecessary cost in custodial fees.)

The groundswell of support exceeded by nearly 50 percent my projections of $400,000 a year to cover the Bureau's assignments, beginning June 1, 1977.[28] By July 1, pledges of $1,753,380 had been received to cover the Project's three-year life span. In addition, the Bureau allocated $100,000 a year from its operating budget, and ANPA reallocated about $300,000 of its annual budget; this included ongoing activities on behalf of the Newspaper in Education program and support from its technical research staff.

Support and Skepticism

Of the roughly 1,750 daily newspapers, altogether about 600 made some donation to the Project, independently or through their group headquarters. Who were the nonparticipants who refused to pledge contributions and who ignored the successive appeals that we sent out? Overwhelmingly they were the proprietors of independently owned smaller newspapers who felt that the circulation problems of the big-city dailies were not their concern. In most cases, they felt remote from the power structures of the Bureau and the ANPA. Many of them were skeptical of the value of general industry activities. Others were reluctant to become involved in an enterprise that held forth the promise of new programs, materials, and things to do, because they felt they lacked the manpower to make proper use of the resources already available through the newspaper associations.

The chains, with rare exceptions, made their pledges at the top management level on behalf of all their papers instead of leaving the decision up to the individual local publishers. Although all of the major groups went along with the fund-raising appeals, they did so with varying degrees of enthusiasm and faith in what the Project might accomplish.

One of the skeptics was Katharine Graham of the Washington Post Company, who (because of Leonard Small's accidental death) succeeded Gannett's Neuharth as ANPA Chairman. She never wavered in her public expressions of support for the Project, but she believed that the root cause of falling circulation was to be found in the inadequacies of many newspapers. She looked around the room where we were talking one day at a social function, and her eye alighted on the animated figure of a highly popular publisher. "Look at him," she said, "a lovely man, but what a terrible newspaper he puts out! I wouldn't read it. You wouldn't read it. Why should the people in his town read it?"

I couldn't dispute her underlying premise, but on the whole, the quality of American journalism had gotten much better—not worse—as the industry had prospered. Following one such conversation, I wrote Graham:[29]

> I accept your contention that the losses in newspaper circulation are largely due to social forces beyond our control. But voluntary cutbacks in circulation, important as they may be for individual papers, are not a significant part of the explanation. . . . [They] can't explain the decline in reading frequency which is behind the substantial weekday audience losses of the '70s. Nor do they explain the erosion of readership among people in their teens, twenties, and (now) thirties. . . .
>
> If we have a problem (and the advertisers have assured us that we do), how can we fail to do something about it? For the past four years we've had some of the best talent in the industry gnawing away at this subject trying to develop programs for action. We've run lots of meetings, distributed thousands of research reports, thousands of ads and commercials, thousands of slide presentations and films. . . . Maybe you're right when you say that for most publishers the material we send out is just part of the massive flow of paper that ends up in the circular file. But if even some of them are paying attention, our message can't be wholly lost. I agree that the real solution to our troubles is to produce better papers and to do a better job of promoting, selling, and distributing them. But

how do we get publishers to produce better papers unless we get them talking? Doesn't it help if we keep up the flow of new things to talk about and to use?

It's not too late to change direction and to get smarter than we've been so far. I know you don't think that this industry should just sit back and hope for the best. I'd like to convert you into a True Believer, but I'll settle for having you in the ranks of the ordinary believers.

Graham replied:

You are nice to be so tolerant of my skepticism. I guess it is based on a deep and abiding suspicion of ideas that are not sharply focused and bureaucracies that are erected seemingly to turn out paper.

I agree loss of readership by newspapers is alarming. To some extent, I fear it is also inevitable. It is a factor of the proliferation of television, cable, and other technologies, the problem of distributing newspapers in cities, changing societal habits, and to some extent an inability or unwillingness on the part of some of the industry to invest in editorial quality or to think hard about what people want to and need to read in a changing society.

There is no doubt, too, that this is a very unreading generation that seems not to feel it needs us.

I guess I think that the answers to many of the questions are self-evident and the answers to the really hard ones will not be arrived at by a Committee.

If you can show me one reader that was added to a paper by the Readership Council, you will have made a convert.

In a futile effort to have the last word, I wrote to V. T. Curtis, circulation director of the *Washington Post*, saying:

While this is a little like asking an editor to find one reader whose mind was changed by a newspaper editorial, I wonder whether this isn't a challenge we can meet. Specifically, I find it hard to believe that we haven't saved at least one subscription as a result of the "Stop the Stops" phone room training presentation that your paper and many others have been using. Would you be willing to ask your phone room supervisor for an answer to this one?

Unfortunately, I never got a reply.

Many of the wiser heads in the industry shared Graham's conviction that readership problems could be faced only by individual newspapers at the local level and that each would have to come up with its own distinctive solution. Yet in spite of such doubts, there was the feeling that "something" had to be done and that a common effort would lead newspapers to tackle their individual local problems more energetically.

In each year's budget, $100,000 was earmarked for the Bureau's overhead and administrative expenses, canceling out our $100,000 pledged reallocation of resources. This was not at all unreasonable, since my own time, my secretary's, and that of a number of other staff members were not charged against the Project. The Bureau staff kept no time sheets. We allocated funds for out-of-pocket expenses and for the salaries and fringe benefits of the half-dozen people who were specially hired to work in the Bureau's Research and Creative Departments.

The handling of the funds and the budgeting for the Readership Project were from the very outset a source of considerable grief to me and to the Bureau's Controller.[30] The ANPA Board insisted that accounts be kept in terms of ANPA's annual budgeting system. This differed from that of the Bureau, which ran on a fiscal year that began in June.

Moreover, under the ANPA's budgeting procedure, it was necessary to show the full cost of each individual project in the program, estimating the value of inside time and overhead, as well as the cost of funds paid to outside suppliers of services and materials. This meant that we had to keep two different sets of books on the same operations, reconciling them semi-annually when we made our reports to the Project's Steering Committee. This reconciliation required a good deal of imagination and much gnashing of teeth.

Diverting Activities

As a not-for-profit business league, the Bureau was restricted to 10 percent in the percentage of its income that could be derived from any source other than membership dues. Normally, however, the sale of publications, presentations, and training programs represented a much smaller amount. Kauffman was determined to bring these extra revenues up to the legal maximum. He exhorted his staff to develop what he called "profit centers" by selling services to the membership or to advertisers. Expansion into the area of circulation could represent such a "profit center." Kauffman considered "profit" to be the additional income the Bureau received over and above any out-of-pocket expenses. Staff salary and overhead did not enter the calculations, as they would by most conventional cost accounting.

Initially, Kauffman was enthusiastic about expanding the Bureau's operations to collect funds from the Project, but his enthusiasm did not extend to its output, in which he was almost ostentatiously uninterested. "The Readership Project is a big fat nothing," he proclaimed at one monthly staff meeting. A considerable amount of my own time was spent defending the interests of the Project within the Bureau and in seeking to expedite its progress.

The period of the Readership Project coincided with intense activity in other Bureau operations. It was essential that the start-up of the Project not interfere with the regular work flow of presentations, publications, and consumer research reports. The Bureau's manpower resources were forever being juggled from one area to another to meet deadlines or to complete priority projects. One project that was particularly time consuming was Newsplan, a program engineered by Kauffman through which national advertisers were offered discounts when they ran advertising schedules of a certain weight and frequency. Before this program was initiated, very few newspapers in the United States offered such incentives to national advertisers, although they were common for local accounts. We faced the task of convincing major newspapers and groups to conform to the scheme. Some of them had considerable anxieties about the antitrust implications, even though the plan had been carefully vetted by a legal firm specializing in the subject.

An even more demanding project was the development of Nabscan (an acronym for Nationally Advertised Brands Scanning Services, which measured product movement in supermarkets).[31] Kauffman envisioned Nabscan—which was jettisoned just before he retired—as a major source of future revenues for the Bureau and assigned the national sales staff to spend a high proportion of its time in selling the service.

Predictably, unpredictable crises were also always in the offing. One that occurred in the summer of 1977 was the threatened failure of Media Records, Inc., a private firm that was the principal source of statistics on newspaper advertising volume and its changes from month to month for individual advertisers and papers. As always, a special INAE subcommittee was convened to take action, but the necessary staffwork was left to the Bureau. To provide a substitute for the essential information that might be lost, I drafted "A Plan for the Newspaper Information Bureau" (envisioned as a new division of the NAB itself).[32] Fortunately, Media Records survived its financial ordeal, and the subject became moot, but not without diverting time and effort from what I considered to be the main task at hand.

People and Work Flow

Not many people would want to leave a good job to go to work on a short-term project, no matter how interesting it promised to be. At the Bureau, finding a staff to get the work done was a real problem, since we could promise only three years of employment at the most. My judgment at the outset was that we should make use of the existing personnel of the Bureau to work on Readership Project activities and compensate for their time by using the Project's employees on the Bureau's usual output of advertising research reports and sales presentations. Everyone who was hired was told that, though the assignment was short term, the job might become permanent because of normal personnel turnover. Several people were transferred to the Bureau's permanent payroll while the Project was in process, and several others were retained when the Project came to an end.

One key executive correctly assessed how the Project would drain energy and patience. Frank Orenstein, who had joined the Bureau as research manager in 1960 and was vice president of research in 1977, decided that the time was right for him to take early retirement. He announced this shortly after work was begun on a new national survey of the newspaper audience, whose intricacies promised to be of nightmarish proportions. When Orenstein moved upstate to tend his apple orchard and write mystery novels à clef that laid bare the secrets of Madison Avenue, he was replaced by the former associate research director, B. Stuart Tolley, a University of Chicago-trained psychologist whose chin whiskers made him an Abraham Lincoln look-alike. Tolley occa-

sionally moonlighted, practicing psychotherapy and teaching statistics—an unorthodox combination. Albert Gollin, a sociologist
who had headed the Washington, D.C., Survey for the Bureau of
Social Science Research, joined the Bureau as associate research
director some months later. Charles Lehman, a senior project
director, became manager of survey research.

All of the Project's slide shows and publications were produced
in the Bureau's Creative Department, where they had to fit into
the regular output of advertising sales presentations. Most of these
had specific due dates because of previously scheduled meetings
and other commitments, while the deadlines for Readership Project activities were for the most part set arbitrarily and were easily
evaded or ignored. To wheedle extra work out of the overex-
tended Creative Department required every imaginable form of
pressure and cajolery.

Henry Simons, the Bureau's Creative Director, was a gentle
soul who would rather go fishing or construct enamel jewelry any
day than deal with the grungy affairs of administration. A former
Stars and Stripes reporter, he was one of the few members of the
Bureau's staff who actually came from a newspaper background.
He had been reluctant to take the top job, much preferring to
spend his office hours writing ingenious advertising copy and
hilarious presentation scripts. Bearded, stately, almost patriarchal
in manner, he presided over a department that had the closeness
and spirit of a large Gypsy family.

The design of our promotional material often departed from my
own standards of excellence, though the presentations themselves
were meticulously critiqued. Art directors appear to have an irres-
istable urge to follow their own aesthetic sense, even when this
leads them in directions that are incongruent with the subject
matter. An administrator learns to overlook such derelictions, lest
criticism damage self-esteem and pride in participation.

This need to soften my own standards was also manifested in
our research, where my proclivity for compulsive perfectionism had long ago given way to a tolerance of what was required to
get the work out. And while an art director or copywriter could
face me down by juxtaposing an expert judgment to my private
opinions, a senior researcher evoked the code of professional col-
legiality, which necessarily made me hesitate to tell him what
to do.

The output of the Readership Project encompassed a wide assortment of products, which came into being only as the result of a process of planning and deliberation. Here the politics of the newspaper associations was enmeshed with the affairs of the four operating committees, which must be taken up one at a time.

CHAPTER 4

A Struggle Over Research

Of what value is it to diagnose an ailment, unless one can also prescribe a remedy? The Readership Project constantly raised questions both about the validity of proferred diagnoses and about the relationship of diagnoses to suggested remedies.

People who should have known better sometimes referred to the Project as a "study." In part, this confusion stemmed from the salience of the research we produced. In part it reflected my own personal identity as a "researcher." Research actually represented a minor share of the Project's total budget and activity. Films, presentations, and publications were concrete manifestations of the Project's accomplishments. Research attracted more attention because it dealt in mysteries. No matter how much was studied and learned, new, unanswered questions always appeared.

The World of Newspaper Research

The evolution of the research program brought to the forefront fundamental questions about the relationship between journalism and marketing and about the real functions of the press in a society gripped by extraordinary changes and increasingly dominated by electronic entertainment. Power struggles over control of research reflected deep philosophical differences. These masqueraded as manifestations of the ancient battle over editorial integrity against the demands of the business office. Sooner or later, most of the research came to center on the content of the newspaper itself and its ability to satisfy the reading public. "They don't care what you put in the news columns," Gordon Strong once told me. "They only read the paper for the ads anyway." Editors believed just the opposite.

The Readership Project required an uncomfortable accommodation of the Bureau's professional research staff to the strongly felt prerogatives of newspaper editors. The progress of this uneasy relationship must be seen in the perspective of the Bureau's research history.

Much of the considerable volume of newspaper research was done in the larger competitive markets. It was proprietary and closely guarded. One of the challenges I saw in the Readership Project was the development of information on a national scale that newspapers would find meaningful on the local level. Within the newspaper business, polls of public opinion were under editors' control, but most research was done to support advertising sales.

George Gallup had begun conducting research on Iowa newspapers in 1932. When Daniel Starch, Carl Nelson, and others started to take readers through the paper in order to see what advertising they remembered having seen, they also covered news items and articles. In the 1940s, some newspapers, like the *Milwaukee Journal*, began to analyze the purchasing habits and brand preferences of consumers in their markets; they released the resulting statistics to advertisers as a form of promotion. Most large city dailies collected census data about their markets and packaged them to show advertisers and advertising agencies why they belonged on the schedule.

In the same period, a number of newspapers, notably the *Minneapolis Star* and *Tribune* and the *Des Moines Register*, initiated statewide opinion polls modeled after the national Gallup Poll. These became established editorial features. Their directors reported to the editors rather than to the advertising or promotion departments. Several of them, like Sidney Goldish of Minneapolis and Glenn Roberts of Des Moines, were of imposing professional stature and were active in the American Association for Public Opinion Research. As a member and then as chairman of AA-

POR's Standards Committee, I was particularly sensitive to the mishandling of reports on surveys in a great many newspapers. I was especially irritated by the failure to differentiate between legitimate surveys and unscientific straw polls, the inability to distinguish between significant and nonsignificant research findings, and the common use of interviews haphazardly conducted by the newspaper's own reporting staff as an index of public thinking on controversial issues.[1] Such sloppy practices in reporting on public opinion would not be tolerated in the advertising and marketing world.

By the mid-1970s, market research occupied an important place in the advertising and sales activities of such newspapers as the *Chicago Tribune* and the *Los Angeles Times*, while at other major papers research was minimal or nonexistent. Many newspapers remained generally resistant to audience research, preferring to stick with the circulation counts of copies sold. Often the research assignment was located within the promotion department, with the promotion manager serving both functions. In other cases, research was an adjunct to advertising sales. Only in a limited number of papers did market research occupy an independent status cutting across departmental boundaries and reporting directly to the general manager or to the publisher.

From the editors' viewpoint, reader surveys, market surveys, and opinion surveys produced dry, dusty statistics that contrasted with the living realities that reporters were taught to discern and describe. Moreover, editors did not want to know too much about their audiences, lest this information be used to dictate to them what they should print.

The Research Advisory Council

The Bureau for years had cultivated close ties with the small fraternity of newspaper researchers. In 1959, Howard Hadley, the Bureau's research director, invited about a dozen researchers from newspapers and newspaper advertising representative firms to a meeting to discuss his plans and the research needs of the business. This gathering irritated the officers of the National Newspaper Promotion Association, who felt that their organization had first claim over the domain of newspaper research, and did not want their subordinates caucusing independently. Lipscomb told Hadley to cease and desist from any further meetings, and Hadley himself departed soon afterward. When I arrived early in 1960, we reassembled the group after carefully assuring the newspaper promotion executives that no secessionist tendencies would be tolerated.

Meetings of what became the Research Advisory Council to the Bureau of Advertising were generally held around the Bureau's conference table. They were devoted to a status report on our own research activities, a review of new presentations, and discussions of research issues confronting the business or on the agenda of individual papers. Other meetings were timed to coincide with gatherings of the Promotion Association, of the American Marketing Association, and of other organizations in which at least a minimal number of newspaper researchers participated. Over the years, the size and sophistication of the group grew considerably. In 1976, its membership, after some nervous genuflections in deference to what they imagined to be our proprietary jealousy, reconstituted themselves as an independent and autonomous body, the Newspaper Research Council. By 1990, this organization had 250 members and was holding two hardworking conferences a year.

Local Newspaper Research

The Bureau's national research on newspaper audiences seemed to require a counterpart at the local level. In conducting surveys of their audiences, newspapers had gone their independent routes. They defined their markets to suit their own competitive convenience rather than by the definitions used by advertisers or the government. They used different questions to qualify people as readers. They classified readers by age or income in different ways. They used different interviewing and sampling methods in their surveys. Although more and more newspapers were doing reader surveys in the 1960s, these could rarely be compared because of the variety of methods and practices. This lack of comparability meant that it was impossible to aggregate information from market to market in a way that advertisers would find impressive and useful.

At the Bureau, we grappled with many of these problems through the 1960s and came up with some proposals for standardization. These entailed (1) adoption of the volunteered "yesterday" response as the basis for defining a reader, as developed in our first Audits & Surveys study: (2) probability sampling; (3) defining markets according to the government's Standard Metropolitan Statistical Area or county boundaries; and (4) classification of readers into groups already defined by the research committee of the American Association of Advertising Agencies.

In retrospect, it seems as though it should have been a simple matter to get newspapers to agree on a standard set of procedures to describe their audiences. This simple goal required, however, the agreement of a number of separate organizations. The International Newspaper Advertising Executives had its own Research Committee. The American Association of Newspaper Representatives[2] had strong interests in the matter, as did the Newspaper Promotion Association. The research suppliers themselves had to be consulted. All had their own preferences and vested interests in the particular procedures they had been following.

It was obviously desirable to place the standardized information in a central data base. The Audit Bureau of Circulations had recently set up a computer facility to store its statistics. Although this organization had no experience or staff competence in the field of audience research, it still seemed logical to make it the repository of the numbers. This required negotiations with ABC's management and agreement from its Board. The venture was both facilitated and complicated by the eagerness of ABC's elected leadership to broaden the organization's scope by moving it beyond its traditional function of verifying the paid circulation of newspapers and magazines. Moving the Audit Bureau from the count of tangible objects to estimates based on subjective reports of readership opened up the possibility that its activities might expand into the murky realm of free publications, broadcast audiences, and trade show attendance.[3]

Then we faced the problem of getting agreement from the advertising customers. These included the Association of National Advertisers, the National Retail Merchants Association, and the American Association of Advertising Agencies. The AAAA contingent was particularly opinionated; they had both a research committee and a separate newspaper committee of media executives (some of whom had an extraordinarily unrealistic notion of their own research sophistication). We also sought the endorsement of the advertiser and agency members of the ARF Technical Committee. As in the case of every other organization, this required additional briefings, presentations, and discussions.

A principal sticking point was the definition of the market. As national advertisers had put a growing proportion of their media budgets into television, they had almost universally accepted the definitions imposed by the two principal television ratings services, A. C. Nielsen and Arbitron. Both divided the entire country up into television areas, which represented clusters of counties in which broadcast signals emanating from a particular central city represented the principal television input.

These Defined Market Areas (Nielsen) or Areas of Dominant Influence (Arbitron) generally covered substantial territories far beyond the limited circulation range of any individual newspaper. This meant that both metropolitan and smaller papers were inevitably disadvantaged. Their coverage or penetration almost always appeared to be a fraction of the market, while television stations, by the very nature of the definition, were watched, at least occasionally, throughout the entire area in which their signal could be viewed.

Since major advertisers were increasingly organizing their own sales territories to coincide with the television market boundaries, the implications of the debate went well beyond the immediate question of what areas newspapers should cover in their surveys. Many newspaper executives insisted that we had to give advertisers information the way they wanted it, while I held out for the principle that the redefinition of the market would place newspapers at a permanent competitive disadvantage, especially with the local advertisers on whom they mainly depended. The compromise solution was to call for marketing data to be presented both for metropolitan areas and also for television areas. (Since the time of these discussions, the television definitions have generally prevailed.)

Before agreement was reached on the modified version of our rather brief proposal, there was meeting after meeting, discussion after often passionate discussion, memorandum after memorandum. Public forums and debates were held as part of convention programs at the Newspaper Advertising Executives Association. The entire process took several years.

Syndicated and Custom Research

Even before the official endorsements, our proposed procedures were followed by a number of organizations that had already entered the field of syndicated local newspaper audience research, offering a standard service to all comers. The syndicated studies were designed to serve the needs of advertisers who wanted to compare audience size and characteristics for newspapers against those of other media and to match these against market requirements and profiles of product use. One by one, these services fell by the wayside. In 1986, Simmons-Scarborough, a merged subsidiary of the two surviving competitors, was providing biennial surveys in 52 major markets. When the merger dissolved after one study, both organizations decided to go it alone.

It proved economically unviable, however, for two competing services to survive. Both companies had been acquired by European conglomerates (Simmons by the British WPP, which owned the J. Walter Thompson and Ogilvy advertising agencies, and Scarborough by the Dutch VNU) and were under intense pressure to show profitable balance sheets. In 1989, VNU's Scarborough-Birch was left as the sole survivor, and the only alternative sources of local newspaper audience data were customized surveys that newspapers had to commission individually. Given the high level of random and human error in survey statistics, this was precisely the kind of situation about which I had long had nightmares.

The syndicated research served newspapers' advertising interests. Several other organizations were engaged in research that was directly oriented toward editors. One was Belden Associates, originally headed by Joe Belden, a pioneer whose Texas Poll of public opinion was carried by newspapers in that state; he had developed warm personal relationships with many editors. (This firm was also bought by VNU in 1989.) Another organization was Market Opinion Research of Detroit, headed by Fred Currier, former research manager for the *Detroit Free Press* and an original member of the Research Advisory Council. (Currier's partner was Robert Teeter, a Republican party activist who specialized in political polling and eventually became George Bush's pollster and headhunter.) Currier, because of his newspaper background, was interested in consulting with publishers and editors on general matters of readership, as well as in providing audience statistics for the advertising department.

As newspapers' appetite for audience surveys grew under the pressure of advertiser demand, both Belden and Currier extended their client rosters beyond their home states. Both began to hold periodic conferences at which their newspaper clients discussed problems of general interest in the industry, exchanged research findings, and discussed their implications for the editorial, as well as the advertising, side. Both Belden and Currier were in demand as speakers on convention programs—offering not only research data but also counsel on how newspapers could attract more readers. Belden, for example, showed the Associated Press Managing Editors a redesigned newspaper front page made up of an enormous number of small tidbit items that were intended to entice the reader into the inside of the paper. Belden also collected newspapers from various places and analyzed their content, passing along word of interesting editorial innovations to his clients and prospective clients.

Across the country, newspapers employed the services of several dozen regional research organizations. Through studies of the readers of specific dailies, researchers were often able to develop useful insights and suggestions that they discussed with editors on a personal basis, independent of any contact with the advertising department. Such consulting relationships had a degree of trust and intimacy that was impossible for an organization like the Bureau to achieve, working as we did with abstract national statistics and dealing with newspaper executives en masse.

The general ferment in newspaper research must be kept in mind as a background to the battles over the Readership Project's research program, in which an altogether different set of protagonists was involved.

A Research Plan

A good deal of existing data had already been analyzed before the Project got under way, but much more remained to be done.

Before the Airlie House meeting, I had drafted "A Program of Research To Help Build Circulation." [4] Under the heading of "Internal Research" it suggested a number of directions for staff-run activity, beginning with a continuing analysis of circulation trends and a search of local newspaper audience studies, to identify case histories of newspapers with striking records of success in building readership and especially to find papers with unusually high and low levels of readership among young people and Blacks. The effects of different levels of rate increases on single-copy and subscription sales would be tracked and used to build a mathematical model to predict the effects of future increases. Surveys of circulation practices would be conducted, with the help of ICMA.[5] Basic data would be gathered on newspaper economics.[6]

Under the heading of "External Research," I listed projects that would require "out-of-pocket" budgets: a systematic content analysis of newspapers with above or below average readership among young people and Blacks; a series of coordinated, depth-interview studies with both readers and nonreaders of specific newspapers; a study of the public's daily exposure to different news sources; and a series of editorial experiments ("a simulated newspaper's content can be varied by taking elements from different papers and combining them in a familiar format, e.g. introducing news summaries, adding new feature material.")

Other research would address the public's reading interests, the media habits of preadolescent children, and the Newspaper in Education program. There would be a systematic review of the current state of knowledge on the decline of reading skills, followed by "a small conference of educators and reading experts to discuss the existing evidence, to propose research tactics, and to suggest remedial steps."

Most of these proposals were carried through to completion in the next six years.

How the Public Gets Its News

We did not wait for the newspaper industry's mills to grind before proceeding on our way. The first step was a large-scale national study of reading habits, launched with the support of the Newsprint Information Committee. This was the eighth substantial study funded for us by the Committee, starting with the Harvard research on advertising repetition. Its members were now increasingly concerned about the possible effects of declining readership on newsprint consumption. I had shown them the same presentations I had made to the publishers, and they were well aware of the urgency of the problem. Now they came up with $100,000 for a survey to update the findings of our earlier studies of the newspaper audience and to provide the diagnostic foundation for the Readership Project. By the time its financing received final approval, the Project was already authorized and the organizing steps were under way.

The Bureau's own research staff were somewhat awed by the size and elusive nature of the problem we were trying to address. As Orenstein put it,[7]

> The Project we are proposing to the NIC is a study of the newspaper as an institution. The other way to go is to study newspapers as individual entities and see what specific attributes make for success in one case and failure in another. Both approaches are probably necessary. Just to concentrate on the latter would, if the effort were successful, tell us what individual papers are doing that's right and wrong. However, we may find ourselves identifying elements that enable a particular newspaper to increase its readership without knowing whether or not this increase represents only a temporary and incidental reversal of a long-range trend or decreasing readership.

Lehman wrote:[8]

> Every time I have the nerve to stop and really think about the problem of declining circulation and readership, I'm struck by its enormity, complexity, and paradoxical nature. . . . The overall problem will necessarily have to be attacked piecemeal, and yet at some point we must attempt to integrate the pieces into a single whole and assess the relative importance of each factor. The claims of model-building researchers notwithstanding, I don't know how it is possible to assign individual weights to the influences involved, or to combine the findings from independent research projects differing in their basic approach, focus, and scope.

But he then gamely proceeded to list a whole series of research proposals. The Bureau's research staff was solely responsible both for the scope of what we chose to investigate in the national survey and for the design of the specific questions. At this stage, there was none of the outside participation that the Project was to cultivate. In planning the study (which ultimately carried the title, "How the Public Gets Its News"), we were able to some extent to build on our previous surveys of newspaper reading and reader attitudes. These studies were geared to the Bureau's advertising interests. Editorial subjects were introduced only as secondary questions to satisfy our curiosity and to serve the conviction that advertising and editorial matter were inseparable elements in the reader's search for useful information. Now the primary emphasis was on reading and interest in the different kinds of news and features.

We already knew from our past research who the nonreaders were, at least the nonreaders of any particular day's newspapers. They were likely to be young, poorly educated, low-income, single, and members of minority groups. The essential objective in the new survey was to see what various elements of the newspaper appealed more to some kinds of people and less to others. The important question was whether newspapers, by modifying their content, might be better able to serve the needs and desires of the nonreaders without at the same time alienating the readers they already had.

We had to start out by measuring the newspaper audience. We needed to know how many people read the paper on a typical weekday or Sunday and who these readers were. We also had to find out how often people read a paper over the course of a week and then to identify those who read most often. We wanted, as in the past, to learn how the newspaper got into readers' hands and why a particular paper was selected over another, when the readers had a choice.

In past surveys, we had made a great deal out of the variation in attention that different kinds of people gave to different elements of the paper—both news and advertising. The traditional measure of attention to print had long been the "noting" score obtained by the "recognition" method. With this technique, readers of a publication are taken back through the pages and asked to identify those items they remember having read or looked at the first time around. A good deal of experimental research had shown that these reports of past readership were subject to all kinds of error. People sometimes falsely claimed to have read items that they actually had not seen. But for every such error, they forgot to mention ten items that they really had seen. Not surprisingly, the items they did not remember tended to be those that didn't interest them. We looked on recognition or noting scores, therefore, as "projections" of the reader's attitudes rather than as actual measurements of behavior.

A direct indication of interest would surely correlate closely with readers' reports of recognition. It could, moreover, be used to measure the reactions of people who had not read the paper, as well as of those who had. But an individual's interest in a particular item might not always fully reflect his sense of its value. There was reason to believe that people expected their newspaper to include all sorts of information that did not fascinate them personally. They might be more interested in a local accident than in a major piece of legislation before Congress, which they probably would acknowledge to be more important. Importance emerged, therefore, as a second criterion by which items could be evaluated. Thus I came up with what the sociologist Robert Park had long before described as the two essential attributes of news—interest and importance. (This may not have been independent invention but a residual recollection of Park's definition.)

Lehman came up with another ingenious diagnostic tool: the "personal newspaper." Through a series of questions, people were asked to select the ingredients of a newspaper that would serve just their own predilections, without regard to whether it left out material of interest to anyone else.

The Editors' Survey

All the information we were collecting about readers' responses to content would make sense, I thought, only if it could be compared with editors' expectations and assumptions. If an incongruity existed between the reality of the public's tastes and editors' notions of them, a playback of this incongruity to the editors would provoke discussion, provide insight, and thereby improve the attractiveness of newspapers.

My interest in this sort of thing had been whetted by a study I had once done on the "operating assumptions" of the U.S. Information Agency.[9] By getting working propagandists to spell out what they thought were the rules of their game, it was possible to see where their assumptions were in conflict and also where they contradicted the available evidence. I suspected that some of the same strategy might be applied to illuminate the editorial practices of the American press.

The result of this was a questionnaire for newspaper editors, along the lines alluded to in the original research plan. I sent a draft of it[10] to the president of ASNE, George Chaplin, editor of the *Honolulu Advertiser*, who, in turn, sent it to several other of his colleagues for their suggestions. Later, after some indignant rumblings from his peers, and to my surprise (given his good nature and initial positive attitude), he objected to the fact that in mailing the questionnaire I said it was being done "with the cooperation of ASNE" and that the officers had "reviewed the material." Pointing out that there was no formal "review" by the officers of ASNE, he distanced the organization from any responsibility for the survey. The final version was mailed out to the ASNE membership, and I was invited to report the results at their annual meeting in Honolulu in May 1977, a few weeks before the Readership Project was slated to begin.

This questionnaire covered the editors' perception of the various elements of content. It also solicited their ideas of what made a newspaper successful with readers and successful by their own criteria of excellence. I wanted to find out whether editors thought that a good newspaper, as defined by their own definitions of editorial quality, would also be attractive to the reading public.

The study seemed to present a splendid opportunity to assert the thesis that the secret to success lay in improved quality, of which most American newspapers were in substantial need. I had been pleased to discover, in an earlier analysis, that newspapers that had won Pulitzer and other similar editorial awards did better than average in the circulation race. I was driven by a missionary zeal to improve the American press—a worthier goal than the service of Mammon to which my career in advertising had ostensibly been dedicated.

In my own naïveté, I underestimated the naïveté of many editors about research, and the depth of their hostility to the advertising sector of their own business, on which their bread and butter depended and of which I was perceived as an infamous representative. Eager to get moving on some concrete manifestations of the

Readership Project's existence, I had neglected to recognize either the significance of the demons I was stirring up or the political necessity of mending fences.

The survey showed that editors of successful and unsuccessful newspapers seemed to be operating by identical editorial philosophies. The inevitable conclusion seemed to be that the forces that made a paper lose circulation were largely independent of its content. Success or failure had more to do with pricing, distribution, and population changes in the cities where papers published than with the character of the editorial mix or the operating practices or theories of individual editors.

When I presented this conclusion to the ASNE convention, it might have seemed likely to evoke the editors' delight. They had just been let off the hook, but most of them had the opposite reaction. To accept my conclusion would have reduced their self-importance, their sense of full responsibility for the fortunes of the papers they directed. They wanted to take the blame, since only by doing so could they be left with the illusion that they had full control over their newspapers' destinies.

Although my report on the survey drew a polite response and even a few plaudits, it also drew some sharp comment centered on the mistaken belief that I thought editorial quality could be defined by an opinion poll.

And the critical comments were not unreasonable. Drake Mabrey, managing editor of the *Des Moines Register* and *Tribune*, wrote:[11]

> I find the enclosed questionnaire rather simplistic and nearly impossible to complete in any depth (nonetheless, I did). For example, what is a feature these days? Is it a story about a family living in a $50,000 home fighting city hall because sewer leaks into their backyard from an unknown source? The point is, the definition of news these days cannot be broken down into simply hard news and features. There are all areas in between.

I replied:

> I can well understand your reservations about the kind of simplistic choices into which the questionnaire forced you and the others who responded. But it was not our intention to take the answers that you and others gave us at face value. Our purpose is rather to see how editors of different kinds of papers differ in the way they

The annual dinner at the ANPA convention, Waldorf-Astoria Hotel, New York 1973.

Co-chairmen of the Newspaper Readership Project, Otto Silha (left) and Joe D. Smith.

The ANPA's President Jerry Friedheim (left) and Vice President Bob Burke.

The Bureau's President Charlie Lipscomb (left) and his successor, Jack Kauffman, in the mid-1960s.

The Bureau's staff: (Clockwise from upper left) Creative Director Hank Simons and researchers Stu Tolley, Chuck Lehman, Thelma Anderson, and Al Gollin.

The Editors: (top left) Mike O'Neill (New York *Daily News*) and Bill Hornby (Denver *Post*), (left, center row) Gene Patterson (St. Petersburg *Times* and *Independent*) and Lester Markel (then Sunday editor of *The New York Times* in 1963). Researcher Ruth Clark.

Facing page: A peaceful meeting of the Research Committee, 1978. (Clockwise around the table, from left): the author, Ken Todd (Indianapolis *Star* and *News*, representing ICMA), Pete McKnight (ASNE), Glenn Roberts (Des Moines *Register*, NRC), Mike O'Neill (New York *Daily News* and ASNE, Chairman), Chuck Hakes (Detroit *News*, NRC), Ed Miller (Allentown *Call* and *Chronicle*, APME) and John Leard (Richmond *Times-Dispatch* and *News-Leader*, APME).

Publishers anointed and appointed. (Clockwise from top left) Frank Batten (Landmark Communications), Alvah Chapman (Knight-Ridder), Bob Marbut (Harte-Hanks) and Bill Cowles (Spokane *Chronicle* and *Spokesman-Review*).

The Editors' Exchange

... Sharing Ideas to Improve Readership

July 1990
Volume 13, Number 6

Dear Editor:

Are you satisfied with your newspaper's policy on identifying people who have been sexually abused? A lot of newspapers have been looking at how they deal with rape and related crimes in recent months. The Des Moines (Iowa) Register (circ. 210,000), which has for years had a policy of not identifying women who have been raped, recently began asking the victims whether they wished to be identified by name. Some have agreed to make their names public. The policy change occurred after Register editor Geneva Overholser wrote a column expressing dissatisfaction with hiding names. "Does not our very delicacy in dealing with rape victims subscribe to the idea that rape is a crime of sex rather than the crime of brutal violence that it really is?" she asked. "Surely the sour blight of prejudice is best treated by being subjected to strong sunlight."

In 1982, Carol Oukrop, now director of the A. Q. Miller School of Journalism and Mass Communications at Kansas State University, studied newspapers' policies on rape coverage. At that time, 68 percent of the 375 editors who participated in the survey said that the names of adult complainants should not be reported in rape cases. Fifteen percent disagreed; 17 percent were undecided. Oukrop found that large papers were more likely to protect the names of rape survivors than small papers.

Some editors — and readers — have expressed discomfort with concealing the name of someone who has been raped but publishing the name of someone accused of rape. If you have changed your policies on reporting rape and other crimes of sexual violence, or have views on the subject, please send them as soon as possible to The Editors' Exchange, ASNE, P.O. Box 17004, Washington, DC 20041. We will publish the results in a future edition of The Editors' Exchange.

Route to:

THE WEEK AHEAD / JUNE 10-JUNE 16

Offer a panoramic view of the week ahead. The Atlanta Journal and Constitution Sunday newspaper (circ. 651,000) does a masterful job of highlighting each week's important upcoming events. *(See example left.)* For information, contact Glenn McCutchen, exec. ed., at the Journal and Constitution, 72 Marietta St. N.W., Atlanta, GA. (404-526-5337.)

Callers jam 'Pediatricians' Hot Line.' The West Palm Beach (Fla.) Post (circ. 156,000) corralled four pediatricians to answer questions over the telephone for three hours one evening. Some 201 callers took advantage of the service; another 374 tried but could not get through. A reporter on the scene with the doctors described the event. The paper also published the "best" questions with answers. Not only was the feature popular with readers; other professionals have contacted the newspaper to volunteer their services for a hot line program. For information on the event, contact Melissa Segrist, features ed., or Lynn Calber, asst. features ed., at the Post, P.O. Box 24700, West Palm Beach, FL 33416. (407-837-4100.)

Above: A recent issue of the editors' newsletter funded by the Readership Project.

Below: Two of the ads in a campaign designed to highlight newspapers' information functions.

*So you left your heart
with someone who works
in newspaper circulation
...and they left you because
they had to run a
carrier recruitment rally.
Have we got
something
for you...!*

*The
circulation
spouse's survival
manual*

What's Inside:

Two simple training formulas:

Whether you want to teach your carriers to <u>know</u> something, or to <u>do</u> something, Roquefort has a foolproof system for getting your message across. After watching the Roquefort Files, your DMs will have the means to train their carriers easily and <u>thoroughly</u>.

How to improve service:

Roquefort says that good service and collection habits start when the carrier sells and signs up a new subscriber. That's why he shows how it's done properly. Roquefort also advocates making sure carriers know <u>exactly</u> what is meant by good service, what they gain by giving it, what they lose by not giving good service.

How to improve collections:

No ifs, ands, or buts, carriers and their parents must know that regular, balanced collections are a condition for keeping the route.

And more!

Like how to help carriers and customers handle problems between themselves. And how to handle a carrier who is continually giving trouble.

Above: Cover of a manual intended to explain circulation workers' irregular hours to their families.

Below: Inside page of the "leave-behind" booklet for a slide presentation ("The Roquefort Files") used in the training of circulation district managers.

Typical small-space advertisements supplied to newspapers to support regular readership and promote subscription sales.

The cover of a promotion campaign booklet addressed to newspapers.

Bureau staffers like Bob Gaines, Claire Lloyd and Jim Rolling were the models.

Are y

A newspaper route is a go

1. *You want to make money.* Is there someth want—something that your parents can't give yc money for college, expensive sports equipmer spending money? A newspaper route is a good wa what you want.

After all, there are lots of ways to spend your ti paper carriers have something to show for their ti

The job offers extra rewards and bonuses, to newspapers run carrier contests that give you a ch earn valuable gifts, sightseeing trips, or substan prizes over and above the regular take from your

And remember that customer tips can add a sizab of change to your bank roll.

The different route leads to profit.

2. *You know what "paying dues" means.* Yc teacher will tell you that profits are the extras you making an investment.

A newspaper route offers real profits. Invest some effort, and the profits are yours. Like anything els "real world," what you get out of it will depend on put into it.

The different route is the road to responsibility.

e of them?

● go. Here are some reasons why.

3. *You enjoy a challenge.* A newspaper route will give you a chance to learn and master all kinds of new situations.

A lot of what you learn will be really useful to you—now, and always. Like how to make sales, how to organize your time, how to handle customers and keep records, how to set goals for yourself, and make decisions.

Mastering the challenges a paper route offers gives you the confidence to face other challenges in other areas of your life. That's a pretty good job benefit.

The different route leads to growth.

4. *You like people.* A newspaper route is a great job for people who like people . . . because serving people is the biggest part of a carrier's responsibilities.

You'll get to know the customers on your daily route, how to keep them satisfied, how to handle complaints. And you'll be seeing many new faces when you're working on sales campaigns.

The carrier sales training most newspapers provide will not only help you make sales—it'll teach you the gentle art of persuasion that'll help you deal with people in all areas of your life.

And it's nice to know that as a paper carrier, you'll really be helping people. A route brings you closer to them, and through your service, the newspaper brings them closer to their world.

The different route brings people together.

Above: Centerfold for a folder to accompany a presentation designed to recruit juvenile carriers.

Below: Ads from a campaign that stressed the utilitarian, money-saving aspects of newspapers.

THE FIRST FREEDOM

"First is freedom of speech and expression, everywhere in the world." Franklin D. Roosevelt

A Guide for Discussion

Cover of the discussion guide for the film, "The First Freedom." The real message of the film was to be left by the teacher or discussion leader.

A frame from the concluding moments of "I Saw It in The Paper." A hard-hat at a nuclear-power construction site gets a copy of *Newsday* and asks, "Can I Keep It?"

answer the questions and also to see how answers on one question relate to the answers given to others.

Another managing editor, Albert Cross of the *Monterey Peninsula Herald*, said he had declined to complete the questionnaire,

> not out of neglect, but rather from a conviction that such surveys are contrived. . . . I consider this form of data collection a waste of time at best and harmful and misleading at worst. . . . I am convinced that journalism is much more an art than a science and that it will continue to be.

One of my main critics was Michael J. O'Neill, executive editor of the *New York Daily News* and co-chairman of ASNE's newly created Readership and Research Committee. O'Neill was a veteran newsman—tall, earnest, bespectacled, gray-haired, and pleasant looking. Coming from an impressive career as a science writer and Washington correspondent, he had worked hard to upgrade the popular tabloid *News* by infusing it with more serious content and toning down its more sensational aspect. His paper, then the largest general circulation daily in North America, had for years undergone a precipitous circulation decline as its working class white ethnic readers moved to the suburbs.

O'Neill's conversation was soft and halting, but he exuded a passionate though highly controlled intensity. He shared with the rest of ASNE's leadership a determination that the editors were going to take charge of the Readership Project's research program.

Markel

Another formidable voice raised on the subject of quality—also with a mistaken notion of what I was after—was that of Lester Markel, the former long-time Sunday editor of *The New York Times*. He had the reputation of being a tyrannical perfectionist. (On one occasion, the writer and MIT professor Harold Isaacs submitted an article to *The New York Times Magazine*. Markel returned it four times, each time with new criticisms. The fifth time Isaacs resubmitted his original text. Markel responded, "Now you've got it!")

Markel had relinquished his power very reluctantly. For years after leaving the *Times* he continued to lecture, write books, appear on television programs, and participate in the extracurricular affairs of journalism, of which he considered himself a senior custodian.

At the age of eighty-two, Markel was actively crusading for "a new newspaper." He had gotten early wind of the plans for the Readership Project and felt that he could play an important part. He wrote to Friedheim offering his services, and Burke had been sent as a special emissary to New York to keep him at bay. Eventually, his offers of help were referred to me. He called to ask me to lunch, and as a main agenda item sent along an article prepared for the *ASNE Bulletin*.

> The publishers grope darkly for remedies; they spend thousands on surveys without result. . . . They fail or refuse to recognize the basic cause of the slump which is this: even though the newspaper's primary task—its very reason for being—is to print the news, it has been doing a far-from-adequate job. . . . Especially devastating has been the trend toward "Gallup-Editing"—the endeavor, through suspect surveys and garbage-fed-garbage-producing computerology, to discover what the reader wants and to supply it in full measure and without question.[12]

I told him subsequently that I could not think of anything in the article with which I disagreed.

> My only question, however, is whether most editors of major metropolitan dailies wouldn't claim that they are trying to fulfill your prescription right now. Ep Hoyt [Palmer Hoyt, long-time publisher and editor of the *Denver Post*] once remarked to me, apropos of some unflattering comments I had made, "The *Denver Post* couldn't survive very long with a 20 percent coverage of its market as *The New York Times* can." The dilemma I think editors have to face is that readers aren't necessarily attracted to what is most useful and relevant for them. I'd like to think that quality is always the answer, but I think there are a lot of conflicting interpretations of what quality is.[13]

Markel retorted:

> No, sir, I do not believe for a moment that most publishers are trying to fulfill my prescription—more than that, I suspect that no more than two or three out of fifty would endorse my program. . . . I do not think the issue is one of "quality" but rather one of objec-

tive and realization of that objective. Quality then becomes the measure of the effort's success and not the effort itself.[14]

Markel proposed to ANPA that a closer relationship between publishers and editors could be brought about by setting up a small working committee that would meet every month or two "to review developments" and by putting out monthly "a well-written bulletin reporting editorial, publishing, circulation, etc." Both ideas were in fact closely similar to those already under discussion by the Project's planners. Markel followed up with what he described as a "stream-of-consciousness" memo on "Publishers Versus or With Editors" in which he suggested that ANPA appoint a "general director of research," covering mechanical, business, and editorial problems, with an advisory committee for each area.

While I told Markel that I was wary of this proposal, I also sent him a copy of the confidential plans for the Readership Project, which had not yet been announced. He was

> disturbed and surprised . . . because for the first time, I understood that the program had been approved in general by a number of publishers and editors—which meant obviously that any changes I suggested would have virtually no chance of adoption. What then, I wondered, was the point of the considerable effort I had devoted to the project?

After reviewing his noteworthy life accomplishments, he confessed that he had held

> high hopes . . . to be part of what I looked upon as the kind of project to which my career had been dedicated. . . . But none of this, I gather, is in the cards. Another dreamer, another idealist, another "radical" I shall be called. . . . And so, I am now aware, I shall have to crusade in other areas. And the newspaper will continue to compete with television for circulation, failing to realize this is a battle it cannot win.[15]

By the time this heart-rending epistle arrived, I was off to the big advertising directors' convention and my patience was becoming somewhat frayed, but I tried not to let my acknowledgment show this: "I think the newspaper industry would be foolish not to continue to take advantage of your experience and wisdom, and I'm sorry if in the pressure of recent weeks I haven't made as much use of it as I might or would like to."[16]

Markel was not to be brushed off lightly. His reply began, "Are you human?" and referred to my "apology for not asking me to do more useless work without compensation." I soothed him by telephone. Within a few weeks he had resumed the correspondence, which was periodically augmented by personal conversations. It was easy enough for me to see him; he and I lived in the same apartment building.

As a member of ASNE, Markel had received my editors' questionnaire, and he was derisive in his comments. His view was that quality defied definition. Like most newspaper editors of his era, he was horrified at the idea that newspapers could be tailored to specifications derived from reader surveys and felt strongly that they had to be edited by informed judgment. As it happened, this was exactly the position from which I started, even though much of my own working career had been spent in the collection and perusal of research data.

Markel discovered a new correspondent, Joe D. Smith, to whom he directed a number of letters focused on the subject of the newspaper in education. Smith responded graciously, but Markel quickly gave up on him too: "I have decided, therefore, that I shall quit these unprofitable and unappreciated efforts, and try to make my views known, not as I had hoped, as an inlaw, but as an outlaw."[17] A month later he came upon our proposal for *The Editors Exchange* and applied for the job as editor.

When Markel died a few months later, his beloved *New York Times* paid him an elegant editorial tribute:[18]

> He was among the first to comprehend that the complexity of events and democracy of the nation required more of a newspaper than the reporting of news. News without explanation was mere entertainment, an empty or even misleading fact. Why, he kept asking, in an age when ordinary journalists were taught to settle for who, what, where, when and how. The man could be ego-shattering or inspiring. But always his message was plain. He was the sworn enemy of journalism of yesterday, of the naive notion that yesterday's speech or yesterday's war had merely to be described to be understood.

Hornby

A forceful advocate for the doctrine of editorial judgment was William H. Hornby, the editor of the *Denver Post* and president of the American Society of Newspaper Editors from 1979 to 1980. Hornby was moon-faced and affable but carried a worried look. More than a year before the outset of the Readership Project, he delivered the Sigma Delta Chi Foundation Lecture at Virginia Commonwealth University. Entitled "Beware the Market Thinkers," it expressed both his suspicions of research and his concerns about the weakening of editorial privilege that would arise if newspapers were designed to meet sales goals set by the business office.

Hornby drew the battle lines with this argument:

> Financial analysts of the press are suggesting that we don't need newspapers, we need use-papers. In nearly any newspaper organization one can find theorists who urge editors to poll the readership, "research the market," find out what the people think they want to know, give it to them in the most effective "package," zingy display, and enjoy heartier sales. "Ask yourself what business you're really in," says one school of management analysis. Maybe, they suggest the newspaper would be better off if it were seen as being in the "communication" business, or the "information handling" business.

In refutation, Hornby argued eloquently that:

> The newspaper is an institution that sets out to do more than just maximize its market. . . . The press has never been and never should be in business to give the people just what they want. . . . its purpose is first and foremost to provide news. . . . If the hard, spot news of what's happening becomes more and more capsuled in easy doses, between columns of matter on how to take a bath, newspapers will move away from the central human need they particularly exist to satisfy. . . . Their product must produce a profit to exist, but the product doesn't exist for a profit.[19]

In practice, no editor could actually edit his paper "predominantly from market research returns," and newspapers since their earliest origins had packed their columns with utilitarian and entertaining reading matter that met no definition of news. But Hornby had made his point, and it was a good one. His sentiments perfectly articulated my own personal opinions; they also appeared to me to be in direct contradiction to the research course on which, I was to discover, the ASNE appeared to be bent.

While the Readership Project's first year was still being planned, Hornby said:[20]

> I am extremely optimistic about the value of this [Readership] project if, and you know my bias from previous exchanges, we use our results to help the news-paper perform its historic function in our society more effectively, and not to lead us into changing that function just because some "market" is said to demand change.

Taking his message into the camp of his marketing adversaries, Hornby addressed the INAME on the theme of conflict between "church" and "state."[21] "The advertising executive's dominant value is to maximize revenue through the sale of the most linage." He contrasted this with "the traditional editorial drive to maximize news content."

> That these values conflict is a truism we all live with. No news there. The degree to which such conflicts are problems must depend a great deal on the strength of a particular publisher and his overall view of his newspaper. The traditional form of newspaper organization has stressed separation of the editorial and advertising departments, making the care and feeding of any overall design in readership viewpoint the publisher's function, a tremendous task for one man. . . . This traditional form of newspaper organization and the modes of education that feed it are no longer entirely adequate to our problems.
>
> On the typical newspaper today I would suspect that the direct, sustained communication between editorial and advertising departments is minimal and that any stress on their common interest in total design and in maximizing newspaper readership is minimal. . . . Nor does the typical management, meaning the publisher, do much about building bridges between them. The time-honored reason for this was the tendency for business considerations, through the advertising department, to be brought to bear improperly on the independent exercise of editorial judgment as to what was news. But perhaps, just perhaps, we are beyond that day.
>
> I can even see on the distant horizon an ad executive who will refuse to sell a page position because of its effect on the newshole or an editor who will refuse to move an ad back in the paper because it has higher readership than a wire story. I can see the day when an editor, asked to move an ad, asks, "What's in it?" or an ad executive, hearing that a shah has fallen, calls to ask, "Should we rearrange the space?" To see that day, I admit, you need pretty good eyesight.

Hornby spoke warmly of the Readership Project:

We've had for the first time on a national scale an organized and formal effort to break through the old walls of newspaper organization, fired by the amazing realization that declining readership and improved product design is everybody's problem.

Hornby's suspicions later made him relatively disinclined to go along with the majority of his peers when they developed research enthusiasms of their own.[22]

Editors and Publishers

Getting editors to be more sensitive to reader interests, according to the publisher of one of the country's biggest newspapers, was "like moving a graveyard." Even the most powerful newspaper magnates sometimes seemed to have the feeling that editors were beyond their control. Thus James L. Knight, a principal stockholder of Knight-Ridder, said,

> I have a quaint feeling that the modern-day editor attempts to dress up the paper with inconsequential junk and heavy special coverage items. It used to be that a newspaper without 15 or 20 front page items was considered rare. Now you get from 3 to 5 stories and they are jumped to inside pages. Your choice is severely limited. I find I can pick up the *Wall Street Journal* with its 40 or more front page items, scan the page and find something that I am particularly interested in. Do you suppose other people are peculiar like myself and find the current editions are becoming less and less meaningful?[23]

Several years after the conclusion of the Readership Project, I found myself in a relaxed dinner discussion with a dozen publishers after a strenuous all-day meeting. The subject at hand was the inflexibility of newspapers in accommodating advertisers who wanted to use units of unconventional sizes and shapes, sometimes in unusual or unfamiliar positions. "Let's face it," said one of the publishers, "we're all afraid of our editors." Although this was said with a chuckle, no one in the room disagreed.

Unlike magazine publishers, who typically are concerned only with the business side, newspaper publishers are unmistakably the chief executives of their organizations, with the power to hire and fire editors at will. This remains the case, even though most newspaper publishers today are not proprietors of the properties they run but appointed managers serving the interests of a larger corporation. In the last twenty-five years, to my knowledge, publishers have actually fired their editors only in a handful of cases. Normal wear and tear occurs in any organization in which executives get pushed out or moved along, but the newspaper business is special.

Those few cases in which a publisher and his editor have publicly clashed over editorial judgments have aroused enormous publicity and indignation. This happened when the notorious John McGoff ousted two of his Michigan editors who refused to carry articles attacking President Carter on the basis of fabricated rumors.[24] (McGoff, it was later shown, acted as an agent of the South African government in an attempted takeover of the *Sacramento Union*.) The editor of the *Dayton Journal*, Charles Alexander, was dismissed when he defied Dan Mahoney, the publisher, who objected to the use of four-letter words in a front page news story that quoted directly from the court proceedings of a sensational local trial. Alexander entered Valhalla and became a journalism professor.

In 1984, the editorial board of the *Miami Herald* chose to endorse Walter Mondale for the presidency while the newly appointed publisher, Richard Capen, preferred Ronald Reagan. The editor, James Hampton, handed in his resignation. Capen refused to accept it and offered him a signed column on the editorial page to present his views in opposition to the endorsement of Reagan that the publisher wrote himself.[25]

This last is a noteworthy case because publishers generally pick their editors, who pick their editorial page editors and writers, who in turn formulate the positions that they want to take on controversial subjects. While presidential endorsements represent the most clear-cut expressions of partisan alignment, most newspaper editorials offer opinions on matters that are far less charged emotionally, ranging from tongue-clucking at foreign potentates to expressions of indignation over local refuse disposal systems. Such commentary often defies classification on the conventional right/left political spectrum.

Publishers are by and large conservative executives who share the views of their counterparts in other forms of business. Journalism has always attracted individuals of a reformist bent. In the last fifteen or twenty years, it has been a particularly appealing profession for idealists who want to change society by investigating its iniquities.

Although surveys of newsroom personnel show them to be centrist in their political leanings, journalists in prestigious news organizations show a liberal inclination. Editors are a decidedly more conservative bunch. Some of this no doubt reflects the aging process. Editors are more mature and settled in their ways than the young reporters who work for them. This often means that they are more tolerant of institutions as they find them and more accommodating to the powers that be in the communities in which they work. They may also tend to become more accommodating to their employers. In any case, they are surely more aware of the line beyond which they cannot deal lightly with their employers' most sacred interests of property and class.

When we speak of editors and publishers in general terms, the typical case is that of a paper of 15,000 circulation in a small community whose values are likely to be rock-ribbed Republican. But the typical reader is not reading a typical paper, because most of the population lives in large metropolitan areas. The editors of big-city papers are more likely to represent a liberal or independent viewpoint, and they have an importance disproportionate to their numbers. One hundred and twenty-five papers with circulations of more than 100,000 represented the lion's share (54 percent) of all newspaper reading in 1990. In fact, fifteen papers with circulations of more than 500,000 represented 20 percent of all the newspaper circulation in the United States.

In the history of American journalism, from Horace Greeley and James Gordon Bennett, through Joseph Pulitzer and William Randolph Hearst, to Allen Neuharth and Rupert Murdoch, the outstanding publishers have been those who have also been editors themselves. But the ability of such individuals to perform superbly both as businessmen and as newsmen is the exception, not the rule. The tradition of editorial independence and autonomy remains a peculiar strength of the American press, despite the inevitable occasional groveling before publishers' prejudices and advertisers' interests or demands.

Editors and Readership

Like those in every other occupation in the business, editors saw themselves at the center of the newspaper universe. But editors assumed this posture with a special certainty. They considered the loss of readership a problem for which they were uniquely responsible. If the editorial product had to take the blame, it would also be the key to regeneration. The decline in circulation, particularly on afternoon dailies, increasingly preoccupied them, both in ASNE and in APME. The APME had a dozen committees that produced reports for its annual meeting each fall, often based on surveys to which, unfortunately, only a small number of members responded.

Incredible as it may seem, forty years after Gallup began reader surveys for the *Des Moines Register,* many large newspapers still had no information on the characteristics of their readers, let alone about their tastes or interests. Papers were designed and edited for "everybody," based on editors' instincts, values, and judgments. Faced with readership declines during the 1970s, some of them turned to market research to discover who their readers were and what they thought of the papers.

As we have already seen, research to describe newspaper readers had already become widely accepted in the advertising department, if for no other reason than that advertisers required it. But editors resisted research because of their long-standing credo that the essence of their craft was precisely in their knowledge of what was right for their readers. This being the case, the content of the paper had to be determined by journalistic canons and not dictated by the readers themselves. Editors were thus determined to take control over any interpretation of research that might mandate a change in their practices.

The Bureau's 1971 study of the newspaper audience included measurements of the reported readership of a large random sampling of items, editorial as well as advertising, in a true cross-section of the American press. The findings had important implications for editors, which I was eager to share with them. But I could get the research before the 1972 ASNE convention only by turning over my slides to a panel of editors to argue about the meaning of the data. They would not sit still for a direct presentation from me because I was a representative of the advertising departments against which they considered themselves to be in a state of perpetual warfare. Neuharth put it to me succinctly in a meeting of the Project's Steering Committee five years later. "You, Leo, are a huckster, and I use the term with great fondness. But no one who represents the advertising side can ever get the confidence of the editors. They spend their days fighting to keep clear of the advertising department." This attitude was certainly reflected in the first meeting of the Readership Project's Research Committee,[26] in which O'Neill and I engaged in a kind of shouting match, both of us insisting on talking at the same time.

In other media, antagonism toward research was not so readily apparent. Magazine editors and broadcast program producers had long made use of studies in which audiences were questioned about their likes and dislikes. Magazine editors knew what kinds of cover photographs were likely to sell more copies, and the resulting guidelines were generally—though not slavishly—followed. In radio and later in television, the networks tested programs as a matter of course. Broadcasters were obsessed with the audience ratings, which determined whether or not shows continued on the air. Research that could predict whether or not viewers would like a show was regarded as the first step to keep rating levels high.

Newspaper editors resisted such uses of research as expressions of the dominance of the business side, against which they were determined to defend themselves. Moreover, they regarded themselves, in a sense, as practicing social scientists. Their own intelligence networks were made up of reporters who kept close watch on the day-to-day affairs of their communities and were sensitive to trends in the popular mood.

The same innocence that caused editors to resist research was later sometimes reflected in a lack of judgment after they were converted into the ranks of the devout. Some editors were induced to use the services of reputable survey research firms that had been employed by their advertising departments. Others gravitated toward researchers who specialized in the kind of qualitative interviewing that resembled the journalistic practice of picking up statements that lent themselves to verbatim quotation. A popular form of this approach was the so-called "focus group," which, in the mid-1970s, was enjoying a vogue in advertising research.

Battling the Editors

The first premise of all who practice the craft of journalism in America is that the First Amendment is sacred. A newspaper's stock in trade—its ability to win readers—depends upon its credibility and therefore on its editorial integrity. In an era of local monopoly newspapers, it is often difficult to know when this proposition is being put to the test. The publishers' fear of their editors was really a fear of compromising their own moral position as guardians of an institution with a sacred mission to report the day's events objectively and interpret them intelligently.

This anxiety was reflected at the very start of the Readership Project by an extreme concern that editors be brought into the planning process. The publishers were inclined a priori to accept the editors' conviction that the problem of declining readership was essentially an editorial problem. It seemed logical, therefore, for an editor to be appointed chairman of the Research Committee.

With great political cunning, the editors were able to double their representation on the Readership Council and the Steering Committees. They accomplished this by insisting that both the incoming president and the new vice president had to serve jointly, in order to maintain "continuity."[27] On the Steering Committee, this brought them to parity with the ANPA and the Bureau, which were represented by both their chairmen and vice chairmen. On the Research Committee two editors were to serve as co-chairmen, further strengthening ASNE's position when a vote was taken.

In his remarks to the ASNE Board in April 1977, O'Neill said:

> Ever since ASNE's founding many years ago, it has essentially been a loose assembly of professionals meeting once a year and concerned about press freedom and journalistic ethics. It was not really deeply involved in the general problem of the newspaper business as a whole. We have been too loosely structured, too narrowly focused, perhaps, to become a really major policy-making force in the council of publishers. The result, I think, is that other groups with other perspectives—whether they be advertising, circulation, or production—have been more influential. This is not in the best interest of either editors or publishers. The challenges that newspapers now face are so formidable that they call for the full and sustained involvement of all editors, not to defend ancient profes-

sional strongholds, but because editors have talents and insights which can genuinely and creatively contribute to common solutions.

O'Neill said the Readership Project

originally was designed in a way in which the editorial involvement was rather more advisory, peripheral, and not really central to the overall organization. I think we've already had a major breakthrough, thanks to the active intervention by Warren Phillips [Chairman of Dow Jones and former editor of the *Wall Street Journal*] and also [ANPA Vice Chairman] Len Small, who are on the ANPA Board and who are in fact members of this committee.

O'Neill told the ASNE convention that responsibility for research had been awarded to the editors. "The full organization and direction of this Newspaper Readership Project was drastically altered to provide full involvement by editorial groups. . . . ANPA and NAB leadership made a very significant concession to encourage the full cooperation and support of the editors of the country." He also announced that ASNE president Eugene Patterson had created ASNE's new Readership and Research Committee "to bring a lot of experience and clout to bear on this central issue."

As subsequently explained by Patterson, the high-minded and high-spirited publisher of the *St. Petersburg Times* and *Independent*,[28]

A natural evolution of ASNE's interest, spanked along by opportunity and by Mother Necessity, propelled us off the bench and up to bat as self-designated hitters in the Newspaper Readership Project. By March, an ASNE Idea Committee under Mike O'Neill huddled in Chicago, learning about research from Ruth Clark of the Yankelovich firm and discussing what the Society might do or could afford to do. Not much. . . . We had launched ourselves in the same direction the Readership Project was taking; but on our own we lacked the money for major news and editorial research of the sort [Joe D.] Smith was saying the Readership Project might make available. . . . In this massive study of the whole news business, editors were either going to step up and take control of the Research Project's research into news content or somebody else would. That content was our business. . . . Our course was obvious.

I found this all annoying, not so much because I regarded the Bureau as uniquely qualified in the realm of newspaper research as because I was skeptical about the research qualifications of most editors. I agreed, however, with some of their prejudices. They detested the term "product," to describe the output over which they presided. It was a crude term derived from the marketing world. They particularly rejected the idea that newspapers could be shaped to fit consumer requirements in the way that a manufacturing business could shape product design.

The Research Committee

"The Consensus Issues as Seen by Research Professionals of the Newspaper Industry" looked somewhat different than they did to the editors. Several months before the first meeting of the Research Committee, I wrote the members of the Newspaper Research Council soliciting their help in evolving a research program. The response was slim. Gerald Zarwell of the *San Jose Mercury News*[29] reported that "readers are experiencing increasing difficulty in 'wading' through most metro newspapers." There was growing evidence, he said, that readers preferred short, punchy stories rather than long, drawn-out analysis. "Conventional" questioning of reader interest appeared to yield very little viable information.[30]

By the time the Research Committee held its first meeting, the editors' survey was already done, and the national survey of media exposure and newspaper reading interests had been set in motion. The other research ideas I originally presented at Airlie House generally met with approval, including one pet notion of mine that was never carried out—a newspaper content analysis based on the editorial quality index to be derived from the editors' survey. High priority went to our suggested study of the media habits of children and adolescents.

Hornby reiterated the editors' concern that market researchers might interfere with their function. He was distressed by surveys that indicated readers were turned off by serious news about government and public affairs and suggested that research might be better applied to test different ways of covering those stories to develop greater interest.

The editors were wary of our proposal to develop pretesting facilities and techniques for evaluating format and content changes.

It was acceptable to show newspapers how to run such tests but not to recommend specific changes. As the minutes put it:

> Interest was expressed in questioning procedures which will get at basic questions of reader wants and needs rather than relying exclusively on the stereotype answers often associated with mass survey techniques.[31]

When the Committee met again a few months later,[32] the editors came up with some new proposals of their own:

> Set up a four-level market size study to test ten basic hypotheses the editors feel will make marginal readers into more involved readers. . . . Start a national monitor of informational needs and changing trends. . . . A three-year study of attitudes toward a significant change in newspaper style or format. . . . Continuous monitoring of content saliency and readership—on a monthly basis. . . . Determine the value of attracting young readers and the tradeoff of losing established readers. . . .

A final proposal made me gasp: "Boil down all research that exists, evaluate it, and recommend how to apply it."[33]

In the editors' understandable determination to call the shots, they had come to the Research Committee from a well-prepared position. The ASNE's Readership and Research Committee, also co-chaired by O'Neill and Hornby, was destined to play an important role behind the scenes. Much of the ASNE group's discussion centered on "the role of the newspaper and the changed relationship with readers"—referred to by the editors as "hostility." In some "Background Notes" on its meetings,[34] O'Neill wrote,

> Most newspaper research has originated with and been financed by advertising departments. It has not been developed to deal specifically with product problems or to guide editors in making content and format changes. There is an urgent need for research that is custom designed to meet the special needs of editors who are trying to improve readership.
>
> As a general proposition, newspaper editors are relatively uninformed and untrained in the uses of research. There is a corollary deep distrust of research findings (often justified). . . . A rapidly spreading new vogue in the industry is the effort to scientifically evaluate the impact of editorial changes on readership and circulation. Related to this is an equally popular fascination with the idea of pretesting new editorial concepts before they are applied. The

methods are still very primitive, particularly in the case of pretesting, and there are a lot of questions about the validity of many of the proposed approaches. Editors should be much more deeply and widely involved in this very difficult but important part of the National [sic] Readership Project.

A fundamental weakness of most of the present and proposed research is that it deals essentially with newspapers as they are today or as they might be marginally modified by relatively conventional changes. It does not attempt to cope with what newspapers might be.

O'Neill commented further,

Most of the projects being mounted in the national readership program are relatively short term and one dimensional. For the most part they are intended to find out what is happening now, not to track deep currents of change, and they rely heavily on opinion surveys, which are limited in the range of information they provide. There is need for more basic research into the dynamics of reading habits, longitudinal studies to spot and interpret change, a system for regularly monitoring social trends, and more variety as well as innovation in research approaches to key readership problems.

O'Neill called for studies of "deep social trends versus psychographic profiles of readers and non-readers." He proposed research on content, on writing, graphics, organization, and editorial attitudes. He argued that baseline data "to find out whether there are serious gaps between editorial instincts and reader interests and needs" required "careful in-depth interviews" and that "the questionnaire which the NAB circulated to editors is not the right way."

To get these hard data in "a study of the changing relationship between readers and newspapers,"

we must search out the underlying motivations of readers, the subtle or even subliminal impulses that turn readers on or off to newspapers. . . . To begin to attack these problems, we propose the use of focus group techniques.

He also proposed "the creation of an ad hoc communications laboratory—utilizing the skills of trained psychologists, sociologists, editors, and survey researchers—but without all of the fanfare, delays, costs, etc. of the usual exercise."[35]

Echoing pollster Daniel Yankelovich in what I regarded as a misreading of Jean-Jacques Rousseau, O'Neill said,

> It has become increasingly apparent that the heart of the readership problem is a changed social contract between the newspapers and their readers. The terms of the old contract were clear: the newspaper decided what was important for the reader, and the reader as a good citizen felt obligated to read it. It was a mark of conformity, upward mobility, etc. Newspapers were not just media, but an institution, a source of authority, etc. If the old contract is pretty clear, the terms of the new social contract are pretty fuzzy. This fact underlies all of the great debates on soft versus hard news, the relationship between television and newspapers, charges of biased depersonalization, etc. There are a lot of general ideas on the subject, but the time has come for some hard data and clearcut definitions.[36]

Further, he proposed an "intensive analysis of all existing newspaper research." The cost was estimated at $10,000, which I considered barely sufficient to conduct a preliminary inventory. Finally he suggested a newsletter for editors.

The ASNE's newly appointed Project Director, C. A. ("Pete") McKnight, the recently retired editor of the *Charlotte Observer*, was to take charge of the *Editors Exchange* newsletter. A former president of ASNE (1971–72), he listed "the basic things editors want to know":

> (1) What is the fundamental mindset of the reader toward newspapers? Is it a hostile stance? Why? . . . Why are newspapers "dull" and "distant" if indeed they are? What would change these perceptions? . . .
>
> (2) What is the effect of writing form and writing style on readers? . . .
>
> (3) What is the effect of newspaper organization of content on readers, etc.?[37]

All of these questions, plus a variety of other subjects that ranged from news about government to TV watching, were to be addressed in a study to be commissioned from the firm of Yankelovich, Skelly, and White, under Project Director Ruth Clark. McKnight said that the sample would be large enough to give solid answers regarding several distinct reader groups, including occasional and loyal readers, mobile readers, community and metropolitan readers, and readers in different regions.

I replied to McKnight's summary[38] with an uncustomary eight-page letter.[39]

All the research done for the Readership Project must be responsive to the practical needs and concerns of editors. . . . Your questions . . . are very difficult to answer in generalized terms. National averages (even broken down—as we do routinely—by different subgroups of the population) may be of interest. But the really important comparisons have to be made of reader reactions to particular papers edited in contrasting styles. This makes it important to define what the crucial differences in philosophy are among editors. About what matters are you undecided or in disagreement? We've got to be able to identify newspapers that are being edited with different objectives or with different notions of what the reader wants or should get. The identification of such key differences in editorial judgment is one of our tasks in the first research phase. . . . It was also one of the objectives of the controversial editors' questionnaire.

I noted that "some of the questions can probably be answered right now in a reasonably satisfactory way on the basis of existing evidence" and proceeded to tackle McKnight's individual questions, systematically referring to the research we had already done or proposed to do.

McKnight had asked, "What underlying social trends among readers are editors missing?" (I commented that this was raising "nothing less than the issue of editorial competence and the degree to which this is reflected in the authority with which newspapers project the world to their readers.")[40] I suggested that "the issue of what our readers are not getting from newspapers that they want can best be addressed by looking at the other printed matter that they are reading now."

McKnight had asked, "What is the effect of drastic change in content or organization on readers? Do newspapers lose many readers habituated to its old ways as they change to gain the new?" (I pointed out that this was "our objective in developing techniques for pretesting content and format change.")

In conclusion, I wrote that

Part of our job right now is to communicate, translate, and discuss the implications of what we already know; part is to specify the problems for future research on possible product improvements. We can't make progress in either area unless we keep talking.

Nothing should be done in the way of research on our readers or on our product that is not responsive to and wanted by the leaders of the editing fraternity. But an effective research program has to be built professionally; it can't be put together by casual proposals and volunteer effort. . . . We expected to continue our established practice of handling the planning, analytical, and report-writing phases of research projects. Field work and tabulations are handled by a variety of research suppliers selected on the basis of their special qualifications. We think this way of handling things is economical and makes good use of the continuing resource of newspaper know-how represented by our research staff.

The exceptions to this practice have occurred (a) when we have subscribed to syndicated media research . . . and (b) where a research company comes to us with an idea that is ingenious in conception or methodology; naturally, we turn to them to do the whole job.

I added that "we would normally never invite any particular supplier to submit a proposal without considering what other suppliers might have to offer." This was intended to be, and was taken as, a protest against ASNE's insistence on selecting the Yankelovich firm without consulting the Bureau's researchers.

By the time of its third meeting,[41] the NRP Research Committee had before it two proposals from the ASNE Readership and Research Committee: "A study of the changing relationship between readers and newspapers" and a testing project entitled "Communicating with readers."

Controlling Editorial Content

Advice on the research program was coming from other quarters as well as from the editors. The head of a substantial chain of newspapers, James Ottaway, Sr.,[42] commented to Smith and Silha,

It isn't necessarily that all the research activities, editorial improvement, better design, better writing, etc. occurs only on the larger newspapers. I sometimes feel that Leo . . . . has a tendency to overlook this. Even in the boondocks there are some bright people. There also are some very dull newspapers. . . . I hope that the Readership Council won't become so entranced with research, promotion, etc. that it forgets that the guts of selling newspapers is the quality of the editorial product. If you put a poor cereal in a box, you can't sell it for hell and high water, no matter how much research is done, no matter how attractive the packaging, and no matter how effective the sales force.

The editors drew the battle lines somewhat differently. What was at issue, they felt, was their professional autonomy to control what went into their newspapers. They were heirs of a long tradition of struggle against publishers who had tried to tell them what to do. Patterson wrote that

> Editors feel they didn't supply adequate input into the first year's programs that affect the editorial product. It's not that we shrink from it; we want to supply it. With much of the research that touches on editorial content coming out of the Advertising Bureau, it seems to us that you need our input to help validate the NAB research conclusions. And editors need at least some research done for them by commercial research facilities outside the NAB to validate their collaboration with the NAB research.[43]

In my drive to get the Project off to a running start, I had annoyed the editors by pressing forward with studies they had no hand in planning. Patterson said it seemed important that the second year's research proposals be presented to the Research Committee "in timely enough fashion and in adequate detail for real review and input" and that

> analyses and conclusions of any completed research projects affecting editorial content be again reviewed by the Research Committee before they are disseminated under the name of the Readership Project.
>
> This does not imply that the originating research agency would be asked to alter its professional conclusions. It's only to make possible critical or supportive addenda . . . in the interest of presenting the findings whole. (Sniping after the fact of the sort we have encountered on some of the first year conclusions seems to be destructive and preventable.)

Replying to Patterson,[44] I wrote,

> If it wasn't quite clear to us a year ago, we are now all well aware of the extreme sensitivity of editors to any intrusion by researchers into their domain . . . When the Readership Project was started, it

seemed like a good idea to launch full steam into an active program without the inevitable delays of starting from scratch and with an open solicitation of suggestions and proposals. In retrospect, this may have been a mistake, as you seem to feel it was. Defensively I must point out that our repeated requests for suggestions and proposals have not really produced much of a response. I'm convinced that no matter how much prior consultation we have, there will always be criticisms afterwards. This is not only unavoidable but all to the good. There is just no way of being all things to all men when you're dealing with a limited budget and an open agenda as we are. . . . We share your concern that our research program not be inbred or monolithic.

I also pointed out that the annual $126,000 out-of-pocket research investment in the Readership Project

> is a drop in the bucket compared with the millions of dollars that are being spent on research by individual newspapers through dozens of research companies. One of our objectives is to get as much as possible of this privately sponsored research out into the open for discussion. When findings or interpretations become a subject of contention, this should serve to advance the debate.
>
> We simply need more conversation and argument about the critical questions that research data always provoke. That means asking busy people to take time off "just" for palaver. Isn't this worth doing? How should we try to go about it?

To relax the pace with which the Bureau had moved into action, O'Neill proposed "a slowdown in dissemination of reports," with time for prior review by committee members. Richmond Newspapers' John Leard, representing APME on the Readership Committee, "suggested that changes in editors' attitudes are more likely than changes in editorial content."[45]

The position taken by the editors created an angry reaction within the Bureau's own professional research staff. Tolley had succeeded Orenstein as Research Director. As he put it,[46]

> It seems that affairs in the Research Committee of NRP now require a clear statement of some very basic principles. Specifically, how the social sciences can be used best in research on applied problems. . . . Unfortunately for the course of social research, few people are able to clearly define the problem to be investigated in terms that can also be used for research. This is the point at which an advisory committee can be most useful—to make the problems

clear—but the farther into the research process a committee goes, the greater are the chances that the research will fail. To get into the details to the extent of choosing a research firm is to court disaster unless the members of that committee are themselves technically competent to do the research. This means, then, that a single professional research organization must direct all the studies of the problems the committee has defined.

The struggle over research methods was obscuring serious substantive issues. I proposed to O'Neill[47] that the ASNE Convention consider the question, "Are newspapers becoming an elite medium and if so, should we just relax and enjoy it?" A report by Loeb Rhodes security analyst, George Adler, "implies that we are going this route, that we can never recover our position as a truly universal mass medium, and that we should therefore charge the reader as much as we can." This was, to my mind, one of the most pressing issues the newspaper business faced. The historic role of the American press, in all its diversity, was a create a universally familiar vocabulary of political and cultural discourse, intelligible at every level of the social spectrum. If newspaper reading were to be limited to a literate and politically sophisticated minority, the consequences would be staggering for democracy as well as for the newspaper business. Why wasn't anyone talking seriously about this?

Other topics for research clamored for a place on the table: (1) "whether the editorial product is significantly responsible for variations in readership from market to market," (2) "whether the difference between readers and non-readers can be explained in terms of how the news is packaged and presented rather than in terms of what is reported" or by "a shift in the public's desire for information," and (3) "is there an incongruity in outlook between editors and readers?"

On behalf of the ASNE Readership and Research Committee, O'Neill prepared a report[48] that said,

> The editors feel that existing research has not provided understanding of some of the subtle and subliminal reader attitudes that build resistance to reading or to picking up newspapers. Most people do not normally try to articulate these attitudes or influences, and new methodology must be developed to give editors better understanding of and insight into these attitudes.

The mysteries of the human psyche are indeed endless, as O'Neill was implying. But in my experience, their exploration depended mainly on analytical skill, and analytical skill arose from insight, scholarship and reflection on sound evidence, rather than from methodological gimmickry.

O'Neill's report referred to the use of focus groups as "a well established and highly acceptable form of research for exploratory studies." Among the subjects to be covered, he suggested "gossip —and the definition of gossip that really counts. 'Are people angry at newspapers, and if so, why?' 'Are newspapers regarded as too commercial?' 'Do readers really distinguish between hard and soft news?' "

The NRP Research Committee took up this document at its next meeting.[49] In the ensuing review of ten proposals, the focus group project was evaluated number one. In response to the Bureau representatives' "skepticism about the value of the yield of focus groups,"

> It was agreed that this phase of the proposal should be con-sidered as exploratory in nature, leading to the development of models for use by others in local markets. No commitment to any particular supplier is implied by acceptance of the focus group or laboratory phases of the work.[50]

The Origins of "Focus Groups"

Editors who came out of a writing background were generally more at home with qualitative than with quantitative research methods, while the reverse was true of advertising and marketing people. Qualitative research begins with the literal transcription of what people say in interviews or in written documents and there-fore somewhat resembles the notes that reporters take in the field. In social science, such "protocols" or verbatim quotations may be systematically interpreted in terms of a body of theory about hu-man behavior and its motivations.

The origins of this art of qualitative analysis may be sought in literary criticism, with its explication of the hidden meanings and connotations that underlie the facade of a text (most recently man-ifested under the vogue term of "deconstruction"). The practice is also rooted in clinical psychology, which digs into the unconscious meanings below the surface of an individual's verbal reports on events both in the real world and in the world of dreams and fantasies. Historians and sociologists have long used documents and intensive interviews to describe human relationships, to exemplify or illustrate social phenomena, and to develop hypotheses on social behavior before they seek corroborative evidence on a larger scale.

Qualitative interviewing in social research has traditionally used a loose or open-ended procedure to elicit insights, verbatim comments, and examples that enrich the interpretation of dry statistics. Such interviews can also suggest more rigorously structured questions that lend themselves to quantification in a subsequent survey.

The practice of qualitative investigation was typified by the work of Robert Park, William I. Thomas, and other sociologists of the University of Chicago school. This tradition received a new infusion of energy with the arrival in the United States of Paul Lazarsfeld, Hans Zeisel, Herta Herzog, Maria Jahoda, and Ernest Dichter, all of the University of Vienna. They became the nucleus of the Bureau of Applied Social Research at Columbia University, which developed close ties with the broadcasting, musical recording, magazine publishing, and advertising worlds of New York. Lazarsfeld and the Columbia school had little contact with newspapers, though they did extensive research on the motivations for radio listening and magazine reading.

The anthropologist W. Lloyd Warner returned from his field research on the kinship system of Australian bushmen and applied the same interviewing and analytical techniques to a community study of Newburyport, Massachusetts, "Yankee City." At the University of Chicago, with Warner's encouragement, his colleagues Burleigh Gardner, Lee Rainwater, and Sidney Levy began to apply qualitative interviewing and social class analysis methods to the study of consumer behavior for clients like Sears Roebuck and MacFadden Publications. Their firm, Social Research, Inc., found a willing and eager client in Pierre Martineau, promotion manager of the *Chicago Tribune.*

A powerful and eloquent speaker, Martineau was a salesman of incredible energy and versatility, relaxing like a compressed coil between opportunities for self-expression. On one notable occasion, to recover from the strain of a client presentation, he downed five dry martinis, each followed by a beer chaser, and reportedly walked away in good form. The studies he commissioned dealt with the motives for purchase of everyday consumer goods. He had the ability to take dry research reports on such dull topics and make the findings sparkle. In his stand-up presentations, he used a minimum number of charts to make his marketing points. His technique was to use the research as a platform from which to suggest new creative directions to advertisers and agencies. Naturally, it was taken for granted that advertising was to be placed in newspapers, and specifically in the *Tribune*.

The motivation researchers of the 1950s and early 1960s were seldom called to task to justify their conclusions on the basis of hard evidence on a large scale, even though they were sometimes held up to ridicule by conventional pollsters like Elmo Roper. The statistician Alfred Politz once hired a hall to deliver himself of a scathing attack. (Dichter retorted, "A thousand times zero is still zero.") The clients regarded their favorite practitioners essentially as brilliant consultants who could come up with bright new ideas that would have to be tested in the marketplace.

Curiously, motivation research was never applied to newspaper content as it was to broadcast forms like the quiz shows. There was no particular demand for this kind of analysis, since the newspapers of that time were riding high. When conditions changed in the mid-1970s, nonquantitative research was to become a major factor in the newspaper business. By that time, motivation research was well past its prime and had largely disappeared from the current working vocabulary of advertising and marketing. However, a successor had surfaced in the form of group interviewing.

This was a long-familiar method in social research, which had entered the field of advertising through the use of the program analyzer, already mentioned, which Paul Lazarsfeld had invented in collaboration with Frank Stanton, the research director (and later president) of CBS. This device was used to evaluate radio and ultimately television programs and commercials. The participants pressed red or black buttons, depending on whether they liked or disliked what they were listening to at the moment. The program analyzer came in two versions—Big Annie, which elicited the responses of 100 or 150 people at a time, and Little Annie, a smaller version used with sessions of about a dozen people, for each of whom responses could be individually recorded on a polygraph.

In the Big Annie version, the responses were all combined to give a composite profile of audience reaction to a program, but the Little Annie system permitted an interviewer to question individual members of the group after the program had concluded. By matching moment by moment reactions to the changing content of the program, it was possible to ask each member questions like, "Number 7, why did you dislike it when the heroine walked to the door?" After half a dozen such sessions, the audience response profile generally stabilized. This made it possible to come up with a reliable diagnosis of a program's strong and weak points and to make constructive suggestions for change. It was much less expensive to conduct such interviewing with groups than to go out and do it with individuals, especially when it was necessary to get immediate reactions to a television or radio program moving forward in real time. The same economies of scale could apply to group interviews addressing other subjects.

Group interviews had been used by social scientists to elicit kinds of information about which a single respondent might show resistance. For example, in interviewing troops in the field during the Korean War, we sometimes talked with four or five members of a unit at the same time. This got them talking among themselves about significant episodes they had lived through; their memories could stimulate each other. The assumption was that people who were functionally related and who had shared experiences would reveal them more comfortably in a group setting and would bring to the surface recollections and feelings that they would not necessarily express in a one-on-one interview.

In the 1950s, respondents for motivation research had been interviewed one on one to get at their feelings about doing the laundry, brushing their teeth, or drinking beer. In the 1970s, some market researchers began to bring groups of people together to talk about such subjects as a way of generating ideas for a survey questionnaire, much as individual depth interviews had been used in the past. Group discussions could not be conducted in the same depth with which a skillful interviewer could probe the thoughts of a single individual talking in confidence. But the technique did make it possible to get responses from a great many people in short order.

The sociologists Robert Merton, Marjorie Fiske, and Patricia Kendall[51] had coined the term "focused interview" to describe a qualitative, open-ended interview in which the interviewer's main task is to keep the respondent's attention on a particular subject, digging away at the layers of memory and association at the back of a respondent's mind, working without a fixed questionnaire but with a strong sense of the topic areas to be covered. Several decades later, the term "focus group" was applied to every group interviewing session. As interview costs climbed, it seemed economical and attractive to bring a number of respondents together at the same time. With ten focus groups, one could easily talk to a hundred people, which to a layman seemed like a sample of respectable size. Yet the nature of both the questions one can ask in a group setting and of the responses that come forth are remote from the rich and searching interactions that can take place in a clinical interview of a single individual. The respondents drafted for group interviews tended not to be typical of the general population. They were often people with time on their hands or "professional respondents" who obliged their interviewer friends by participating in session after session on different subjects.

Apart from the atypicality of their members, group sessions tend to be dominated by a few assertive voices (as Merton, Fiske and Kendall had pointed out). As a source of hypotheses and ideas for further systematic investigation, group interviews are a valuable resource. They sometimes provide interesting or humorous quotations and anecdotes that can be cited to illustrate a valid point. However, gradually the practice developed of letting the group interview findings stand alone, without the trouble and expense of large-scale field work to corroborate the hunches.

In spite of its failings as scientifically valid research, the "focus group" technique had an overpowering advantage. It lent itself to observation of the proceedings. Individual interviews are conducted in privacy, and their results are amassed into abstract statistical form. But at a group interview, usually conducted behind a one-way mirror, the client could be present and could even participate in the questioning, usually at the final stages. (One client I have heard of wanted to watch two focus groups simultaneously.) Most important, the client could see the interviews and hear people saying what was later quoted back in the report. The resulting reports thus had an appearance of authenticity that hit much closer to home than the usual kind of disembodied statistics. Advertising agencies and sophisticated marketers learned to use group interviews with caution and restraint. In the tradition of the Program Analyzer and adaptations of it employed by other networks, television stations had used group interviews to assess the formats and personalities of many types of programs, including newscasts. Since many newspapers are owned by organizations that are also active in television, it did not take long before the same researchers were called in. Newspaper editors suddenly found themselves fascinated, even overwhelmed.

To a journalist, the main question was not whether what respondents said was typical or projectable to a larger population; it was whether or not the quotations were accurate. Had they actually said it? For generations, newspapers had been quoting "the man in the street." Interviews with taxidrivers, doormen, bartenders, and other accessible individuals were often used to enliven news stories or to illustrate interpretations of the changing political scene. It is not surprising, therefore, that editors were attracted to the "focus group" technique and more receptive to the resulting advice than they were to the columns of statistics generated by large-scale surveys.

Clark

The research firm of Yankelovich, Skelly & White was known for its imaginative application of catchy phrases to describe social trends and to differentiate groups of consumers under unconventional labels. O'Neill in particular liked to refer to Ruth Clark's "credentials," which he linked with those of Yankelovich, who held a doctorate from the Sorbonne.

Clark had been a project director at the Louis Harris research firm before moving on to Yankelovich, where she conducted studies for a number of major newspapers who were contemplating editorial changes. She began to acquire a following among editors who admired her feisty style. She translated her findings into specific pieces of advice in a plain language unencumbered by the technical jargon that editors, and perhaps clients in general, associated with much market research. I knew her through occasional social contacts at meetings of the American Association for Public Opinion Research but was unfamiliar with her professional work.

In 1976, while plans for the Readership Project were being formed, Clark was retained by Harte-Hanks Communications' Bob Marbut (a director of the Bureau) to look at the question of why the newspaper reading habit had declined among young people. The three of us lunched in Regine's, a nearly empty discotheque exotically decorated in ancient Egyptian style. I mentioned to her that the Bureau had done a number of national surveys on newspaper reading among young people and that we maintained extensive files of studies done for individual newspapers. We were eager to give her any help she might need. Although she never took me up on this offer, the introduction to her report listed me among the sages with whom she had consulted and who had provided invaluable assistance. I considered this rather peculiar.

Among the editors who had used Clark on their local newspaper surveys were Patterson and O'Neill. Her studies for the *Daily News* were instrumental in the decision to launch an evening version of the paper called *New York News Tonight*, whose agonizing and notably unsuccessful history coincided with that of the Readership Project.

In her various studies for individual newspapers, Clark reported generally similar findings. Readers found newspapers dull; young people thought they were not "with it;" the articles were too long and boring; people weren't really interested in the news as much as they were in entertaining flashes of the kind to which television had accustomed them. The response was, in fact, the formula adopted by Clay Felker, the editor of *Tonight*.

Before the Project got under way, but with the expectation that research funds would become available, Patterson reported that Clark was about to "undertake a survey for the American Society of Newspaper Editors to determine the relationship between television and newspapers in the citizen's mind."[52] This would be research that editors could understand and control, in contrast to the studies that they saw being imposed upon them by an alien force, the Newspaper Advertising Bureau.

Ruth is critical of the massive 3,000 sample survey which Leo Bogart of the National [sic] Advertising Bureau is plunging into in the same general area. She feels his approach is so mechanistic and demographic—measuring time use with the different media—that he is going to achieve quantifications before he knows what he wants to quantify. She feels the modest ASNE survey can complement Bogart's undertaking and give meaning to the figures he'll produce by providing some qualitative findings on how people put together their various sources of information into the package they live by. . . . The idea is to get a pattern of a typical person's day that should give us a "fix on how people relate to newspapers in relationship to the other media." This, she thinks, has not been adequately explored, particularly with respect to her suspicion— and mine—that people are more likely, not less likely, to want to read some news in the newspapers after seeing it on TV or hearing it on radio. . . . ASNE is enthusiastic about the possibilities and is going to proceed, at very little cost.

In authorizing the research ("twelve focus groups to develop 'our newspaper reader's contract,' and 'ad hoc communication labs' "), McKnight wrote Clark:[53] "I would emphasize the point that these will be ASNE projects and that the ASNE Board is holding me responsible for their successful completion."

In each of the twelve cities where a group interview was conducted, editors sat in as observers. They were fascinated to hear what people said about their papers and were able to testify later that they had really said it. Clark's original report (which was augmented by cartoon illustrations provided by the Bureau) was edited extensively by O'Neill and McKnight. "Changing Needs of Changing Readers" became the most widely circulated document yet produced on newspaper research. An initial run of 5,000 copies was mailed to the ANPA, the NAB, the ASNE, the APME, the National Conference of Editorial Writers, the Newspaper Research Council, and the Canadian Daily Newspaper Publishers Association (CDNPA).

The report contained no forbidding statistics. It was short enough to be read by every editor and publisher in the country. To all intents and purposes, its conclusions were endorsed by the ASNE. By proclaiming the message that the public wanted fun rather than facts about the world's grim realities, it legitimized the movement to turn newspapers into daily magazines with the pelletized, palatable characteristics of TV news.[54] In this respect it contrasted with the conclusions of the large scale survey the Bureau had conducted with the financial support of the newsprint companies.

Our report, "How the Public Gets Its News," was to be presented publicly to the APME in October 1978. A few weeks earlier, in September, I traveled to a meeting of the ASNE Board at Chatham on Cape Cod to preview the findings. Clark was also there to present the results from her focus groups.

McKnight later told Gollin that my presentation "left them wondering what they could do with all those statistics." Clark's on the other hand "seemed to have struck a highly responsive chord." As Gollin put it, "Gene Patterson mentioned to Pete that one thing that gave Clark's work added conviction was that she had involved editors from the start, had them in the focus groups so that they could form their own impressions." McKnight himself attended five of the seven groups, "which made her recommendations aces high with him."

> Pete took this opportunity to stress again that NAB-type studies suffer from lack of editorial input and interpretation of results in a manner that would carry conviction with editors generally. All those statistics—what do they tell editors about what to do (even assuming they would be credited as accurate and revealing, given their anti-quantitative biases)?[55]

"Changing Needs of Changing Readers"

In the foreword of the Clark report, which he signed along with Hornby and McKnight, O'Neill sounded his favorite mystical theme:

> The phenomenon of declining newspaper readership is an extraordinary mosaic of social and behavioral influences that still lie beyond the reach of definitive researchá. . . we know very little about the subtle forces that seem to be weakening the emotional ties of many readers . . . analyzing the chemistry of individual relations is difficult enough; explaining group attitudes is even more challenging. . . .
>
> One of the central conclusions of this study is that there is a gap between editors and readers and that the best way to close or at least to narrow it is to improve communications.

The report itself suggested that "the new social contract between newspapers and readers" required five areas of information. "(1) serve us and help us to cope, (2) don't just tell us about the world—help us to understand it, (3) cover our lives, our communities, our towns. We are just as important as Washington, London, Paris, or Peking, (4) be our surrogate, (5) remember we are hungry for good news, not just bad news." The report also stressed "the importance of 'me' " saying "for many readers, 'self' is an important newsbeat not being adequately recognized or served by editors." "Newspapers are hard work," said Clark.

Under the heading of "Other Insights," she noted that "an overview of the profile of occasional readers indicated the following: Most are young and well educated, most are readers of magazines, particularly special interest magazines, among women housewives are less likely to be regular readers than working women." (The Bureau's surveys showed consistently that better educated people were most likely to read both newspapers and magazines frequently rather than occasionally).

Apart from the statement that there were twelve group interviews, the report included no description of methodology. "The depth guide" for the group discussions had the interviewer asking what I considered to be a loaded question: "What we're going to talk about are some of the reasons editors feel people don't read or like newspapers as much as they used to."

Clark gave a verbal summary of her report to the 1979 ASNE convention, in tandem with our report of the Bureau's national survey, which was delivered in somewhat unpracticed fashion by the team of research analysts who had worked on it. As reported in *The New York Times*,[56] she told the editors that "Readers want more self-oriented features with no loss of hard news, more news about their neighborhoods, more personalized journalism, clear explanations of complex issues and good indexes so that they can find what they are looking for quickly." They expected newspapers to be "more caring, more warmly human, less anonymous."

The study became the lead item in the "Talk of the Town" section of *The New Yorker*.[57] The article began by referring to the new buzz-term, "social contract." The old contract's terms were "simple and clear." Formerly "editors decided what readers should know and readers read what editors thought they should know." But now the contract had to be amended, because readers found their newspapers to be "aloof and unresponsive to their needs."

The study speaks of an old contract and a new one, but the idea of a social contract that binds newspapers and their readers is itself new. At first glance, the idea seems attractive, for it suggests an extension from the governmental sphere to the journalistic sphere of our much-cherished democratic principles. . . . Should not newsmen also be accountable to somebody—namely, their readers? Don't they, too, have an obligation to supply what their public wants? The reasoning may sound plausible, but under the Constitution their role is conceived differently. They are given not a contract with sovereign voters but virtually unbounded permission to present facts and opinions. They fulfill their obligation to the public when they say what they think needs to be said, not what they think readers want them to say. . . . American newspapers are only *offered* to readers, not forced on them. . . .

[Readers'] great wish was to read about their own private lives. One of the two themes of the Yankelovich findings is . . . "today's emphasis on self-fulfillment and self-gratification." It quotes one reader as complaining, "Newspapers stray too far from my life." There was a time, of course, when the main purpose of newspapers was precisely to bring the reader tidings of events far from his life. It was assumed that he was deeply absorbed in his own life already; he didn't need the newspapers, of all things, to help him with that. Newspapers were a window, not a mirror. *His* life became newsworthy only when he did something that might be of interest to *other* readers. . . . In this closed world, obeying the dictates of "the social values of today," writers and readers hold forth about their own lives, in an uninterrupted one-to-one relationship from which word of events in the larger world—what used to be called "the news"—is shut out.

A number of Clark's findings accorded well with the conclusions we had drawn earlier from our large-scale national surveys, but some of the most publicized results were directly at variance with our own. Our study made it clear that people came to the newspaper primarily for news. The analysis of their reactions to thousands of individual articles showed that, while they wanted news of all kinds, they were more interested in the news of the nation and the world than in news of their own localities. These conclusions fit with the trend toward improved education and a more cosmopolitan outlook reinforced by exposure to network television news. It also jibed with the shifts in population and the heightened daily mobility that made it increasingly hard to define the territorial boundaries of an individual's local concerns and sense of identity within a sprawling metropolitan region.

Clark reaffirmed the editors' traditional notion that local news was what people were most interested in. She stressed a point I had made in my own report: that much of the hard news is disagreeable. In her view, readers had to be cheered up and reassured by entertaining features. In reporting to the group of editors and researchers whom we assembled to review the evidence on young people's readership of newspapers, she reported (of readers in general), "They all love the *National Enquirer*." (To this I felt impelled to retort, "I know that's not so, because I'm a reader and I don't love the *National Enquirer*.")

As a panelist at an ANPA conference a few years later, Clark reported that the readership of sports pages had increased "tenfold." The publishers who heard her took careful notes of this point, although the readership of sports pages had not changed significantly over the years. I found such statements offensive, not merely because they were untrue, but because I was aware that if I had made them myself there would have been hell to pay.

What was more serious was that Clark's advice was being followed. During the period of the Readership Project—and for years afterward—American newspapers were greatly expanding their total newshole (that is, their total nonadvertising pages), but they began to devote a smaller proportion of this editorial content to news and a greater proportion to features and other entertainment. They cut down the proportion of their editorial space devoted to news of the nation and the world at large in favor of emphasizing local content.

There were, of course, other forces behind this trend. It occurred at a time when many newspapers may have been trying to eliminate boilerplate and build up their own staff-written content. Also in the same years, many papers were dropping United Press International as a second wire service and making do with the Associated Press alone. Sometimes they substituted a secondary service like that of *The New York Times, Los Angeles Times-Washington Post*, or Knight-Ridder.

In 1982, as the Readership Project was closing shop, Clark approached ASNE with a proposal to repeat her earlier study. (She had now left Yankelovich to start her own firm.) I commented more openly to the editors than I had previously felt I could.

The "gap" of perceptions between readers and editors was not revealed by the earlier Yankelovich study. It had been well documented by previous research. And it has always struck me as being a kind of commonsense notion, like the fact that doctors and patients or lawyers and clients have different perspectives on the same events. There is always a difference of view between laymen and specialists. . . . Since there was no systematic sampling or questioning procedure used in the first study, there is no way to use it as a benchmark. . . . Some people would say things similar to those said by the first group of respondents, and some would say different things. But there would be absolutely no way anyone could accurately say that this was because things had changed in the past five years rather than because they were different people. This would, however, not prevent anyone who wanted to from saying that there had really been a change, and citing as evidence the actual spoken words of respondents, attested to by editors eavesdropping on the other side of the one-way mirror.[58]

Since the Readership Project was no longer a funding source, Clark got her study paid for by the soon-to-be-bankrupt United Press International. Her new survey of the reading habits and attitudes of the American public was in many ways directly redundant with the Readership Project's final 1982 national study. This time Clark's group interviews were supplemented by a national sample, though she had characterized our own large-scale surveys as "sterile." Not surprisingly, her survey produced results closely similar to those we had reported five years earlier. Clark did not acknowledge that her original twelve group interviews were an inadequate foundation for her conclusions. Instead, her explanation was that the readers had changed; whereas in 1977 they had been interested in entertainment, they were now miraculously interested in news.

By the fall of 1984, Clark was telling the Newspaper Research Council that "hard news is back in vogue" and that "the trend is back to a two-paper household." Two-paper readership was actually going down, but Clark was concentrating on more profound observations: "You should remember that readers are people too," she told a 1986 editorial conference of the Suburban Newspapers of America.[59]

Testing Content

In the world of marketing, the testing of alternatives is taken for granted. Products, package designs and advertisements are routinely compared and modified to enhance their consumer appeal. In broadcasting, as I have described, programs and personalities are constantly being researched. But a daily newspaper is an assemblage of such complexity that there was —and still is —a serious question about the validity and applicability of product research.

Dramatic changes were taking place in newspaper formatting and content. I felt that "a useful role for the Readership Project would be to work up a number of different possible alternative methodologies that could be simply and inexpensively applied by individual newspapers to pretest proposed changes before they incur the inevitable expense and risk."[60] Considering two subjects that had come to the fore, public affairs reporting and writing style,

> our immediate task now is to come to grips with the preparation of specific alternative versions of stories that could represent significant choices for an editor and to prepare them in a context that makes the comparisons realistic.

An example might be

> A contrast of (a) the conventional expository style of writing a news story with all the 5 W's in the lead, the highly restrained "objective" style that we associate with the wire services, with (b) personal, subjective, novelistic interpretation of events and personalities, a style that aims for dramatic effect, grabbing the reader's attention rather than quickly informing him of what he's going to find out.
>
> In the area of public affairs reporting, it is very hard to disassociate the subject matter from the writing style. We must start with different versions of specific news stories dealing either with local or national events. We can compare the way readers react to these stories told in different ways or with different strategies of attracting the reader and conveying the essence of the news. But the appropriate contrast of techniques for reporting the Senate debate on energy may be very different from the significant choice of tech-

niques reporting the Senate debate on Medicaid abortion. The problem of infusing interest, drama, and excitement into the presentation of news is different again when we're dealing with some local civic issue which may not even have reached the point of public debate.

I asked editors to have a story prepared about the same events in one or the other of two styles. This would permit us to go out with a random selection of twelve stories set in type, six written one way and six another way, all on different subjects, in a portfolio test among readers.

Average reaction across all stories would show which style is preferred; average reaction per story would show which story is more appropriately written in one style or the other. The story by story analysis may suggest that some styles are more appropriate for one story than for another.

The problem with this approach is that a comparison of twelve specific stories written two ways is not the same as a comparison of two newspapers which consist of stories written primarily in one way or the other. The analogy might be in the observation that if we find people are interested in crime news more than in obituaries, we should fill the paper with nothing but crime news and eliminate the obituaries. An editor looks for a balance of content, and we might assume that a balance of writing styles is equally important.

With the cooperation of the Richmond newspapers, the Bureau conducted an experiment, using two sets of stories (one national, one local), one of which used the traditional pyramid approach and the other of which employed a narrative approach."[61] A "concept memorandum" submitted by Belden Associates, a leading newspaper research firm, also proposed the need for a laboratory design to study such questions as the "hard-soft mix in content, the dynamics of single-copy sales, and the problem of appealing to young people."

But the editors wanted to retain direct control of research in the vital area of content. In July 1979, the ASNE Readership and Research Committee, with funding from the Readership Project, gave Clark and the Yankelovich firm an assignment that directly duplicated our original proposal. Its execution was facilitated by the *Chicago Tribune*,[62] which produced experimental "papers designed to test reader reaction, color versus black and white, graphics versus non-graphics, big pictures versus layouts and smaller pictures, biographical information which humanizes reporters, etc."[63]

Max McCrohon, the *Tribune*'s editor, eventually submitted the report of the "Ad Hoc Lab" to the 1981 ASNE Convention. Entitled "Pretesting Readers' Reactions to Format and Content Changes in Newspapers," it expressed the results in somewhat qualified form; for example:

> Younger readers like the narrative style, but weren't quite sure that it was good for a newspaper. Other readers consistently and strongly preferred the traditional journalistic writing style. It should be stressed strongly, however, that the test was very limited: only one page in the prototypes incorporated the narrative style; the rest of the paper was written in traditional style.

The report was essentially devoted to an exposition of the methodology, with suggestions as to how newspapers could use it. None did. But testing continued to surface as a subject of discussion and of occasional experiments, by the *Boston Globe* and other papers. The introduction of *USA Today* in 1982 was preceded by extensive research on a number of prototype versions. Editors remained divided between their wish to be responsive to readers' preferences and their urge to package and present the news as they had traditionally done, guided by their instincts and professional training.

CHAPTER 5

From Research to Action

In the spring of 1981, the ASNE Readership and Research Committee, now chaired by Robert Clark, issued a report entitled "Editors and Readers." It began,

> From time immemorial, editors have been blithe spirits—largely untouchable, unteachable, and utterly independent. They listen to the dicta of few except their publishers. Vox populi be damned. The editors knew what was right for newspapers and what was good for the public to read. All this until there began to be ferment in the newspaperland. Many readers tended to grow restless, to turn more to television, to find newspapers perhaps not as interesting as before, and perhaps not as needed as before.

The report went on to say that

> Editors have come a long way in the last few years. Great reams of research have now come out of this joint effort. . . . One of the problems of all this research has been how to make the results known to editors. How many editors' desks are piled with materials of many kinds? How many unread reports sit on their shelves?

The News Research Center

Converting research into action was not a puzzle unique to the Readership Project. The question was not just one of how to communicate but of how to make the leap from knowledge to a creative response. The problem was tough in the case of the studies devised by the editors themselves. It was even tougher when it came to translating the findings of research that originated in other quarters.

In addition to newspaper editors and researchers, academia provided another set of participants whose interests were touched by the Readership Project. Schools and colleges of journalism were regarded by some publishers as training grounds whose primary purpose was to produce a steady supply of fresh recruits for their newsrooms. Some journalism professors were content to settle into this role. Others—especially those who had enjoyed active careers as working journalists—took seriously their responsibilities as students, critics, and conscience of the press.

The annual meetings of the Association for Education in Journalism and Mass Communication (AEJMC) were Spartan affairs even by the standard of most scholarly societies. They were generally set in midwestern or southern campuses baking in the mid-August heat and with programs replete with topics so obscure and arcane, so remote from the day-to-day realities of American mass media management, that most editors regarded them with bewildered bemusement. The field had evolved into an uncertain blend of the traditional trade-school orientation of journalism faculties and the trendy, broadcast-oriented world that had emerged from what before World War II were called departments of speech. Far more of its students embarked on careers in advertising and public relations than in news work.

A scattering of journalism school professors and deans attended the conventions of publishers and editors. But many journalism educators seemed to pride themselves on their insulation from the fevered pace, corruption, and incompetence of the media. One, who held an endowed chair at a major state university, told me proudly that he never read newspapers. At an AEJMC session devoted to career opportunities for journalism graduates and featuring a panel of senior representatives from seven mass media organizations, the panelists outnumbered the audience.

Yet for all this unworldliness, a considerable volume of useful research information came out of the major journalism and communications schools. With rare exceptions (notably in television research), the studies were done with meager resources and small, often unrepresentative samples. Some of the best of them were secondary analyses of data collected for other purposes. *The Journalism Quarterly*, the principal outlet for this research, had a total circulation of 4,100, and by all indications very few of its readers were practitioners.[1]

Commercial research, as practiced by private market research firms and advertising agencies, moves at a totally different pace than it does in the academic world and for a very good reason. The serious scholar looks upon data as building blocks in constructing the never-to-be completed temple of truth. Evidence acquires meaning only insofar as it finds its place in a network of theory that must constantly be expanded or rewoven. The design of a research instrument, the preparation of an analytical plan, the writing of a report—all require serious reflection and consultation of the literature that provides a context for the investigation and its findings. This takes time and often a lot of conversation.

The commercial researcher works under cost pressure to finish the task at hand and get on with the next one. But there is another critical distinction from the academic approach: most commonly, the data are valued for their own sake, as a straightforward description of what is here and now, rather than as an element in an ever-changing tangle of hypotheses proven and unproven.

The Bureau's research staff was a mixture of people who came with one orientation or the other, though most of the new hires for the Readership Project came from the academic side. There was, therefore, a startling disparity in the pace, productivity, and quality of the reports prepared by different analysts.

To overcome the barriers imposed by scholarly jargon and formalities, ANPA (which had no research professional on its staff) had set up a News Research Center in the early 1960s, under a retired journalism educator, the venerable Chilton ("Chick") Bush. His task was to abstract the findings of studies reported in *Journalism Quarterly* and other academic journals, boiling them down to a palatable essence that even the most Neanderthaloid editor might not reject out of hand. These summaries were issued in a bulletin format and ultimately compiled as a series of volumes. Under Bush's successor, another professor (and later dean) of journalism, Galen Rarick, the Center began to sponsor some original research.

With the third director, Maxwell McCombs, Jr., the John Ben Snow Professor at Syracuse University, the Center moved into a more ambitious phase. McCombs, a soft-spoken Alabaman, was catapulted to a position of great power in the underfunded domain of academic communications research. Under McCombs, the Center provided grants to support a number of university-based projects. These tended to be done on a small scale in individual communities. In my judgment, many of the findings had already been well documented in our national surveys.

In the original planning of the Readership Project, ANPA sought to assign a significant part to the News Research Center. They were to run the "academic research program," while the Bureau was to handle the "commercial research." For the research staff at the Bureau, this distinction seemed unreal. While the first steps were being taken to bring the industry's leaders together for the Airlie House summit meeting, McCombs proposed that his News Research Center should sift through the existing scholarly literature to identify significant questions for future investigation. I thought this would be useful but was not where the design of a new research program should begin.

It reflects a very methodical approach to the subject of readership from the standpoint of communications theory rather than from that of management. It is wholly appropriate procedure for a scholar to start with a theoretical framework, systematically consider alternative hypotheses that have been advanced to explain how mass media are used, and look for ways in which those hypotheses can be tested and, if necessary, restated. This is what Max's memorandum does, and his inventory of existing studies is the logical place to begin. However, a good many specific and actionable research questions can be confronted immediately from our knowledge of the problems, without waiting to determine where there are gaps in the theory. (Just as an illustration—and it has nothing to do with the immediate situation we face—consider the potential of the Reuters' I.D.R. System [an information data retrieval service for owners of home computers] for supplementing and perhaps expanding the information utility of the daily newspaper. It would be realistically possible, within the next year or two, to conduct an experiment, with the I.D.R. in a cable TV community, to see what actually happens to newspaper reading habits when people have access to a wire service on their television set. This is an important matter for us to investigate, and yet there is no way in which we could arrive at it by considering what is omitted from existing studies of newspaper reading.)[2]

ANPA authorized McCombs to proceed. He approached his new task intelligently and in an admirably systematic fashion by reviewing the research literature on readership and circulation from 1950 through 1976. He examined 222 different articles and research reports, of which 50 were private studies provided by individual newspapers.[3] A third of the studies dealt with the measurement of readership for items appearing in a given day's issue of the paper. Another one sixth of the studies dealt with the choice of a newspaper rather than another news medium. McCombs set up a grid that included what he described as focal questions set against analysis perspectives ("structural attributes, social categories, psychological characteristics, uses and gratifications, and attitudes").

Altogether, he identified 469 findings and 72 different types of research in the existing literature; only 11 were represented by a significant number of studies. This led him to conclude that, "The state of knowledge about newspaper readership and circulation is quite uneven," with "many gaps to be filled."

McCombs later[4] proposed the formation of an "NRC Mining Company" to cull existing research, much of it proprietary, in the files of individual newspapers. "The data files of most newspaper research operations are an untapped goldmine of information about newspaper readership." He proposed "the creation of a small, highly trained task force of research specialists who can spend one to three months at participating newspaper research operations . . . [and] analyze the available data on topics designated prior to their visit."

The NRC Mining Company project received a high rating from the Readership Project's Research Committee and was under way early in 1980. McCombs and his associates at Syracuse obtained more than 300 proprietary research reports and produced two documents of their own from secondary analysis of the data. One examined the characteristics of morning and evening newspaper readers in 36 markets that had both kinds of papers.[5] This showed morning readers to be higher on the social scale—an understandable finding, since more of them lived in the suburbs (though this connection was not drawn in the report). Evening readers showed greater interest in "soft" news—again understandable, given their lower education (though the report did not offer this explanation). A second report compared subscribers and nonsubscribers in 34 markets.[6] It concluded, not surprisingly, that "subscribers more frequently cite the newspaper as their primary source of news and . . . tend to have more positive images of the newspaper."

My own main concern about these analyses was that they sought to mine generalizations from the individual newspaper studies instead of treating them as case histories. After all, the limitation of our national surveys was that they necessarily aggregated information about reading habits and attitudes in many different localities. A case history approach might have made it possible to connect variations in reader opinion and reading behavior with the attributes of specific newspapers and communities. What would be really interesting would be to find out why a particular newspaper generates a distinctive reader response. (Years later, Robert Clark, with ANPA funding, moved in this direction with a collection of twenty-eight "success stories" of papers that had increased circulation, but this was done without the benefit of survey research.)[7]

The termination of the Readership Project also brought an end to the Newspaper Research Center. Lee Stinnett, who succeeded McKnight as ASNE's Project Director in 1981, commented somewhat ambiguously on its closing: "I don't really think that editors pay much attention to the reports that were produced, although I am sure they served some purpose."[8] But this judgment might have been applied to all the Readership Project's reports, as we shall see.

The Bureau's Research Program

Research initiated by the editors and the ANPA News Research Center actually constituted only a fraction of the studies done for the Readership Project, which produced nearly 100 research reports altogether. (They are listed in the Appendix). A few suggestions also came from other outside sources. (For example, API proposed[9] a series of workshops on newsroom communication.) But most of the research was initiated at the Newspaper Advertising Bureau, in the form of proposals that were accepted by the Research Committee and then implemented directly by the Bureau's research staff.

The studies conducted by the Bureau (described at length in my book, *Press and Public*) investigated both the reading habits of different kinds of people, and the response to different elements of the newspaper itself. We learned that the essential problem we faced was one of reading frequency. Only a small minority of the public never looked at newspapers, but more and more people were relinquishing the habit of everyday reading. We compared subscribers with single-copy buyers (they were not all that different), and looked at the outlets where newspapers were bought. We examined the characteristics of the frequent and infrequent readers and probed for a better understanding of what made people increase or decrease the regularity of their reading. (The ones most likely to be heavy or light readers were the ones who moved in the expected direction.)

The Sunday paper had a growing appeal, and we examined its special attractions. (By 1990, its audience actually outstripped that of the weekday press.) We looked at the people who read more than one paper a day and examined the factors that made them choose one competing paper over another. Newspaper readers, we learned, were more active participants in the political process and in the affairs of their communities.

We studied how newspapers were shared by members of a household and how they figured in conversation and in the affairs of everyday life. We looked at the changes in reading habits that occurred as individuals moved through the life cycle, and especially at the evolution of reading habits among children and adolescents. We confirmed our hunch that people who moved a lot were less likely to be readers. Those who underwent major life events, like a marriage, divorce or job change, might be expected to undergo some change in their media patterns; this was the subject of a long-term study. But we were interested in the broader question of how newspaper reading related to the consumption of other media and looked at their use around the clock. Our analyses did not indicate that TV news viewing cut directly into newspaper reading. It turned out that heavy consumers of television news included both news "junkies," who were heavy newspaper readers too, and also people who just watched a lot of TV in general and who came from parts of the population where newspapers were less widely read. We took a particular look at the appeal of news magazines to young adults.

We researched how the public felt about newspapers as institutions and how they were compared with television along a variety of dimensions. Were newspapers understandable? Were they fair? (People generally agreed with the editorial policies of the papers they read.) The public's attitudes were examined in detail, both with respect to the medium in general and for the individual papers with which they were most familiar. News interests differed among different kinds of people; we sought to understand how they developed and why they differed. We tried to account for the wide variations we found in the response to specific papers in specific markets.

We looked at individual personality differences and how they influenced media habits. Newspapers served entertainment and information functions; our research examined both aspects, in relation to the motivations for reading and the "uses and gratifications" (a popular social science buzz phrase) they offered. We examined people's general life concerns and related them to the elements of the newspaper.

The actual patterns of reading were a major focus of research— the way people went through the paper, the likelihood of exposure to different kinds of sections and content, including the advertising as well as the news. (Readers went through their papers systematically, though smaller papers got somewhat more thorough readership than larger ones.)

Newspaper content was a major focus of our attention, both through analyzing successive cross-sections of the American press and by periodically polling newspapers to find out what kinds of material they covered on a regular basis. We looked at the variations, by type of paper, by day of the week. And we used a number of different approaches to determine how different kinds of readers responded to different elements of content, what they found memorable, what they wanted more of, and what they felt they could do without.

Preparing and planning research proposals was, in itself, a substantial task. Our suggestions for studies to be done in year three of the Project ran fifty-one pages in length.[10] In carrying out its research assignments, the Bureau followed its usual practice of designing the study plans and questionnaires, farming out the field work and tabulations to outside suppliers, and then preparing the analysis and reports.

In using vendors of research, we naturally gravitated to those who were familiar to us, who were conveniently accessible, and who seemed especially qualified to do the particular kind of study we had proposed. The normal procedure, as with all Bureau studies, was to secure bids from a number of research firms and then select one based on the quality of the proposal, with price as an important but secondary consideration.

Although news of the Readership Project appeared widely in the trade press and was talked about in many newspaper meetings, we received remarkably few unsolicited research proposals. On one occasion, an old colleague,[11] Fred Currier, of Market Opinion Research, addressed an indignant letter to the officers of the Bureau and of the ANPA, accusing us of favoritism and of ignoring research firms not located in New York, his own in particular. Naturally, this required the preparation of a detailed rejoinder, which then had to be sent to the dozen or so people who had received copies of the original letter. Surprisingly, not one of these individuals ever raised the subject directly with me. This may have been a sign of their confidence in us, their boredom with the subject, their indifference, or their reluctance to take sides in a matter that they knew nothing about. In any case, coping with unexpected irritations is an inevitable part of an administrator's job. Given my own impatient nature, they were particularly unwelcome because they deflected me from the main task.

Confronting the Root Causes

I concluded very early in the game that newspapers could best handle the problem of declining readership by improving the quality of their product in strictly professional terms. Yet large and excellent newspapers continued to die of complex causes that seemed to reflect the changing character of their markets more than their own editorial shortcomings. (In 1981 and 1982, they included the *Washington Star*, *Philadelphia Bulletin*, and *Cleveland Press*, as well as the *Buffalo Courier-Express*). Great newspapers like *The New York Times*, the *Los Angeles Times*, and the *Washington Post* survived very successfully. But the biggest circulation growth story of all during the period of the Project was that of Rupert Murdoch's *New York Post*, hardly an exemplar of journalistic virtues. Its gains were achieved at great expense by that oldest of circulation promotion tactics, the game or lottery. (When the *Post* finally dropped its Wingo game in 1985, its circulation fell precipitously by 140,000.) The *Post* continued to post $10 million a year losses, since its large circulation could not be translated into increased advertising.[12]

The editors wanted research to explore the ways in which content could be reshaped to fit what they perceived to be the changed interests of the reading public. Yet our research findings seemed to suggest that the real problems lay in areas over which editors themselves had no control. They showed that the interests and tastes of people who were infrequent readers of newspapers were not dissimilar from those of the frequent readers—except that the infrequent readers seemed to be generally disengaged from society and less interested in everything. Changing the balance or mix of what was in the newspaper would not, therefore, seem to offer much chance of attracting them; moreover, it carried with it the peril of alienating the faithful. I became increasingly concerned that perhaps we were looking at content in terms of the wrong dimensions. Perhaps the critical factors were attributes of symbolism, style, or expression that would be extremely difficult to check out.

The real reasons why readership had declined appeared to be rooted in the changes in society itself or in the changed media environment. Our studies seemed to confirm many of the observations and analyses I had offered the Bureau Board for years before the Readership Project began: the weakening of urban culture; the lost sense of identification with the central city; the growth of the underclass; changed family structure, with more mobile one- and two-person households; and the time pressures that followed entry of women into the workforce. Television was occupying more and more hours of the day, and news was an increasingly important component of television.

As the cost of a newspaper to the reader kept rising, many people came to regard it as a discretionary expenditure rather than as a necessity of life. In a bygone era, lively metropolitan newspapers slugged it out, forced readers to take sides, and aroused a general sense of excitement. Newspaper mergers and disappearances had changed this competitive atmosphere.

As the research information from the Project came in, the considerations that appeared to take precedence were those that had nothing to do with editorial content: pricing, the timely delivery of the paper, and the number of places where it was available for sale. Yet there were editors who believed strongly that newspapers could flourish in spite of rises in price and greater difficulties in distribution. To survive in the face of great social changes, newspapers would have to be adaptable, be able to assure readers that they provided real value, and be lively and interesting enough so that readers continued to regard them as indispensable.

In the ongoing discussion, serious questions were being raised regarding the relation of newspapers' circulation and advertising income. In their early days, circulation had provided most of the revenues. In the middle of the nineteenth century, the balance shifted, and by 1990, four fifths of newspaper revenues were from advertising. To maintain this ratio entailed a delicate balance. Advertisers wanted the maximum audience that they could get at a given cost. But that audience was maximized only when the cost to the reader was kept low. By raising their subscription rates, newspapers would reduce circulation and thereby increase the advertisers' "cost-per-thousand"—the magic number by which the dollars spent were related to the size of the audience delivered.

Circulation directors insisted that they could expand their numbers if publishers were willing to pay the price. It was easy enough to sell subscriptions, they said. The problem was collecting for them. As they sought to expand sales in low income inner-city areas, they encountered credit risks that raised the cost of each unit of additional circulation well beyond any possible return. They also faced increased delivery costs when they went farther from the newspaper's home market base. The subscribers who were harder to get required a greater investment in selling and promotion and were more expensive to service.

Apart from the economics of distribution, there was a question of whether advertisers actually wanted the additional circulation. Local merchants were generally interested in reaching only the people who lived near their stores and regarded copies sent farther afield as wasted. Many advertisers, retail and national, were doubtful about the value of low-income readers who accounted for only a minor part of total consumption for their products or services. Reacting to these tendencies, as I have already mentioned, some security analysts suggested that newspapers would be most profitable if they followed the lead of the magazines, concentrated on the upper half of the market, and ignored the less desirable customers.

Then there was the other side of the coin when newspapers were charged with discrimination or insensitivity to minority needs. (The *Washington Post* was accused of cutting back its distribution in black neighborhoods in order to upgrade the quality of its demographic audience profile for advertising purposes.) At the same time, chain retail advertisers were demanding that newspapers offer them higher levels of market penetration. Some turned to direct mail to provide them with saturation coverage of the areas from which their customers were drawn. Newspapers responded by offering "total market coverage," with preprinted inserts, usually wrapped in a tabloid of mixed advertising and feature material, distributed free to nonsubscribers, especially those in upper income neighborhoods.

The movement of chain retail advertising from the paper's regular "run of press" pages to preprints had many causes: cost advantages arising from economies of scale, excellent color reproduction, and flexible distribution. But it was partly spurred by the concern over newspapers' failing ability to maintain the nearly universal level of readership that most advertisers wanted for their ads.

The Impact of New Technology

While the Readership Project was focused on the existing challenges to the press, there were others still in the offing. New electronic information systems like videotex and teletext could hardly be blamed for newspapers' readership losses. Yet their impending rise was bound to have great implications for the press in both its advertising and journalistic aspects. I wanted "a study of a Video Information Service."[13]

The impending feasibility of supplying wire service news through a pay-TV facility (like Reuters' Monitor or BBC's Ceefax) carries important implications for the newspaper business both as a potential source of competition and also as a possible avenue of diversification or as an alternate form of delivery. . . . The potential exists to provide a considerable amount of special interest input from regional services throughout the world. The evolution of satellite communications technology will eventually make it possible to transmit 24–hour, up-to-date news service directly to home receivers without the intervention of a cable.

We propose that a year-long experimental study be undertaken to observe how the public responds to this kind of a video information system. . . . The video news service would be offered at a very modest subscription price to a portion of the households on the cable, and a matched selection of those not offered the service would be used as a control group.

The proposal never received a very high priority from the NRP Research Committee. However, in February 1980, Arnold Rosenfeld, then editor of the *Dayton Daily News* and chairman of an ASNE task force on editorial content and new technology, proposed

a coordinated, on-going industry look at the total field, one that would deal not only with the technology involved but also with its content, competitive, legal, and sociological implications. This kind of study, which would be comprehensive and require regular updating, stretches the capacity of a small task force of editors originally designed merely to keep colleagues in touch with interesting trends.

Under the direct auspices of the Bureau, rather than as part of the Readership Project, I organized a one-day conference[14] under the title of "Newspaper Marketing in the New Era of Telecommunications." The program was designed to call attention both to the competitive challenges of teletext and videotex and to the opportunities for newspapers to find additional profitable uses for their vast data bases. Some 300 newspaper executives attended, and a book of proceedings was published.

At about this time, the Bureau also joined the Associated Press and ten newspapers in a pilot study launched by a company called CompuServe,[15] to provide input through a telephone-linked home computer network. (Characteristically, the effort was abandoned after only one year, just as the last of the participating papers were coming on line.) In the following years, a number of newspaper companies (Knight-Ridder, Times Mirror, Field Publications) made large investments in unsuccessful experiments with videotex, and the Bureau itself set up a small New Technology Department.

The breakup of the telephone monopoly in 1984 brought the

advent of electronic classified advertising much closer. With competition eroding their retail base, newspapers drew a growing percentage of their advertising revenues from the classified sector. It was increasingly apparent that they were vulnerable to competition even in this arena, which they had come to regard as their private preserve. However, in the planning stages of the Readership Project this still seemed like a remote concern, and my research proposal was never pursued.

Chewing Over the Findings

The Readership Project was, among other things, an exercise in the translation of research findings into action. Applied social research is always initiated for some pragmatic reason, even when that reason is vaguely conceptualized—as in, "Let's find out what the hell is going on out there." Honest researchers are imbued with the ethos that they must seek out the truth, and this dictates limits to their interpretations of the evidence.

Researchers who are commercially successful are those who manage to convince their clients or employers that what they learn is of practical value. This requires clarity of expression, an ability to distinguish between the important and the unimportant, and a willingness to take the next step beyond reporting, which is to give advice. In the decision about what advice to give and how much, some serious questions of professional ethics arise. Researchers steeped in a particular subject that they have studied repeatedly develop personal opinions that they should carefully distinguish from their scientific observations. Researchers themselves disagree about how and when these should be labeled, but they generally agree that it is part of their function to communicate.

Users of research commonly want more than data and their interpretation; they want to be told what to do next. Good researchers find this frustrating, both because it pressures them to step beyond the bounds of their own sphere of competence and also because they know that the users are really the best qualified to come up with solutions to their own problems.

To come up with solutions, however, is a creative act, which may be more successful if it is preceded by immersion in the evidence. Knowledge does not automatically point the way to practice. The translation process requires reflection and discussion —what Silha liked to call "grinding away" at a problem. Sustained discussion of serious problems did not occur often in the newspaper business, with its breakneck, day-by-day tempo. It was important to take the research to the next step of generating proposals for specific activities to increase readership.

The problem of translating research into action was hardly unique to the Readership Project, but it seemed particularly acute because editors were impatient with the usual qualifications and boring technical details embodied in research reports. This sometimes led to clashes at the meetings of the Research Committee, in which several of my associates expressed themselves more caustically than I was likely to do.

The editors' long-standing discomfort with research arose from a number of interrelated causes. Researchers poached on a traditional journalistic domain—sensitivity and response to shifting public interests. Researchers toiled long and expensively to come up with restatements of what was already commonplace and well known. Researchers posed problems without presenting solutions. And researchers wrote their reports in an unintelligible gobbledygook of the kind that editors would never tolerate in their own papers. For O'Neill, who had once specialized in the translation of scientific reports into lucid layman's prose, this was a particular challenge: "The most critical need at this stage in the NRP program is the analysis, communication, and application of results."[16] He proposed publication of a series of "sophisticated and well-written analyses" that would

> carefully analyze and synthesize all the research done so far on key issues important to editors. Relate the NRP's findings to other readership research, social trends, demographic facts, etc., so that the results are put into a meaningful context. Discuss the significance of the research, and where possible suggest the practical implications for editors. . . . The first priority now must be to present the knowledge that we have gained in ways that are both persuasive and practical. . . . A highly qualified science writer—with good knowledge of both research methodology and newspaper problems —would be assigned to each major research subject.

He illustrated his point with a criticism of the Bureau's report on "Women in the '80s":[17] "In angling, writing, etc. it fails to mold the facts, etc. in a compelling, fresh way that would encourage readership. A good magazine writer searches for new insights and fresh observations that set a piece apart from what has already been written." The criticism might have been leveled at almost any research report. The report's author, Clyde Nunn, was, of course, not a professional writer but a sociologist, with a recent doctorate from the University of North Carolina. (Perhaps in rebellion against the harsh commercial world he had encountered, when the Readership Project ended he and some confederates opened a coffee house and art gallery in the Bohemian precincts of lower Manhattan.)

O'Neill was prompted by the idea that an editor speaking to editors could take dull, dry information and bring it to life in a meaningful and compelling way. At his urging, a budget was set aside for the preparation of some popularized conversions of the research reports. To refurbish the report on women, O'Neill gave a free-lance assignment to Edwin Diamond, a media critic who had recently worked for him as an associate editor of the ill-fated *Daily News Tonight*. I was never shown Diamond's text, and it was never published.

When I prepared a review and summary of the extensive data we had assembled on the subject of young people's media habits, O'Neill chided me for my "little tendency to summarize the discussion and raise questions rather than suggest your own conclusions. I'm wondering if it wouldn't be more effective if you were to cut through all the research . . . and then say what you think the situation really is. It would . . . perhaps be more subjective than a good researcher likes to be. But . . . it might be more provocative and stimulating."[18]

He proceeded to illustrate his suggestion by raising a point that he and I had debated a number of times, and for which I told him I knew of no evidence:

> One of my own hunches, for example, is that young people have developed much greater skills at receiving impressionistic communications, i.e. images and emotional stimuli, as a result of their massive exposure to TV. They are less verbally skilled than pre-TV generations so that there is a fundamental dropoff in reading in this entire group. I believe the massive sales of magazines and books may be more a function of dramatic new merchandising techniques (e.g. supermarket distribution) than a reflection of actual reading

growth. I admit that it might offend your professional sensibilities to attempt to project subjective conclusions without conclusive data. But . . . it might actually be more effective in stimulating thought and discussion, leading to new insights.

Somehow I failed to convince him that new insights were worthless if they were wrong.

Editors and Researchers

In my years at the Bureau, I had learned the difficulty of getting newspaper people to pay attention to our advice, even when its implementation required very little effort and promised immediate benefits. The greatest challenge was to get them to read their mail as they drowned in an unremitting avalanche of paper.

The principal vehicle of communication with the editors was *The Editors' Exchange,* the ASNE newsletter funded by the Project.[19] Its objective was to publicize bright ideas emerging from papers around the country, but it also disseminated research findings from the Project and other sources. The first issue (January, 1978) had a front-page signed memo from McKnight headed, "Why This Newsletter?" The answer was that "It should be crammed with research results, new ideas, editorial experiments, snippets on who's doing what, where, tips on new projects, and everything else that will help editors improve their papers—and improve readership."

But written communication was only the first step. From the beginning of the Project, it seemed important not merely to communicate our research findings in an easily assimilable format, like booklets and slide presentations, but also to initiate the process of generating actionable ideas by bringing newspaper executives together with researchers. Just bringing researchers together would be of no avail, since experience indicated that this would only be likely to produce suggestions for further research.

Both editors and researchers seemed to feel a need for closer communication, particularly as the pressure—and the budgets—mounted for newspapers to do individual studies of their own readers. The evolving relationship called for yet another get-together.[20]

My original idea for a meeting of editors and researchers was to organize it as a trial workshop that could serve as a model for regional meetings of editors. O'Neill wrote, "Because a number of editors have not been deeply involved in the national project, we decided we'd be better to drop back one step and simply have a free-wheeling discussion of the whole communications problem." He suggested some questions to put before the group:

> How can valid research be presented to promote maximum credibility among skeptical editors? What findings have we already developed in the national project that would be most saleable to editors as relevant and practical, so that they are not turned off? How can we raise the consciousness of editors so that they are more receptive to readership research and are more likely to apply it?

Following this initial meeting, a series of editor-researcher seminars was run with the cooperation of the ASNE and the Newspaper Research Council.[21] In each of these sessions, the Bureau's Gollin, a skilled lecturer and facilitator, presented some fundamentals of research practice and led discussions of the major findings of our national studies. Burke wrote in the ASNE *Bulletin*, "We were searching for the missing link. Not the link between ape and man. The one between research and editorial action."

One editor commented, "It reinforced my belief that research can be a good tool to back up gut feelings. You've got to have an idea first, a gut feeling that something should be changed. Then you use research to confirm you're [sic] gut feeling." Reporting on reactions by a dozen participants, Eric Wolferman, managing editor of the Saratoga, New York *Saratogian*, described the sessions as "a consciousness-raising experience."

> For the most part editors felt the workshops were useful. But the general feeling seems to be a desire for more concentration on the "how to" aspects of applying research and less emphasis on the academic theory of research. Editors, as you know, are an impatient lot and want quick answers.[22]

Whatever reservations the editors may have had, the joint meetings evoked the enthusiasm of the researchers, whose relatively lowly status was greatly enhanced by these egalitarian encounters with the journalistic elite. In February 1980 an NRP Review and Evaluation Committee set up by the Newspaper Research

Council proposed that a workshop program be set up "to bring editorial and research people from individual newspapers together under the rubric of building newspaper readership"—to interpret and develop applications for the research that had been done.

The honeymoon between editors and researchers was not without its difficult moments. Stinnett commented that many editors "take the studies based on statistically valid samples from the nation and apply them blindly to their markets without local verification. It's quick, easy, doesn't cost anything—and dangerous."[23]

The researchers had, of course, their own, and different, perspective. At a Newspaper Research Council meeting[24] in the Project's last days, Copley Newspapers' research elder statesman, Tom Copeland, delivered his critique of the Project: "Our industry has accomplished a great deal with the NRP." But he added,

> I think the NRP has blown a lot of money simply because of all the chefs in the kitchen—many with unrealistic ideas of what research can and cannot accomplish—and the political necessity of keeping all of them happy. But as a realist I know that that's the way things work. . . . I think we can be very satisfied with the large research studies the Bureau has handled over the years. They tend to be very well designed and well administered. But they also have to have an immediate payoff, and this precludes the type of basic or experimental research I personally would like to see occasionally.

But proposals for basic research invariably received a low priority from the Readership Committee, which wanted immediate, actionable answers to the pressing problems of the business.

Issues Workshops

How does one move from knowledge to action? The intermediate stage is concentrated thought and argument. Meetings of editors and researchers were intended to make each group more familiar with the perspective of the other, rather than to zero in on the solution of specific questions facing newspapers. This second purpose was addressed in a series of "issues workshops" that reviewed research on these critical subjects: the drop in reading among young people, the changing role of women and its implications for the press, the national state of reading skills, the special interests and resistances of black readers, and the responsiveness of journalists to the reading public.[25]

In every case, we used a similar format, starting in the evening with cocktails and a get-acquainted dinner followed by an exposition of relevant research summarizing material that had previously been sent to the participants in report form. For the following day, I handed out assignments that set off a series of discussions focused on different aspects of the overall subject. The objective was to come up with actionable ideas that went beyond the research.

In retrospect, it is doubtful whether any of these discussions had particularly valuable direct consequences, although the conversations were intelligent and the participants appeared to find them highly stimulating. We released summaries of the deliberations, but this kind of educational experience was hard to transform into programs that the entire newspaper business would accept. At the same time, newspaper practices continued to undergo changes that may in some part have been influenced by the ideas set in motion among the industry leaders who participated in the workshops.

Youth Readership

Youth readership was the first subject we tackled, a few months after the Project got under way.[26] It took as a starting point a report by Ruth Clark on her pilot study of young adults, for Harte-Hanks.[27] Clark announced that the young were the "front wave of the future." In the words of the *Detroit News*'s Charles Hakes, she said that "while young people represent a new phenomenon, they also stand for the vanguard of changes throughout our society: concern with self-understanding and individual freedom, relations with the external world, a strong anti-authority position, the women's movement, physical ease and convenience, and finally music. They are very active, they're fascinated by color."

Harte-Hanks' researcher Richard Hochhauser advanced the idea that since the young were not news oriented, perhaps the industry should talk about "papers" and not "newspapers." Broadcast researcher Frank Magid pointed out that television news was not popular among younger people either. (Magid had begun to do research for newspapers, but his main specialty was acting as a "program doctor" for TV news shows.) O'Neill suggested that the "primitive methodology used in research came out of advertising and was not very usefully framed."

In fact, a good deal of the discussion at this meeting revolved around the relationship between editors and researchers rather than about the substantive issues of reaching young people. Magid said that a favorite editors' theme was, "Why it won't work." John Timberlake, research director of the *Chicago Tribune*, pointed out that it took one and a half or two years for a new newspaper section to catch on. He suggested that this time lag should be used to analyze the situation and the effects.

I tried to focus the debate with a question: Was Marshall Mc-Luhan correct in arguing that the public's perception of the world had been permanently changed by television and that the "linear" form of acquiring information from print was outmoded? Or were we simply observing discontinuities in interests and values between different age cohorts? This question remained unanswered, as my summary of the meeting indicated:

> Younger people are always different from older ones, in newspaper reading habits as in other ways. Our immediate concern lies in the widening of the gap. Does it mean that young people are getting information and entertainment differently than their predecessors and that future generations will continue to fall farther behind? There is no agreement on this point.
>
> Young adults are no more homogeneous than their elders. . . . [They] are especially caught up and affected by social change. . . . They change residence at a much more rapid rate than anyone else, and this mobility and rootlessness may have more to do with their comparative disinterest in the community and its newspaper than their position in the life cycle or the unique historical perspective of their particular generation. . . . They may be especially sensitive to the "information overload" of metropolitan life. But youth, with its intense sociability, dating, and entertainment-seeking, is a time of life when all kinds of non-media activities compete for time. . . .
>
> Do newspapers repel young people because they're so dull? Are they so poorly organized that they waste readers' time? Some researchers, and even some editors, would admit this, but others argue that most young readers find their papers good looking, convenient to handle, and easy to read, though less acceptable in terms of their credibility or in the pertinence of their content to

youthful interests. . . . Young people are interested in news personalities, but then, who isn't? Young people's reading interests are typically confined to a somewhat narrower than average range of topics. Still they are more critical than the average reader.

The discussion raised issues that were still being debated over a decade later.

Editors say that there is a need for tighter writing (even without the newsprint crunch), but some who feel this way also believe that young readers are aroused by vivid imagery and by a colorful, emotionally tinged writing style. Can abbreviated stories make elegant use of adjectives, adverbs, and independent clauses? The "new journalists" who go in for this kind of thing may have a huge youth following, but since some editors consider them to be less reporters than politicians, there is some question as to how much they should be encouraged. . . .

If editors wish to be responsive to the changed values of the young, as expressed in both the substance and the style of what they print, how can they avoid antagonizing the mass of present readers? And how much of what may be categorized as avant-garde or "with it" is merely trendy and ephemeral?

Many editors seem to be complacent in the faith that the problem will go away as young people get older and wiser. They resist change because they're not really convinced that it's necessary. The crux of the problem may not be young readers, but old editors. One solution: Fire all over thirty!

Editors define what's news, and each one defines it differently. The staffs respond to these definitions. News that readers (young or otherwise) may want to read about may remain uncovered by the press because it lies outside the traditional beats, or because the reporters assigned to those beats have not broadened their scope as the territories themselves change boundaries. In one staid Southern town the weekend police blotter report in the Monday paper gets high attention from the youthful set eager to find out which of their peers got high, drunk, or cracked up on Saturday night. A paper in Oregon that prints marriage license records, including addresses of brides and grooms, is read avidly by those curious to know who was living in sin with whom prior to the event. This obviously means more in a small town than in a big metropolis. Still the point is that various kinds of "subterranean" news may be compelling to many people and yet remain unrecognized as newsroom assignments. . . .

A corporation like General Motors conducts research not only to help decide how many of next year's cars should be red and how many blue; they also must think in long-range terms about fundamental changes in the use of transportation. Similarly, research for newspapers should not merely deal with the immediate questions of content and readership, but with the larger ongoing social trends that will ultimately and perhaps profoundly affect both. Our difficulties with younger readers might have been anticipated by an early warning system of research.

The seminar produced, inevitably, a number of suggestions for further research.[28] It was evident that this kind of discussion could be highly enjoyable for the participants. But it was far from clear that it could give direction to the industry.

Women and Newspapers

What were the implications for newspapers in the rapid movement of women into jobs, the development of their new career interests, the sharing of domestic chores with their husbands, the broadening of their daily horizons? For the first time, women journalists were beginning to ascend into the ranks of newspaper management, mostly as editors, but in a handful of cases as publishers.

Experts from outside the newspaper business joined an assortment of newspaper women and men for a workshop on these issues. It covered such questions as these: What have editors already been doing to respond to the change in women's roles? Should the present mix of newspaper content be reoriented? What changes are indicated in the traditional women's news and features? Does sexism turn off readers? Is there a danger of alienating traditional full-time housewives?

Newspapers printed far more material oriented to men than to women, according to our analyses of content, yet our recently completed survey of women with and without outside jobs indicated that they did not seem to be conscious of this. The study repeated many questions we had asked in previous research we had done in the early 1970s and documented a remarkable transformation in the perception of the female role.[29] In a short period of time, work had become the norm, and the perception of the traditional stay-at-home housewife had become far less flattering, both to those who fit the description themselves and to their sisters in the workforce.

The discussion repeatedly returned to the point that reading interests were less and less defined by gender. Many women followed sports and business news; men were interested in home decoration and cuisine. As with so many aspects of the Readership Project, it is difficult to assess the specific catalytic effect of this discussion and its reverberations. The topic was placed on the editors' agenda, through the ASNE *Bulletin* and convention programs. As time went on, more newspapers reoriented and relabeled their women's pages, consciously looked for ways to cover the new career interests of their women readers, and took feminism seriously as a political movement.

The Problem of Reading Skills

Was the drop in readership a unique ailment of the newspaper business, or was it merely a symptom of a more general decline in the ability and will to read? The mid-1970s were a period of accelerated concern over the dropout rate in urban school systems, and the drop in academic achievement scores like the S.A.T. examination for college admittance. Anecdotal accounts were freely traded to support the view that the "cancer of illiteracy" was spreading.

Public opinion surveys sometimes included tests of the public's ability to perform simple tasks (like successfully filling in a driver's license application form). The results were, predictably, deplorable, but since there were no benchmarks, it was impossible to say whether the results represented a change and, if so, whether this was for the better or for the worse.

It appeared unreasonable to me to assume that falling newspaper readership merely reflected an actual decline in the public's ability to read. However, a good many prominent publishers saw illiteracy as the root of their own problems. (Joe D. Smith addressed FIEJ (the International Newspaper Publishers Federation), on the subject of "The New Illiteracy: The Threat to Newspapers.")[30]

Educational philosophy had changed during the late 1960s and early 1970s when the doctrine of doing one's own thing was prevalent. In those years, schools placed less emphasis on the basic skills that involved memorization and perfectionism, like penmanship, spelling, and the arithmetic tables. However, now the pendulum seemed to be swinging back in the direction of more structured education.

Arnold Grisman, an executive vice president of the J. Walter Thompson agency (and occasional mystery novelist) had prepared an elaborate multimedia presentation called "The Desensitization of America," which he took about to newspaper conventions. Its thesis was that the insistent noise of rock music was hypnotizing America's youth and that reading was becoming a lost skill. Years later this theme was sounded in an advertising campaign by the Advertising Council, a group that has harnessed the talents of the advertising business, along with donated space and time, to promote worthy causes like Smokey the Bear and Radio Free Europe. (The 1985 campaign warned that two out of three Americans could be illiterate by the year 2000, implying that most of the people now alive would either be dead by that time or would have totally forgotten the alphabet.)

The improvement of American educational standards was surely a high priority, yet it was not urgently related to the specific problems confronting the newspaper business. I thought it could best be addressed in the context of Newspaper in Education activities rather than through a major independent thrust.

The problem called for yet another conference, though this one was not officially a part of the Readership Project. I organized it in collaboration with Robert Ellis, a vice president of Time, Inc. For a one-day meeting on reading abilities and skills, we brought together representatives of the book and magazine industries, along with academic specialists, officials of reading organizations, and government functionaries.[31] There was little agreement among the experts, either in their assessment of the state of reading skills or on the proper strategy for improving them.

The participants brought a wide variety of viewpoints and observations to this discussion. To take a sampling: "Reading skills may be improving while reading habits decline." "Illiteracy can be both voluntary and involuntary." "The key target is the parent and not the child." "Fiction has almost disappeared from magazines." "Japan has a sustained silent reading program in schools." "There is no reason why information can't be more efficiently handled by television than reading."

The "net conclusions" from the meeting[32] were that there was "a heightened sensitivity in recent years to problems of reading ability, academic achievement, and educational test scores," because "expectations have been going up as our national level of educational achievement has been raised." Formerly "invisible" minority populations had become urbanized and highly visible to the media and to public officials.

> Changes in academic achievement scores can probably best be explained by changes in the characteristics of the populations being tested. . . . There has been an enormous expansion of educational opportunity. . . . As the pool of those taking tests is expanded and the background and capacities of those taking the tests is diluted, it is inevitable that scores should change. . . . For a period of some years, many school systems shifted their primary orientation from the traditional disciplines of the 3R's to social studies, self expression, and other educational objectives. The pendulum now appears to be swinging back. . . . At any given level of schooling, children today are on average doing at least as well as they did in the past. But apart from that, far more children than ever before are achieving higher levels of schooling.

It was noted that the media represent only one aspect of reading matter and that "there is a tremendously increased amount of casual utilitarian reading that people are required to do on the job and to handle personal affairs." I found the consensus of the experts reassuring and managed to keep the Readership Project focussed on the practical and immediate needs of expanding the use of newspapers in the classroom and away from any wholesale assault on the broader question of reading skills. Yet the problems of big-city school systems continued to generate alarm in the newspaper fraternity. Poor school performance and high dropout rates were inherent in the breakdown of the family, and could not be dissociated from the illegitimacy, drug abuse, crime, unemployment and welfare dependency of the underclass —matters that cried out for a huge social investment. Publishers were being warned constantly that 30 percent of the adult population was functionally illiterate, even though the latest surveys showed that 85 percent were newspaper and magazine readers. There were periodic calls for "the private sector" to come in and straighten out what was widely regarded as a moribund educational establishment, and newspapers were urged to join in.

In 1986, three years after the Readership Project ended, the ANPA embarked on a campaign against adult illiteracy and hired a staff director for this purpose. Many papers set up their own adult reading programs. These well-intentioned efforts were not wasted. But the greatest contribution the press could make to the struggle was through its editorial support for adequate school budgets and teachers' salaries, its intelligent reporting of educational issues, and its support of the Newspaper in Education efforts to which the Readership Project was heavily committed.

Blacks and the Newspapers

Reading of newspapers by members of racial minorities had, according to our research, always lagged behind that of whites. Our 1977 survey plans provided for an expanded sub-sampling of blacks, to permit a special analysis of their reading habits and interests (which resembled those of whites at the same educational and income levels). It had always seemed to me self-evident that the matter of readership was inseparable from the larger question of black involvement in the daily newspaper business, which had been minimal.

It was not until the early 1970s that the subject of equal opportunity employment began to appear on the newspaper industry agenda. I tried to discourage the leadership from lumping together "the task of recruiting and upgrading women employees . . . with the problem of racial and ethnic minorities" which I argued was "primarily a social class problem."[33]

> The major target is the twenty-four million Negro minority. . . . the toughest problem and the one to concentrate on. . . . Newspapers must tackle the problem of minority recruitment out of self interest, not because it is the right thing to do, or because EEOC requres it. . . . The survival of metropolitan newspapers requires them to draw readers from a black population that is far more youthful than the white . . . and in considerable degree suspicious or hostile toward the white majority and its institutions. . . . To the extent that the newspaper misses them, it loses its special character as the media voice of the entire community or market, and advertisers begin to look for alternatives.
>
> The aging and inbred structure of newspaper craft unionism has

been an impediment to change. However, the obsolescence of most traditional craft skills because of the rapid evolution of newspaper technology has opened up a large number of new job opportunities not covered by union contracts.

I proposed that a structure be set up as a high priority assignment for the ANPA to "coordinate what is now being done by a number of organizations, part-time and in bits and pieces." Newspapers should "look at the minority hiring issue as just one aspect of a much more comprehensive problem in editorial content, circulation, and readership." I suggested an inquiry into Newspaper in Education programs in black neighborhoods, a special effort directed at high school journalists, and a search for success stories in affirmative action. (ANPA set up a minority affairs committee in 1986 and moved into an active program soon afterward.)

On one occasion when I suggested that it might be appropriate to study the problems of boosting newspaper readership among blacks, McKnight lectured me that, "We Southern editors know the blacks, and we don't need any research to tell us what they think." (McKnight's deliberately cultivated crustiness was almost crocodilian. Under his editorship, the Charlotte newspapers had courageously fought the die-hard segregationists.)

I had prepared an "Outline for Discussion on Black Readership of Newspapers" even before the Readership Project began.[34] With the completion of our research report on black readership, it was high time to move to the stage of generating some specific suggestions.

For the workshop on blacks and the newspaper, the "issue workshop" format was broadened to include other newspaper specialties besides the editors. I submitted 45 questions in advance to the twelve black and five white participants.[35] These covered in detail the problems and obstacles amenable to action within the newspaper business, in the areas of editorial content, circulation, and employment. They encompassed such specifics as:

Can there be full participation without ownership participation or economic clout? Does the existence of the black press illustrate that daily newspapers fail to cover significant news beats? Are there unconscious symbolic expressions of racial bias that enter newspaper articles or features? What can be done about problems of payment and collections with low-income subscribers? What types of newspaper functions (e.g. circulation, advertising) represent critical areas for increased black involvement? What specific steps might encourage this?

The main direction of the discussion was to stress the need for more research rather than to suggest specific actions that could be taken by newspapers to increase black readership. Robert Clark, summarizing the proceedings,[36] concluded that "Although city circulation problems were readily acknowledged, a more important problem was seen as the newspaper itself." One participant, Charles Pittman, promotion director of the *Erie Morning News* and *Daily Times,* insisted that, "If the product is what black people want to buy, they'll find a way to buy it." Lionel Barrow, then Dean of the School of Communications at Howard University, said he could afford to buy more than one newspaper, "but why buy two or three? That would be just as demeaning to me as the first one." Barrow said that newspapers cover the black community "mostly in connection with sports or crime" and gave emphasis to black failures rather than successes.

The *Oakland Tribune*'s black publisher, Robert Maynard, commented that "loyalty and interest among minority readers improved in Oakland when coverage of the minority community improved, but we also found that increasing the quality of local news improved the interest of whites as well."

Booker Izell, circulation manager of the Springfield (Ohio) Newspapers, suggested that black employees should not be put to work only in black areas. His view was that white supervisors "think all central city areas are made up of irresponsible blacks. . . . They have no knowledge of the conditions of these areas first hand. They assume that these are the problems because of the things that they have read in newspapers, heard on the radio, or seen on television. . . . They must go into the area, talk to the people, and see the areas to determine if this area is really in the condition of no return."

Edward Bennett, the white circulation manager of the *Baltimore Sun* newspapers, remarked that the problem is "not that less affluent minorities will not or can not pay. The problem is finding carriers and carrier families responsible enough to follow good collection routines—routines which meet the needs of subscribers."

Bennett wrote me later[37] that "A common problem is that the carrier cannot take his collection money home without a member of the family using it for some other purpose, and these problems are more associated with the economic levels of the neighborhood rather than race."

Dr. Chester Pierce, a black psychiatrist on the faculty of Harvard University, noted that all blacks were very interested in racial issues, regardless of their income or education. After the seminar, Pierce raised the question of

> whether blacks are more likely to read papers they didn't purchase. . . . Compared to whites, do we do more "impulse reading" perhaps with brevity, relative lack of concentration, but in more socially interactive circumstances? . . . On a more subtle and psychodynamic level, I would suggest the possibility of focusing on the role of possible gratuitous, repetitive micro-agressions as a turnoff for black readers. That is, such reportorial consequences of predictably tyrannizing or minimizing blacks' time/space (overtly, covertly, by omission or comission) may be as important as the racial staffing patterns at a newspaper . . .
>
> Incessant negative or despairing communications from a near ubiquitous variety of socialization forces must make it more difficult for any black not to succumb to feelings of helplessness and hopelessness. These feelings are the nidus for depression. Part of the symptomatology of depression would be to constrict one's interest and concern about the rest of the world. . . . Hence, as more depression reigns, less concentration on newspaper reading would be present. At the same time, TV might be a more conducive medium for many reasons.

He went on to describe the following incident.

> About a year ago I sat on a bus next to a young man about 20. He was reading the *Boston Banner* (our black paper). He was so absorbed by the want ads that I read them surreptitiously in order to understand his intensity. There were many, many job openings. They were for process engineers, computer scientists, physicians, systems analysts, etc. For him to get one of these jobs, they could have as well demanded that he should be twelve feet tall. . . . I was devastated by the pitiable and unforgettable look of dejection the young man had as he closed the paper.[38]

Maynard, his wife, Nancy Hicks (administrator of a minority journalism program at the University of California), and *Philadelphia Daily News* Managing Editor Jay Harris volunteered to serve as a follow-up committee. Citing our findings that blacks and whites have similar news interests and use television news in the same way, they wrote,

> A possible if not probable explanation for the consistently lower level of newspaper readership among blacks may be that newspapers simply do not serve the needs and interests of black readers as well as they serve the needs and interests of white readers. There has been insufficient research on this possibility. Instead, the primary focus has been on "explaining" the differences in newspaper readership. . . . Little effort has been devoted to identifying or developing more effective news, circulation, and promotion policies which can help close the readership subscription and service gaps.

Their report went on to suggest that "such information can more effectively be gathered in individual newspaper markets than in a national sample survey." They suggested an inquiry into differences in interests (already rather fully explored by our national surveys), "how from the point of view of blacks, newspapers can best serve black readers . . . how the attitudes or perceptions of blacks and of newspaper staffs shape the relationship of each with the other and how newspaper content and staffing patterns affect readership habits."

They concluded by recommending (1) new analysis of existing data on minorities and newspapers, (2) a replication of the 1977 national survey with no change in the questions, (3) research for newspapers to "determine what kinds of content have the greatest appeal for black readers in their area," and (4) coordinated studies to be conducted concurrently in a representative set of communities.

The national survey was already scheduled for repetition in 1982. The other proposals were presented to the Newspaper Readership Council but were never funded. We prepared the suggested uniform questionnaire for individual newspapers to use and urged them to conduct the recommended studies. None ever did. However, under prodding from ANPA and ASNE, newspapers began to make more systematic efforts to hire and promote blacks. The major groups, led by Gannett, Knight-Ridder, and Times-Mirror, made affirmative action programs a major management responsibility. More blacks were entering the executive ranks, and the handful of black publishers was growing. Surely, though very slowly, American newspapers were becoming racially integrated, but the black-white gap in readership persisted, like the larger social gap it reflected.

Research in the Newsroom

In the increasingly marketing-oriented newspaper environment, editors remained preoccupied with the "gap" between journalistic values and reader interests. The last "issues workshop" centered on another major piece of research conducted at the insistence of the editors and by a research team they selected. This was a substantial survey of the attitudes of newsroom personnel in which editors' views were compared with those of rank and file reporters, writers, and copy editors.

The ASNE contingent never made it clear how the opinions and morale of newspaper employees were directly related to the decline of the newspaper reading habit. However, a plausible case could be made that part of the problem was the failure of those who produced the news to understand their public and its tastes. Many of the editors were convinced that the journalists who worked for them were "out of touch" (the operative phrase) with the readers. A survey of their opinions would check on exactly how far out of touch they were. I tried to provide some direction for this newsroom study:[39]

The object . . . . is to discover clues as to how newspaper editorial staffs can be made more sensitive and responsive to the outlook and interests of readers. . . . As we descend the hierarchy of any large metropolitan newspaper's editorial staff, we should expect to find differences in awareness and perceptions of the readers, differences in conceptions of the newspaper's social function, differences in the value and meaning attached to one's own job. We can translate these expectations into a series of researchable questions:

At various levels of rank, staff assignment, age, experience, and professional training, what are the differences within editorial staffs in the notions of what a newspaper is and does and in the notions of what readers want and expect from it? In fact, to what degree is there any conscious awareness of the readers at all? If there is any, how does it enter into the process of gathering, writing, and editing the news? What fundamental assumptions, professional and practical, underlie the allocation of editorial space and energy? Where do these assumptions conflict and by what kinds of judgments are such inconsistencies resolved?

To what extent are news-related decisions made with some anticipation of reader interest, and on what basis of evidence or judgment is that level of expected interest defined? How do such expectations of reader response affect major decisions on space use, establishment of new beats or bureaus, subscription to supplemental wire or feature services, design and format changes? How do they influence day-to-day newsmaking decisions on specific assignments and stories?

I suggested that the study of newsroom attitudes and assumptions should look at "the social organization of the whole newspaper and of its editorial department," supplementing interviews with "sustained and systematic observation."

To what extent do editorial staff members think of themselves as professionals serving a higher social purpose? How do they define their future career lines? How compatible are their personal opinions with the newspaper's editorial position? In what social circles do they move, within the newspaper and in the town? How rooted are they in the community?

Finally, I argued that the task called for the collection of case histories of a number of different newspaper organizations of contrasting types, rather than a national cross-section of newspaper staff members.

We should try to include papers whose editors have accepted a marketing philosophy and made extensive use of research in redesigning or reorganizing what they do and others whose editors are reluctant to relinquish their traditional reliance on judgment and instinct. There should be papers where circulation is gaining (and where editors may not feel they have a problem) and others where it continues to drop off (and where the editors feel the hot breath of the publisher against their necks).[40]

This proposed strategy was not adopted. The Research Committee appointed a study group to define the project more precisely. The discussions produced what Gollin called[41]

two closely linked goals: the first is "diagnostic": what are the prevailing attitudes and values in the newsroom?. . . the second goal is more change oriented, how can newsroom values and practices be made more sensitive and responsive to readers' needs and interests as these have been defined by a growing body of evidence from readership research?

The study group was in "general agreement that editors are finding it more difficult to exercise effective supervision or control of the newsmaking process, a development that hampers efforts to achieve a more coherent reader-sensitive newspaper on a daily basis." The final product was an attitude survey, with all the data aggregated without differentiating among the newspaper sites.

The research on "The World of the Working Journalist" was conducted by Michael and Judee Burgoon and Charles Atkin of the School of Communications of Michigan State University. This team had been doing a considerable number of reader surveys for Gannett Newspapers. (Gannett's top editor, John Quinn, was at this point climbing the ladder to the ASNE presidency.)

In combining their academic duties with commercial research work, the Michigan State researchers were following a not uncommon practice. Although full-time commercial researchers regarded it as unfair competition, employing university facilities and low-paid graduate student labor, university administrations generally accepted the argument that outside consulting assignments kept faculty members in touch with the "real world," added to the prestige of the institution, and provided both staff and students with the opportunity to acquire valuable data that could be reanalyzed for scholarly purposes after their initial utilitarian function had been met.

The Michigan State research used written questionnaires completed by 489 news people at eight papers and 187 personal interviews from which quotations and insights were drawn without quantification. The fact that some of the report's conclusions were based on these qualitative interviews aroused concern from some critics among the editors, who wanted statistical evidence to support the statements. This stance was ironic, since no such demand had been made when more revolutionary conclusions had been drawn from the "focus groups" a few years earlier.

The Michigan State researchers did find that most reporters and editors had a very vague conception of who their readers were and tended to misperceive many of their interests. The study uncovered a certain amount of disengagement on the part of most young reporters, both from their newspapers and from their communities. The research team interpreted this to be a serious problem. They stressed this aspect of the findings in a series of speeches and convention presentations.

Even though 76 percent of the respondents disagreed with the statement that "readers are gullible and are easily fooled," the report said that "a majority of journalists appear to hold a patronizing and unflattering view of their readers" and that "news people underestimate their readers' dependence on newspapers, especially for hard news, and overestimate the public's use of television and interest in fluff." It also noted that "most journalists do not believe their paper has an identifiable or consistent news policy."

These interpretations were disseminated in the form of convention speeches before the report itself was completed. They confirmed the worst fears of some editors but irritated the hell out of others. Michael Burgoon was sensitive to the critics. He wrote Gollin,[42] "I am just a simple soul from Kansas trying to figure out the best way to do the right thing. It ain't always easy, is it?" Gollin replied,[43] "It would be most unfortunate if you felt this was turning into an adversarial proceeding."[44]

At our "Issues Workshop,"[45] the Burgoons and Atkin joined a group of editors and several journalism professors and deans to present and discuss the findings of the research. The first evening was given over to an exposition of the findings by the authors. The participants had already read the report ahead of time and two of them were assigned to comment on each chapter for five-minute lead-ins to the general discussion on the second day. I asked the discussants

> to dissent (if you feel impelled to do so) from the authors' interpretations of their data, to refer to any additional evidence that sheds light on that particular subject, and most important, to offer your own suggestions as to what editors, newspaper managements, or the newspaper business might do about it. Remember that the purpose of the workshop is not to critique the report (though that's within bounds) but to talk about the present state of newsroom attitudes, morale, and sensitivity to reader interests. This leads into

larger issues of editorial staffing, organization, communication, training; journalistic principles; the challenge of competitive media; whither the newspaper business, etc.

The Burgoons' demeanor was grim and academic, in contrast to that of the naturally extroverted editors. In preference to simple percentages, they made extensive use of advanced statistical analysis techniques that abstracted and clustered the answers received to their questions. At the same time, they were ready to extract impressionistic observations from their field visits. During the discussion, I tried to differentiate among three types of observations: those based on the self-administered questionnaires, those based on the depth interviews, and those that represented the authors' impressions. The discussion was lively, with Michael Burgoon's blood pressure rising steadily throughout. At the conclusion of the day-and-a-half-long session, I assured the authors that the vigorous questioning reflected the importance of the subject and the value of their research, which had important implications for newsroom management as well as for journalism education.

A few days later,[46] I sent out a list of forty "action suggestions" that had either surfaced in the discussion or that occurred to me independently. Ideas that had aroused controversy were asterisked: "Provide incentives to journalists to become involved in community activities; encourage more newspapers to set up ombudsmen; alert editors to the dangers of succumbing to the 'new journalism' and the attrition of traditional news values." Among the other suggestions were:

- Get every newspaper management to prepare a mission statement that clearly sets forth the newspaper's objectives and its role in the community.
- Make editors aware of the need to set clear directives on news policy, while at the same time giving reporters maximum autonomy to operate within those directives.
- Make editors aware of the importance of giving reporters a sense of greater participation in decision-making as they move along in their careers. (Transfers and job exchanges between reporters and desk people or between the daily paper and the Sunday news magazine staffs represent one way of keeping them stimulated.)

- Encourage more newsroom programs to improve writing skills.
- Try to identify the "cynical one-fifth" of the newsroom staffs before they are hired and handle them with special sensitivity. (The people who are most talented and move ahead most rapidly also tend to be the ones who develop the most elitist work attitudes.)
- Make editors aware that some isolation from the surrounding community is inevitable in a business where many of the reporters are young, highly mobile, unaffiliated, and are working at odd hours. If reporters themselves are made aware of this peculiarity of their job, they may be more encouraged to make up for it by expanding their contacts.
- Prepare a presentation or booklet to improve the planning of work-flow systems in newsrooms and the training methods now used to master those systems.
- Encourage wider reading of material that is produced not by journalists but by other types of writers.
- To cope with widespread dislike of VDTs and anxiety about their medical effects, prepare a booklet that (a) reviews the evidence on this subject, (b) explains the safety precautions that are taken in installing new equipment (to relieve any lingering concern about radiation), and (c) provides tips on how to avoid visual strain.
- Prepare another booklet for management describing the concern of newsroom staffs about (a) sharing VDTs (where individuals formerly had their own typewriters), (b) the "isolation booth" phenomenon and its effects on the sociable newsroom atmosphere, (c) the difficulty of establishing accountability for particular changes in text, and (d) the reduction of editorial feedback and criticism to reporters. Suggest ways to anticipate and eliminate these problems.
- Prepare a discussion guide on the subject of "What is News?" Get editors to run discussion meetings with their staffs away from the newspaper premises. (Most staff meetings are devoted to housekeeping matters; they should be directed more to issues of real substance.)
- Promote the positive findings of the MSU report both to newspaper people and to the public at large. E.g.: (a) journalists adhere strongly to professional criteria in making their news judgments and don't to any significant degree feel

themselves subject to improper outside influences. (b) Accuracy is almost universally accepted as the number one criterion of professionalism.

- Make editors aware that reader response can not be accurately judged by phone calls and letters, particularly critical ones.

Neither ASNE nor ANPA ever took any action on these proposals. Since by this time the Readership Project was ending, the subject never arose again.

The study generated considerable publicity, controversy, and even passion. Robert Stiff, then editor of the *St. Petersburg Evening Independent,* was scathing in his comments on the Burgoons' presentation to the APME:[47]

> The conclusions the Burgoons draw are not always backed up by the data. The survey results and the information picked up in group interviews are weaved together throughout the report in such a way that they're often difficult to separate—and there is nothing to back up the conclusions that come from selected interviews. . . . Michael was particularly outrageous as he addressed an audience that had not seen his report and was in no position to challenge anything he said. He said some things that the report doesn't say and . . . . spent a big block of his time attacking journalism educators and discussing the First Amendment, both of which are chapters in his report, although no survey questions were asked in these areas.

The study also had its enthusiasts, notably Larry Fuller, publisher of the Sioux Falls, South Dakota *Argus Leader,* who chaired the Newsroom Management Committee of the APME. He stressed for his colleagues the report's conclusion that "many journalists are out of touch with the communities they serve. And for many, this is a state of affairs they would prefer to maintain. . . . A fair number of journalists feel aloof from the public and have little regard for it."

The report never had the impact on rank-and-file editors that its sponsors had hoped for. At the same time, however, it may have accelerated a new movement to train editors in the managerial aspects of their work—best symbolized when Michael Fancher, the editor of the *Seattle Times,* made the considerable effort to acquire an MBA degree while he continued on his job.

Once again, it had been demonstrated that research can rouse strong emotions when it touches the established ways of great institutions and their dedicated practitioners. It was appropriate, perhaps, for the Readership Project's research program to wind up where it began, with an examination of the values and practices of journalists and their relationship to the reading public. The discussions inevitably returned to the same underlying question: What was the real mission of the press, and how should that mission change as other media assumed some of its historical functions, and as sweeping changes occurred in the society on which it reported and on which it depended for its continuing vitality?

Our research had pinpointed newspapers' weaknesses and strengths. It showed in what parts of the population readership was slipping; it identified the elements of the newspaper that attracted different kinds of readers in differing degrees. It tracked the trends in reading habits, in the use of broadcast news, and in the content of the paper itself. But the research did not in itself offer newspaper managements the magic solution they were seeking, nor did it give them tangible means of boosting their circulation. Providing the tools for action was the assignment of the three other operating committees of the Project.

CHAPTER 6

Circulation: People, Hardware, and Software

Newspaper circulation was an arena where practical actions could be taken immediately, with or without the benefits of research. These actions involved both the people involved in the distribution process and the machines and systems they used in their work. Here the Readership Project managed to be constructive without being controversial.

Delivering Newspapers

Circulation departments were the field troops in the great competitive wars of the yellow press in the late nineteenth and early twentieth centuries. The game was played rough, often by strong-arm men like Hearst's Moses Annenberg, later the owner of the *Philadelphia Inquirer.* Although that era was long over, the distribution of metropolitan newspapers was still in many cases dependent upon the compliance of the Teamsters Union and of wholesalers who sometimes had to accommodate the pressures of organized crime. Circulation people dealt with large amounts of money dispensed in nickels and dimes. They bore a social stigma: they were "truck drivers." Circulation was a matter of manual labor; it was heavy work to toss bundles of papers around.

To outsiders looking at the newspaper business, circulation executives appeared to be inbred, somewhat demoralized by the declining sales figures with which they had to cope, and concerned about the lack of top management interest and attention to their work. The circulation department was not an arena in which publishers had traditionally taken much interest. Circulation careers rarely led to transfers to other responsibilities within the newspaper, and only a few circulation directors had worked their way up to become publishers themselves.

By contrast to the Bureau's wary relationship with newspaper editors, our dealings with the leadership of the ICMA were extremely cordial from the start. As more papers adopted the concept of a unified marketing operation, circulation directors became somewhat fearful of being taken over by the advertising department and anxious to preserve their autonomous status. The Readership Project brought them direct attention from the top. We were constantly pointing out to publishers that circulation was a neglected function and urging them to give it more interest and investment.

The circulation department was an autonomous realm into which employees of other newspaper departments rarely ventured. Circulation management had a different orientation in big cities, where most of the sales were in single copies, and in smaller markets where home delivery accounted for virtually the entire distribution.

As a child growing up in Brooklyn, I loved going down to the newsstand in front of the local subway station in the early evening to see the bundles of first editions come in on the delivery trucks. A substantial little crowd of people were always waiting to see the headlines in the next day's *News* and *Mirror*, to get the sports results, and perhaps to check the "numbers." There was considerable immediacy, excitement, and a sense of the impact of the great world beyond. But bulldog editions have long since vanished under the impact of television's early evening news. As competitive newspapers died off, it became increasingly difficult for news dealers to survive.

For years, newspapers had been largely delivered by "little merchants," boys of ten to fifteen, and, more recently, girls as well, who were earning some money and learning the ways of the world by running a newspaper route. In an era of increasing affluence, carriers became harder to recruit. Papers got heavier, particularly with inserts, which the carrier was usually expected to stuff into the paper for a nominal fee (like a penny a copy). Youngsters always found it especially uncomfortable to solicit and sell subscriptions and to collect money from customers. The exodus of the American population from cities to suburbs had increased the distances between residences and lengthened carrier routes. Moreover, as readership and subscriptions declined, the distances between one customer and the next became even greater. This made it more difficult for a young carrier to cover the route in a relatively brief time.

Studies of discontinued subscriptions found that poor service was very often cited as a reason. However, carriers attributed stops to reader dissatisfaction with the product rather than to poor service. High turnover among carriers was generally translated into a high turnover among their subscribers. And turnover among carriers was, in many cases, itself a reflection of the turnover among those who supervised them. (A 1975 study of circulation district managers by the Belden research organization showed generally low morale.) Turnover at every level increased the newspaper's operating costs. The task of recruiting, training, motivating, and supervising carriers remained essentially as formidable as it had always been. Yet individuals with the necessary skills were finding a greater array of alternative career opportunities.

Training Tools

A key objective of the Circulation Training Committee was to cut into the spiral of turnover by producing better trained district managers and carriers. The Committee was headed through its entire lifetime by Albert Dilthey, the director of personnel and public relations for Knight-Ridder's Miami Herald, who was, when we started, president of the Newspaper Personnel Relations Association. The projects generated were, however, essentially set up to serve the interests of the ICMA, and many of them funneled through the Training Committee after prior discussions by the ICMA Board. Before the Project began, ICMA already had a number of its own training presentations, which struck us as somewhat unsophisticated in tone and technique. The Bureau's staff were restrained in expressing their criticism, being highly conscious of sensitivities, but we found that the leaders of the circulation group regarded the help of the Readership Project as manna from heaven. They actually wanted us to remake the basic presentations from scratch and were eager to have us do new ones.

A wish list prepared by ICMA, even before the Project formally got under way, called for sixteen different district manager training films, including such memorable titles as "Enthusing Newspaper Carriers To Sell," "Public Relations Through the Circulation Carrier Leader," and "Second Follow-up with the Carrier When the Customer Receives His First Bill."

The Bureau came to the Training Committee's first meeting[1] armed with proposals to develop materials aimed at district managers, carriers, and phone room personnel, "as well as presentations dealing with specific targets or prospect groups like blacks, young people, apartment house residents."

A recent survey had indicated that there were approximately 6,000 people employed in circulation phone room operations. We proposed that our first two training presentations be addressed to telephone technique. One would deal with the fundamental principles of selling, handling subscriber complaints, and heading off cancellations. A second presentation would deal with the practice of selling subscriptions through cold calls to nonsubscribers and upgrading sales on voluntary calls.

Bill Jardine, ICMA's ebullient president in 1979–80, worked for Silha in Minneapolis. He wanted a film "on the free enterprise system, the backbone of the American economy" that would "give a good lesson to youngsters, probably fourth and ninth grades, and could be readily accepted in schools" and "help the image of newspapers." He felt they could "learn a great deal about business and the free enterprise system by having a newspaper route." Although the Committee was inclined to be supportive, I derailed the proposal. Commenting on it afterward[2] to his fellow officers in ICMA, Jardine said ruefully, "I still like it, and I think it would be very helpful to all circulation people, but Leo is wondering if we're getting a little bit off their goal." I knew how he felt.

Jardine kept coming up with additional suggestions. He proposed that we "do something in human relations for district sales managers and supervisors on working with people both young and old on how to respond to certain situations." Tina Novaseda, a newly hired writer with a knack for elemental comedy, was assigned to prepare a presentation to show district managers how to motivate youngsters. She began by going into the field to visit circulation departments and attend carrier meetings, at the suggestion of Creative Director Simons. As he put it, "This recasts the show as an on-location demonstration of good technique rather than our prescription for what that should be. It relieves us of the onus of being industry experts."[3] The results delighted Jardine. He was "pleased and impressed" and "most enthusiastic about the people in your organization that I work with . . . people that are most cooperative and excited about what they are doing, which means we just get that much better work."[4]

Carrier recruitment was a major problem. We designed a presentation that could be shown in schools and community gatherings to glamorize the job of the juvenile carrier. A growing number of newspapers had moved from juvenile to adult deliverers, many of whom were moonlighting part-timers. Another set of presentations was aimed both at the carriers themselves and at their supervisors. The job of a district manager involved long and irregular hours. A "Spouse's Manual" gave family members a sense of what the circulation job was all about and endowed it with importance.

The training materials were developed for use in the newspaper's own plant, but the Bureau's training staff also developed a circulation workshop along the lines of its established activities with advertising sales people. William Solch and Steve Van Osten normally spent their time teaching newspapers' retail sales personnel the rudiments of salesmanship, of advertising budgeting, scheduling, and planning, and of advertising design, layout, and copy. They had no prior background in newspaper circulation, but they were seasoned trainers, accustomed to a routine that encompassed entire days of high-pressure, stand-up performance and evenings in motel rooms at the side of interstate highways. Using the slide shows and publications developed for the project, they devised role-playing sessions to heighten selling and managerial skills. A TV camera provided feedback and allowed the participants to critique each others' performances. In a training session at one middle-sized paper, Solch asked what the circulation was and got the reply, "The publisher won't tell us."

At Knight-Ridder's Miami headquarters, Byron Harless, the company's personnel vice-president, had developed a circulation sales training program that included a slide film and cassette, a videotape, and three manuals. Jardine and ICMA proposed purchasing the rights for other newspapers to use. Caught in the relentless cost pressures of the corporate world, Harless was anxious to recoup some of the company's substantial investments in this material. We could never agree on a price.

One way of reducing turnover among district managers was to hire the right ones in the first place. This could be done with the help of a weighted application form that would identify those job applicants who were likely to be successful or unsuccessful. Nunn, of the Bureau's Research Department, developed a screening device (later adopted by many newspapers) based on what circulation managers considered to be the attributes they were looking for. (Not to our surprise, the most desirable characteristic turned out to be a genuine interest in working with young people.)

Studying Practices

One of the first obstacles we confronted in developing our plans was an absence of basic facts about the circulation business. Ignorance of industry practices was not unique to circulation; it applied to all newspaper departments. Competitive sentiments and the antitrust laws had inhibited the exchange of this type of information among publishers. The ICMA itself periodically ran informal membership surveys, but as in most newspaper associations, these were not done professionally. The returns (which came disproportionately from larger dailies) were not adjusted to reflect the distribution of newspapers across various size groups.

Working with the leadership of ICMA, we began to generate information about the state of training activity and circulation practices across the country. The first source was a survey of circulation directors that the Bureau designed and analyzed. It covered such subjects as the availability of zoned editions, publication of Total Market Coverage products or shoppers, distribution of advertising sections to nonsubscribers, operation of alternate delivery systems for magazines or packages, presence of a subscriber information system, use of adult carriers, use of contractors or fleet employees, assembly of newspaper components for delivery, and use of specialized delivery vehicles.

By disseminating the findings of this study, we were able to give both circulation executives and their publishers a better sense of the rapid changes in the industry's operations. It was also a way of heightening their awareness of the tasks that still had to be faced.

A high priority for newspapers was to recruit more black employees and executives. While editors complained about the shortage of qualified black writers, the job skills required in the circulation department posed fewer obstacles to the educationally disadvantaged. From the start, our presentations featured black participants both as presenters and as role models. I revived my earlier suggestion that each newspaper association establish a committee on minority employment and got the Training Committee's endorsement of this idea. Ten years later, ICMA moved to set up such a committee as part of the industry-wide minority recruitment effort launched by ANPA.

Professionalizing Circulation Management

Unlike newspaper advertising, the craft of newspaper circulation lacked academic credentials. Courses in advertising generally, and in newspaper advertising, were widely taught in American colleges, both in journalism and business schools. Employees in circulation learned their skills on the job. There was no academic preparation, not a single course or textbook,[5] no scholarly articles or journals, no professors of circulation. Therefore, no one assumed that circulation was a field complicated enough to warrant study, as advertising did. Yet circulation was rapidly being transformed from the business of manipulating bundles of products to a business of manipulating computerized data on sales, returns, personnel performance, and subscriber histories and characteristics.

There were some 4,000 jobs in circulation management and 400 openings a year in a growing job market. As graduation from high school and going to college became more common throughout American society, newspaper personnel at all levels were better educated than in the past. Before World War II, college graduates were a minority in most newsrooms. However, by the start of the Readership Project, few new hires in newspaper editorial departments did not have a college degree. Even at this late date, circulation executives were likely to have advanced directly out of the field force. They were less likely to be college educated than their counterparts in advertising and far less likely to have done any graduate work. (In 1969, Knight-Ridder Newspapers made a move to change this, by recruiting recent MBAs and immersing them in a circulation department as the first step in their management training program.)

A chance conversation in 1975 between Scott Chisholm, a teacher at Empire State College, and Ron Anderson, the circulation director of the Rochester newspapers, brought about the creation of the Empire State College program in circulation. This unit of the State University of New York specialized in individualized programs of adult education through which students were given credit for their work experience.[6] Chisholm's academic field was English literature, and his avocation was cross-country hiking over the forgotten trails of the Mormon trek westward. (He eventually moved to Brigham Young University, where he set up a similar program.) Somehow or other, the prospect of enlightening the circulators captured his imagination. The Readership Project gave his program strong support.

One of my pet ideas was to launch a graduate level program in circulation management.[7] The starting premise was that

> More sophisticated and better trained personnel are needed to improve distribution and selling methods, to handle subscribers' servicing problems, and to reduce delivery costs. The newspapers of the United States are engaged in a distribution operation second only to the Postal Service in its scope. Newspapers employ thousands of workers in their circulation departments and have millions of dollars invested in trucks, vending racks, stuffing machinery, computers, and other circulation-related equipment. However, most jobs in circulation have been comparatively low-paying within the newspaper business. Typically, they have been regarded as dead-end jobs which have not logically led to promotion elsewhere in the organization and which have not been easily translatable into career lines in other industries.

After reviewing the major changes in progress and prospect, I argued that these would

> heighten the need for better trained and more professionally oriented circulation personnel. In advertising, a comparable move-

ment toward professionalism has been met by the development of specialized graduate studies. An MBA in marketing with a concentration in advertising is offered by many universities, while others offer an MA in communication or journalism with a concentration in advertising.

I proposed a master's program in circulation management and offered a prototype curriculum.[8] Finally, I traced a connection between the creation of a degree program and "the evolution of scholarly interest in the field and of a body of research literature." The great unanswered questions of newspaper distribution cried out for systematic scholarly investigation. But research would follow teaching and fellowship opportunities that would open up only when the field carried academic legitimacy.

The Training Committee liked the idea but debated whether a school of business administration or a school of journalism was the appropriate place.[9] ASNE's McKnight suggested that the program could be run at the community college level, but the Committee felt that "the interest of a prestigious university was needed to make the program successful."

ICMA circulated the proposal to journalism school deans and got noncommittal replies, except for one, from John R. Wilhelm of Ohio University. He wrote back that the problem

> would be how to fund a new program which would cost in the neighborhood of $1 million a year; that is, we would need at least one endowed chair of $600,000 to provide salary for a permanent professor. . . . The proposal set forth is to me descriptive of what is wrong with much of higher education today. It proposes a specialty in circulation management. Why not management of an advertising agency or of a wire service or magazine? What is needed is to develop individuals who are educated, not individuals who are trained in an occupation.

By that token, I might have said in rebuttal, what was the rationale for having schools of journalism? But the criticism came not only from the academic side. William Attwood, the publisher of *Newsday*, wrote,[10]

> It encompasses more than our own circulation managers would require to do their job well. We have found from experience that on-the-job training in the topics that you list is the most effective way of training competent people to perform as we expect them to.

Whether or not he was right, Attwood apparently spoke for the majority, both of newspapers and in academia. The proposal remained dead in the water.

Homegrown though they were, circulation executives were swiftly becoming a different, technology-minded breed. There is no identifiable point at which an occupational craft may be said to cross the line and become a profession. Perhaps it occurs when practitioners think of themselves as engaged in a higher calling that transcends the day-to-day demands of the job. In this respect, those who distributed newspapers were not yet as far along as those who worked at the trade of journalism. For this reason the debates that accompanied the Project's activities in circulation systems and training were far less passionate than those that involved newspaper editors.

Raising Hard Questions

At least some of newspapers' circulation problems were rooted in the complexity of the distribution system itself. These problems began in the plant, where a product of larger bulk and with more components than in the past had to be printed and assembled in timely fashion to meet transportation schedules. The mailroom, in which papers are bundled and shipped forth by truck from the loading dock, was the starting point for the process that took them into the field, assigned in proper quantities to the individual carriers or distributors, and eventually placed at the reader's door or at a point of sale.

Of the Readership Project's four working committees, the one on circulation systems and equipment was the hardest to get off the ground, and yet it may have left the most enduring legacy. In the early stages of planning the Project it seemed to me that the personnel aspect of circulation management was distinct from the mechanical and production areas and that two separate committees were needed.

The efficiency of newspaper distribution could be increased by introducing technical improvements as well as by better selection and training of people. Circulation systems and equipment was the smallest committee. It was chaired by a circulation manager (initially the *Phoenix Republic*'s Donald Martz and later Kenneth

Todd, his counterpart at the *Indianapolis Star and News,* another Pulliam newspaper). The ANPA Research Institute (which was later merged directly into the ANPA) was represented by Erwin Jaffe, an engineer of great competence and versatility. There was also Uzal Martz, publisher of the Pottsville, Pennsylvania *Republican* (and not a relation of Donald's), who represented the Institute of Newspaper Controllers and Financial Officers (INCFO, later renamed the International Newspaper Financial Executives, or INFE). We wanted to get this organization involved because their members were in most cases responsible for the computer information systems in newspaper plants. Martz insisted on "proper reference to INCFO's participation" when I inadvertently forgot to mention this in a script prepared for a major convention presentation. This kind of sensitivity was understandable, since each constituent association was engaged in a continuing battle for recognition.

As with every other facet of the Readership Project, a certain amount of staff effort had to be diverted from the substantive tasks at hand to the stroking of Committee members who were dissatisfied with the rate of progress or were critical of the direction taken.

A weekly publisher who had been designated as the National Newspaper Association's representative on the Committee missed an early meeting but wrote afterward that his study of the minutes made him feel that "they are a bit over 'our' head." At another point, he threatened to resign because he felt that discussion of advertising was out of bounds, —even though advertisers' wishes were actually a key determinant of distribution patterns. One active member of the Committee told Silha privately that the operation "was producing booklets that aren't worth the paper." [11]

Asking the Questions

The agenda that seemed appropriate to me as an outsider was on a more rarefied level than the practical subjects that confronted working circulation and financial people who had to get their papers out to the public every day. As the Project was getting under way, I addressed a series of questions in a memorandum to the Controllers:

1) We need more cost benefit analysis. . . . What is the ideal ratio of advertising-to-circulation income? Those rare newspapers that have deliberately kept down their price to the reader to the pre-inflationary level seem to have generally held on to their circulation. Has the resulting advertising gain outweighed the additional circulation revenues that might have come through raising the price and maybe losing some readers in the process?

2) . . . Do we know as much as we should about the economics of handling inserts, especially when newspapers' basic distribution and editorial costs are factored into the package? Are they as profitable a source of revenue to our business as many of us have supposed? The answer to this question relates directly to the subject of zoning and to the nature of the product we put before the reader. . . .

3) More and more newspapers are computerizing their subscriber lists as a way of facilitating customer invoicing and servicing. . . . What is the payout experience from the very substantial investment required in hardware, programming, and personnel? How can this type of system be instituted in complex, competitive metropolitan markets? Isn't there an urgent need now to put all these computer systems on a single, uniform, nationwide basis, with the same basic codes and programs, so that they can talk to each other?

4) Can we develop more systematic knowledge about the economics and logistics of circulation; the cost of getting a paper to different types of readers through different distribution methods and in different types of urban and suburban environments; the cost of selling an order and the cost of keeping it going; the cost of stopping and starting; the cost of delivering and servicing? Can we develop more information about the merits of different types of circulator compensation and incentive plans to develop circulation that sticks?

5) What have been the cost and benefit consequences in those newspapers where the carrier's traditional job has been limited to delivery of the product and where sales, collection, and servicing of subscribers have been handled as separate functions within the circulation department?[12]

6) Can we develop more precise assessments of the advantages and the true expense of different home delivery methods, with turnover, supervisory costs, and productivity factored in? Can we spell out with greater precision the comparative virtues of using

adult versus juvenile carriers, employees rather than independent contractors? What types of situation are most suitable for each system? How will the equation change if newspapers move more aggressively into the field of alternative distribution for shoppers and magazines, in competition with the Postal Service?

7) For papers of different sizes, how do newsroom budgets relate to circulation growth and to overall profitability?[13]

In the course of the following six years, the Readership Project was to make some progress in facing these questions, but many of them remained unanswered years later. The controllers themselves had no institutional mechanism for coping with questions of this order. Like other newspaper associations, they operated through a series of standing committees that met infrequently and briefly, mainly at conventions, and that generally grappled with matters that affected their members immediately on their day-to-day jobs rather than as participants in a great industry.

From the start, the Equipment and Systems Committee felt more comfortable talking about the hardware of the business than about the murkier type of operations research that I felt was needed.[14] The agenda for its first meeting did take up the topics I had raised with the controllers, but it also covered a generous assortment of other subjects: vending machines (or racks)—both their design and location, stuffing and bundling equipment, trucks, and other equipment.

While some meetings of the other operating committees meandered off into long philosophical discussions of the social changes governing the fate of daily newspapers, the Equipment and Systems Committee meetings were comparatively mundane; they focused on finding solutions to immediate shortcomings of the machinery already in place. The problems seemed to cry out for substantial engineering investments, for which the Project lacked funds and which ANPA, in spite of its original good intentions, was unable to make.

The meetings rarely drew more than six or eight participants, including staff, but an effort was made to draw ideas from the constituent organizations. INCFO was requested to study the economics of inserts, ICMA to develop initial computer specifications for a newspaper circulation system; the ANPA Research Institute was asked to develop design parameters for an effective newspaper delivery vehicle.

The Research Institute's preferred method of introducing technical change was to offer suggestions to equipment suppliers. In some cases its staff carried this out to the stage of actual laboratory experimentation and prototype development. The big decisions on the investments necessary to create new equipment were left to market forces. The normal practice was to present proposal requests for specifications to equipment suppliers and encourage them to develop commercial products on their own entrepreneurial initiative. Initial plans for the Readership Project had called for the ANPA Research Institute to add several engineers to its staff to work on circulation equipment and systems. The Committee endorsed this idea, but the necessary funds could not be allocated.

The absence of additional engineering support placed a heavier burden on Jaffe, who had been given the staff responsibility on top of his regular assignment as ANPA/RI's manager of technical research. As a result, a number of the intriguing ideas that were brought up in Committee meetings were never pursued to the next stage.

Vending Racks and Other Points of Sale

As the number of newspapers had declined, so had the number of street vendors and newsstands. This made coin-operated vending machines or racks more important to the sale of single copies. An estimated 150,000 newspaper racks were in the field. They were subject to direct vandalism and pilferage from the coin box and had an annual attrition rate of 22 percent. Rack stocking by employees who belonged to the Teamsters' Union had become vastly more costly.

An additional complication occurred as a result of extra sales on "best food day" (Wednesday on most papers), when the paper carried valuable coupons. Someone inserting coins for a single copy could usually open the box and take away the remaining copies. Far more expensive machines fed by gravity might dispense only a single copy of a newspaper at a time. This problem did not lend itself to an easy mechanical solution, since newspapers were of very different thickness on different days of the week. Sunday newspapers represented an even more difficult problem. Because of their very heavy bulk, many papers did not sell them through racks at all.

Only a handful of manufacturers produced vending racks. Jaffe took on the task of contacting them and of keeping abreast of their progress, but the matter had little urgency for the vendors, who doubted newspapers' willingness to pay the necessary price. More satisfactory racks seemed likely to be so expensive that the investment would be difficult for newspapers to make up through savings in lost sales. The committee concluded that progress would be determined by the demands of the market rather than by any technical research of our own.

The Research Institute had already developed an improved single-copy vending machine called ANPA/VEND, but a proposed field test of it foundered. Donald Martz wrote that[15] "newspapers have been reluctant to take enough vendors for a full route operation even though we have agreed to subsidize. They feel after the test they may very well end up with a white elephant and just won't make a commitment for a full load." A year later ANPA/VEND was still awaiting a test in Phoenix, Oklahoma City, and Wichita. The machines were eventually withdrawn from the market, since there was no prospect that a manufacturer would develop a satisfactory model that was commercially viable.

Our discussions of racks led us in another direction. Newspapers lost potential sales when a rack sold out early in the day, and they lost money on unsold copies in racks that were oversupplied. About one-quarter of single copy distribution (as opposed to subscriptions) was unsold and wasted. Given the high cost of newsprint, there seemed to be promise in a systems or operations research approach to the measurement of rack sales, with the objective of reducing both overstocking and understocking.

Few papers kept records of sales for their individual racks. In a past era, when papers had put out successive editions, they reloaded racks during the day. This practice had virtually ceased because of the cost of vehicle operations. We struggled with the idea of placing portable timing devices in the racks to determine when the last copy was sold; the goal was to provide the optimum number of copies for each machine—never too few or too many. Donald Martz conducted some experiments on rack replenishment in Phoenix, with inconclusive results. The subject never generated the energy that might have elicited funding to pursue it more seriously. (A dozen years later there was still periodic talk of a "smart rack" that would automatically signal headquarters when it was depleted.)

The meetings were an opportunity to exchange experiences and comment on innovations;[16] the discussions of racks often wandered into related subjects like the challenge of finding new single-copy sales outlets. Supermarkets seemed to offer promising opportunities, but their resistances had to be overcome on a local level. What could the Readership Project accomplish nationally that would persuade individual grocery chains to purvey newspapers within their limited floor space? The discussions went around and around.

Trucks and the Delivery Mechanism

Inevitably, problems that were typically defined in purely mechanical terms actually originated in human relationships: circulation executives interacting with truck drivers and ultimately with the general public. Machines were merely instrumental to the series of transactions that gave the reader convenient access to the paper.

The vehicle fleets that carried newspapers to the points of distribution represented the largest single capital investment in circulation equipment, except in those comparatively few cases that relied entirely on independent distributors to take the papers from the plant and get them out. The daily newspaper fleet in the United States held 17,000 trucks in 1977. They were changed at a rate of 6,000 a year.

In addition to the trucks that were used to transport newspapers in bulk to field offices or distribution points, individual adult carriers on motor routes used cars or vans—usually their own— as they made their rounds of subscribers' homes. Papers were generally tossed onto the driveway or lawn—an awkward and time-consuming task when done from an ordinary left-hand drive vehicle. (This represented a problem similar to that of the Postal Service, which eventually came up with a right-hand drive vehicle that allows rural deliverers to reach into a roadside mail box without getting out.)

The motorized carriers were not the only ones who generally

failed to put the paper at the subscriber's doorstep, where it was wanted and expected. Juvenile carriers on bicycles generally threw their papers while on the go. Not surprisingly, discussions of this point led both to the subject of plastic wrappers to protect papers from rain and dew and also to the possibility of a bazooka-like device that might propel them to their destination with greater accuracy.

The prospects for vehicle redesign seemed more immediate and practical, and the Committee prodded Jaffe to turn his attention there. He prepared a lengthy description of the requirements for a newspaper delivery vehicle.[17] It was expected to take between a year and a half and two years after field tests of experimental models before final specifications could be published for manufacturers to follow in mass production, and then individual newspapers would have to order the new delivery vehicle from their own dealers. The Readership Project could not afford the luxury to think in such long-range terms.

Another proposed study that never got off the ground was to be an evaluation of mailroom procedures and systems. (The misnamed "mailroom" is the newspaper's distribution center, into which the conveyor belts feed from the presses.) The Committee discussed the possibility of setting up a low-cost computer information system geared to small newspapers.[18] Other items proposed were a single-copy wrapping machine and a bundle distribution system.

We tackled the question of how newspaper components are assembled for delivery. (This might be done entirely in the plant, partly at regional distribution centers, or all by the carriers.) There was talk of a booklet (never produced) on packing and shipping inserts.

The growth of preprinted advertising inserts posed new problems for production and for the mailroom. We argued the comparative merits of collating versus insertion. (Collating requires assembling components only; insertion—or stuffing—requires both assembling and wrapping.) We discussed specifications for the development of an on-line inserting machine, which was expected to cost $200,000 over a five-year period. And a more fundamental query was raised: what were the readers' reactions to inserts?

Somehow, when we talked about possible actions, we were always faced with the need for more information. For example, to design the interior of a delivery vehicle, experience data were needed on the weight and size of newspaper bundles. A few years earlier, in association with MIT, ANPA/RI had conducted a test on the computerization of newspaper delivery systems to plan the organization of routes. This sixteen-month test had failed primarily because a number of the factors involving the practical realities of fleet management had not been considered.

Circulation departments often kept no records of the replacement papers that they delivered and of the percentage replaced on an average day. How could such records be kept and assembled? We talked about the handling of apartment house deliveries, the collection of historical records on the effects of price changes on circulation, selective market coverage programs (in which advertising was delivered to only parts of a paper's total distribution area), the use of contractors (rather than the paper's own truck fleet employees) to haul papers, and the question of whether the fleets should be owned or leased. This grab bag of practical issues seemed remote from the great sociological question of declining readership, but they reflected the day-to-day realities of distribution with which circulation managements had to contend.

Subscriber Information Systems

The Committee's most important accomplishment arose from its discussions of subscriber information systems. Early in my encounters with circulation executives, I had been struck by their inability, in most cases, to identify individual subscribers. It was patiently explained to me that there was no way of getting this information, because the subscriber list on each route was the property of the "little merchant," and newspapers had long been exempt from the child labor laws on the grounds that the carriers were not employees but independent entrepreneurs.

Yet the absence of subscriber information was placing newspapers under several heavy handicaps. For one thing, it made their solicitation of new subscriptions extremely inefficient, since there was no way of identifying those people who were not already customers. Even more important, it limited newspapers' ability to fight two new and growing competitors for advertising: the mail and free publications or shoppers.

It had been apparent for some time that one of the most pronounced trends in marketing was the increased importance of targeting. Marketers and advertisers for any particular product or service were highly conscious of who their customers were and anxious to direct their promotional efforts at them rather than to diffuse messages to the general public. Direct mail had undergone a spectacular growth based on the development of lists of individuals with specific characteristics. "Telemarketing," telephone selling based on similar target lists, was also on the rise.

The development of lists was facilitated by the emergence of the computer, with its capacity to store and manipulate vast files of information about individuals or households: their past purchase records, their membership in organizations, their subscription to particular kinds of publications, and their demographic characteristics, or at least their residence in neighborhoods that could be described by distinctive attributes. This last application took a new turn as a number of organizations emerged to manipulate information from the census. The data were arranged by census tracts or postal zip codes, which were grouped through a statistical technique known as factor analysis into clusters with shared characteristics across the country.

Although newspapers' local identity had always been their major attraction, both for advertisers and for readers, national marketers were interested in reaching people of a particular type, whether they lived in Maine or in California. Where they could go after them by name and address, they would do so individually. But in the absence of that type of specific information, they could target their promotion by ascribing to households and addresses the prevalent characteristics of their geographic area. Since the geographic area could readily be defined in terms of the zip code, this became a tremendous boost to direct mail advertising. Large retailing organizations were analyzing their own charge account customer lists on this basis, and they began to ask newspapers to classify circulation by zip code so that it could be matched against the geographic location of their customers. The next step was to match subscriber names directly against charge account customer names.

For the most part, newspapers found it impossible to respond to such requests because they did not know the names of their own individual subscribers and readers. Many newspapers, especially larger ones, did not deal with their subscribers through their own distribution networks, using employee zone and district managers. Instead they worked through wholesalers or independent distributors who had their own district managers and carrier supervisors.

"It can't be done," was the characteristic response of the circulation department to the suggestion that newspapers begin assembling and computerizing their own subscriber lists. Yet since the late 1960s, computers were taking over more and more functions in every newspaper plant. They handled accounting, billing and payroll. They set type and made up ads. Eventually they were making up entire pages.

It seemed inevitable, and also imperative, to accelerate the process of applying the computer to the management of subscriber information. This provided an opportunity to target telephone solicitations more efficiently to nonsubscribing households. It facilitated the development of direct payment systems that took the disagreeable burden of collection out of the hands of the carrier. And it provided a basis for comparing the field performance and service levels of individual carriers and district managers.

A good deal of the impetus for computerization also came from the advertising department. As I have already mentioned, falling audience levels had prompted retailers to divert newspaper advertising budgets into other media.

Big retail chains wanted total coverage of their markets. At a time when newspaper penetration was dropping, they could get this through occupant-addressed mailings or by placing their inserts in hand-delivered shoppers. Newspaper managements quickly learned that, even if they could not supply the level of market penetration advertisers wanted, they could still distribute advertising inserts to their subscribers at a lower cost than the mail. If the newspaper could identify its subscribers and match their names against a complete directory of all the households in the market, advertisers might be persuaded to limit their mailings to nonsubscribers in the areas that they wanted to reach. By putting subscriber names on the computer, a "merge/purge" program could match them with household directory listings to produce lists of nonsubscribers. With this kind of a system in place, the newspaper could retain its position as the basic advertising buy, and mailings to nonsubscribers could be kept as a mere supplement. The result would be a considerable saving for the advertiser. Advertisers brought mounting pressure to have circulation shown by zip code in the ABC reports. Some newspapers resisted, fearing a growth in "cherry-picking"—concentration of inserts in only the most desirable neighborhoods. The effect, they feared, would be not merely to reduce their advertising revenues but also to weaken their traditional function as a voice for the entire community, including the low-income neighborhoods in which advertisers had no interest. Sears and Penney's were unwavering in their demands. Although newspaper representatives on the ABC Board prevented a move to make zip code reporting mandatory, it was included voluntarily in the ABC reports of some 700 papers by 1990. Many other dailies supplied the same information informally to advertisers who asked for it.

Matching subscribers to households is, of course, a task that made sense only for those papers that distributed primarily through subscriptions. For large metropolitan papers that had a high percentage of circulation through individual copy sales, advertiser pressure on this point was far from welcome. It seemed to carry with it the implication that a single-copy purchaser was of less value than someone whose newspaper was home delivered, even though it could be argued that a single-copy purchaser would be highly motivated to read. Still, national advertisers of packaged goods grocery products, who used inserts, were fearful that their valuable coupons might be misredeemed. They commonly supplied fewer copies of their inserts to newspapers than the audited circulation would require, to keep them out of copies sold at vending machines or stores. Advertisers delivering preprints through a combination of newspapers and the mail (or other forms of distribution) were concerned about what they saw as wasteful duplication in the case of single-copy purchasers.

The Bureau's expert on inserts was James Hollis, who had started as a trainee at the S. S. Kresge Company, had managed a K-Mart store, and had gone on to become national advertising manager before Kauffman hired him to head the Bureau's discount store contacts. Although he had changed affiliations, Hollis continued to view his domain from the merchant's point of view and to press newspapers to introduce the changes that he felt were necessary for them to retain the insert business. Somewhat to Hollis' dismay (he had an aversion to unnecessary discourse), I asked him to participate in the Equipment and Systems Committee's discussions. His first step was to initiate a test in Bryan, Texas, matching a direct mailer's computerized list of all residents in the market with a newly assembled list of the newspaper's subscribers. The results were encouraging enough so that the Committee proposed additional testing in other markets.[19]

At about this same time, the *Los Angeles Times* moved to take over direct control of its circulation field operations and became engaged in a nasty battle with its independent distributors, who had no relish to become employees. Impelled by the talk at meetings of circulation managers and controllers, pressured by advertising considerations, newspapers began to collect subscriber lists from their carriers. They discovered hardly any resistance. This was not too surprising, in view of the frequency of turnover among carriers. It was customary for a youngster to turn over the list to the circulation district manager when relinquishing a route, so that it could be handed over to a successor.

Centralizing and computerizing the lists, moreover, was to encourage the practice of billing customers directly from the newspaper's own office. This tended to reduce the carriers' tips, but it relieved them of what they generally considered the most onerous part of the job.

From Concept to Action

How does one translate a concept into an action program? The evolution of subscriber information systems may represent a useful illustration of the steps to be taken. In 1977, no more than a dozen newspapers had on-line computerized circulation systems. The first task was to teach all the others the rudiments of what could be done. This took the form of publications and conferences. Neither format aroused much enthusiasm at first.

Preparation of an introductory booklet on subscriber information systems might have appeared to be a very simple task. Actually, every proposed text had to be reviewed by every member of the Committee. They were not always in agreement, and the process was time consuming. The three booklets eventually prepared reflected contributions both from staff (Jaffe and Hollis) and from Committee members.

Uzal Martz wrote,[20] "I do think that we are at the beginning of a very important project 'for the good of the order.' " Martz was himself preoccupied with the development of a uniform identification system for occupied dwelling units that could be used to store subscriber information.

Todd, ICMA's representative, also wanted to publish specifications for the listing of occupied housing units in the form of a booklet or manual. This would show newspapers how to approach the problem, state their objectives, identify the possible sources, weigh the relative cost advantages and disadvantages, standardize their procedures, and handle off-route deliveries.

To give newspapers "the ABCs of how to approach this problem," I raised the following questions for Hollis:[21]

> What are the objectives [newspapers] have in developing a list of occupied housing units? What are the possible sources they can use? What are the relative costs, advantages, and disadvantages? How can they achieve standardization in the procedures to be followed, for example, by following postal routes? What procedures should they use for handling off-route deliveries? What do they do when there is more than one copy delivered per household? What is the status of the nine-digit Zip Code? [This was not introduced until 1983.] What provision should be made for postal carrier numbers?

The indefatigable Todd also drafted a proposed pamphlet (never produced) on the packaging, shipping, and handling of inserts.[22] Our booklets were rather elementary in content, yet they seem to have had a pronounced effect, alerting newspaper managements to the changes under way and creating an impression of momentum to which they had to be responsive. Significant progress came about as computer software companies recognized that this was an area that promised profits. A number of circulation management information systems began to be displayed at the annual production conference.

The conference did not normally draw many circulation executives. We decided that the way to speed up the adoption of subscriber information systems was to sponsor a seminar.[23] The first circulation computer systems symposium was held in Dallas[24] and drew more than 400 participants. The meeting was held under the joint sponsorship of the Readership Project, ANPA, INCFO, and ICMA, which took the leading role in planning the program. It was hard to realize that the entire organizational process, efficiently implemented by the ANPA, had been set in motion by the seemingly unfocussed discussions of the Equipment and Systems Committee.[25]

The second circulation symposium, held a year later[26] featured presentations by representatives of smaller papers using inexpensive and simple Radio Shack equipment. This was instrumental in overcoming the impression that only larger papers, with their mainframe computers, could apply electronic data processing to circulation systems. Significantly, a score of equipment and software suppliers were on hand to exhibit their wares and to legitimate the importance of what was happening. A decade later, almost all newspapers had developed computerized subscriber lists. Creating them was a herculean task—*Newsday* keypunched 750,000 names and addresses in a two-week period—and maintaining them on a current basis was no easy matter either. Subscriber names were routinely being matched against directories of households and against the name lists supplied by advertisers.

Newspapers would surely have expended the money and effort required to go this route even if there were no Newspaper Readership Project. But the process would probably have taken a good deal longer, with many more false steps along the way, if there had been no systematic exchange of information or the perception that what each paper did was part of an industry-wide endeavor. If the tasks faced by the Committee were hardly concluded when the Project's funding came to an end, substantial progress. had been made.

The circulation department and its functions were being transformed by a number of concurrent developments, quite apart from the advent of the computer. There was a great growth in the number of newspapers offering zoned editions designed to tap local advertising that was being taken over by shoppers, yellow pages, and other new competitors. Many newspapers also introduced total market coverage programs to bring advertising to nonsubscribers, using the regular carrier force, the mail, or special carrier forces.

It seemed to me important to stimulate the process of change by making circulation departments aware of what was going on and also by bringing that transformation to the attention of top management. One way to do this was by assembling a number of case histories on different newspaper circulation departments. The result, after a series of field visits in 1982, was a report, a casebook, and a slide presentation, "Circulation: Key to Successful Newspaper Marketing." Among the conclusions, I presented a management dilemma.

> A critical issue that remains unresolved is whether circulation is to be regarded as an independent "profit center" within the newspaper organization, or whether its primary job is to maximize the numbers that the advertising department can sell to advertisers at a profit. Ideally both objectives should be exactly compatible. In practice they rarely are. Newspaper managements must face up to the continuing dilemma of whether they want to encourage advertising by building the largest circulation figures they can, whatever the price, or whether they want to operate the circulation function with the greatest possible economy.

In the ensuing years, newspapers continued to face this enigma, as they did most of their problems, from one day to the next.

CHAPTER 7

Promoting the Medium

Improving distribution methods was essentially a preliminary step to building the circulation numbers. The Promotion Committee had the rather unenviable assignment of finding new ways to do what newspapers had been trying to do all along—to persuade readers that they were worth buying. It might seem that this task could be handled in a fairly straightforward way, yet here again the Project was caught in cross-currents of conflict between the judgments of the professional staff in New York and those of the newspaper people in the field who were paying to get the job done. The regular job of promotion directors was to extol the merits of their individual papers, often in the battle against competing dailies. It was not always easy for them to adapt to an industry-wide perspective. The Promotion Association (INPA) had its own subterranean political currents, but all newspaper promotion specialists shared a desire to be recognized as peers of the advertising directors to whom most had formerly reported and to whom many still reported.

A Public Relations Dilemma

The promotion directors were a merry crew, younger and more informal in manner than the editors, advertising directors, or circulation managers. The scope of their activities varied from paper to paper, in some instances defined narrowly as a service to the advertising department, in others encompassing a broad domain that included community relations, research and marketing. Some papers maintained two separate promotion departments to support their advertising and circulation functions. (When the INPA renamed itself the International Newspaper Marketing Association in 1986, expressing its members' aspirations to higher status, the INAME [itself renamed to incorporate the term "Marketing" in 1981] objected strenuously, but the promotion directors stood fast.)

From the very outset, the Promotion Committee struggled with the public relations aspects of the campaign to build readership. Ambitious plans were laid[1] to develop and place special articles, to service the press with information, to develop case histories of successful readership efforts, and to maintain information files and records.

We had a strong urge to promote everything we were doing, in the hope that it would give the whole industry a sense of optimism and forward movement, a feeling that someone was in charge. Yet by publicizing our activity, we were also publicizing our problems, and not just within the newspaper fraternity. As the committee expressed it (in the words of one of its chairmen, the *Toronto Star*'s dignified, goateed promotion director, John Taylor),

> The public relations program should at all times maintain a positive stance with respect to the newspaper business and its efforts to increase both readership and circulation. This means putting the stress on upgrading and improvement rather than on stemming losses and erosion.
>
> By its nature, the focus on readership and circulation can result in emphasizing some negative developments in the newspaper business. It is therefore important to present the activities of the Newspaper Readership Project in a positive way. This is particularly important since competitive media have shown that they will quickly exploit any chinks in the newspaper armor. The competition between media is particularly keen with respect to advertising, and it is important that the readership story be presented in ways that strengthen and protect the newspaper position in this area.

As a matter of fact, sophisticated advertisers were quite well aware of newspapers' circulation problems and did not need to be reminded of them by the competition. Typically they were irritated by what the trade termed "negative selling." In any case they placed advertising in specific newspapers at a given cost and found it difficult to translate broad generalities about all newspapers into their own advertising prerequisites.

The Project's public relations problems were not just with the world at large. They began within the newspaper business, to which we were trying to communicate the sense of urgency we felt on the subject of readership. The first task was to get the various associations to cooperate, with space in their newsletters and time on their convention programs. This took constant goading, which was not always appreciated.

James Pauloski, the public relations director of the Indianapolis Newspapers and president of INPA, told the members of the Readership Council that INPA had not had a program segment devoted to the NRP.[2]

> By shifting one or two items on our program, we were able to clear a slot . . . We're reporting this not to pat ourselves on the back, but to underscore the need for having newspaper association meetings continue to promote the Readership Project and also to point out that oftentimes NRP is not included on the program through an oversight.

Pauloski added later,[3] "With all due respect and some sense of modesty, we in INPA feel very strongly that we are the only organization that cuts across traditional newspaper organization lines and whose members traditionally work with all elements of the newspaper organization." He therefore suggested "that INPA should be represented on three of the four committees into which the Project is organized, adding representation on the Training and Research Committees."

A change in INPA representation brought a shift in attitude. The new president, Donald Towles, promotion director of the *Louisville Courier Journal* and *Times*, wrote Burke[4] that he could not attend the Readership Council meeting in Washington; he added, "Very frankly, Bob, if this meeting isn't any more productive than the meeting of the Promotion Committee in New York a few weeks ago, it won't be worth the time. I'm getting a bit weary of listening to Leo Bogart berate the INPA for failing to promote an effort these past years that actually didn't deserve some of the promotion it got." Burke sought to mollify Towles,[5] saying that Bogart was not "singling out INPA when he lamented the declining attention given to the Readership Project on convention programs. I thought he was describing what he saw as a general problem and one that is perhaps less applicable to INPA than to most other newspaper associations." I covered much the same ground later, saying "the difficulties are universal."[6] Appeasing sensibilities was an essential part of getting the job done.

Advertising To Win Readers

As advertising professionals, it would have been unthinkable for us at the Bureau not to make advertisements an important part of our promotional efforts. A number of campaigns were prepared for distribution to newspapers to run in the form of house ads, filling vacant advertising space.

As Simons told the INAE convention, "At first glance it may seem a contradiction in terms to try to build circulation with in-paper ads. . . . But on closer examination it is not so illogical. First, you need to convince occasional readers to become regular readers, convert newsstand purchasers to subscribers, and reassure regular readers and subscribers that they are getting good value."

Even before the start of the Readership Project, the Bureau's Creative Department had prepared a booklet entitled "Idea Starters for Newspaper Promotion Campaigns" suggesting ads to promote circulation. We had also prepared a series of small space ads under the heading, "Jack Saves" (the headline of one ad). The photographs, which dominated the space, used members of our own staff as models. The copy was made up of two-paragraph statements with a punchline like the following: "Listen to Jack, this newspaper can save you money every day." Another campaign used headline words like "Foxy," "Handy," "Canny," and "Sporty" and featured closeup head shots of people who typified the adjective. The copy stressed the various elements of the paper that might appeal to this type of individual.

A series of ads under the title of "Queens and Beans" was prepared with funding from Harte-Hanks Newspapers. In "Sales 'n Nails" the copy "suggests that the newspaper can save the reader money by providing information on the best buys in the stores and by providing do-it-yourself home improvement tips."

"Mitts 'n Grits" dealt with sports and politics, "Looks 'n Hooks" with fashion and beauty features.

These ads were widely used, so much so that they came to the attention of powers in Buckingham Palace—the Queen shown in "Queens 'n Beans" being Elizabeth II. A stern letter informed us that Her Majesty could not be used in any advertising or promotion for private commercial purposes. By that time, the campaign had already run its course.

In some cases, promotion kits for the ads included planning guides suggesting how they should be scheduled and merchandised. Under a policy of seeking the widest possible use of our output, "the Committee agreed that the NRP should continue the policy of pricing the ad campaigns and other promotional materials to recover out-of-pocket costs of reproducing materials and mailing [without including the more substantial expenses of the original production], and promotion campaigns should be made available to all newspapers, without restrictions."[7] This meant papers that had not contributed to the Project and that were not even Bureau members.

Simons also produced a series of ideas for newspapers to use in their local promotions: "Say you've got a feature writer who's an authority on needlework and antiques and she has an upcoming feature on quilts. Write her up in a promotion ad. 'Colonial cover-ups: How to overcome quilt feelings.' "

Simons and his art director, Tom Clemente, prepared layouts for promotional campaigns on the relevance of newspapers to everyday life, the benefits of newspapers to their readers, and the newspaper as a "machine for coping with life's problems." Another series of ads was designed to support Newspaper in Education activity. Prototypes were developed for two other promotions: one based on our national survey ("How the Public Gets Its News"), the other from a new Bureau study of food planning and shopping.

Other series of ads were proposed (but not prepared), with such disparate themes as promoting newspaper readership by young people, freedom of the press, the need to increase advertising during recessionary periods, and the newspaper's role as a catalyst for community action. At one point, to encourage everyday readership, we suggested a campaign for newspapers to run with the heading, "If you think today's paper is interesting or exciting, wait until you see yesterday's." Some promotion directors reacted negatively to this idea. "We're only going to create more frustration for those who didn't read yesterday, if time was the reason."[8]

The Asner "Lou Grant" Campaign

In the course of a meeting, demonstrating that real life imitates art, O'Neill (whose public persona was that of the hard-boiled editor of the *New York Daily News*), expressed admiration for the depiction of the newspaper business in a then popular TV series, "Lou Grant." We were able to enlist the voluntary cooperation of Ed Asner, who played the title role as the managing editor. This came about as the result of a personal connection. Steve Sohmer, a former creative director of the Bureau, was at the time the promotion vice president of CBS.[9] He was a man alert to any opportunity for additional publicity for his programs and their stars.

The resulting television commercials, produced at minimal cost, showed Asner, at his fictional editor's desk, talking about the necessity of keeping up with the world through the newspaper. In one commercial, Asner, holding up a newspaper, said, "I wish teachers had used this textbook when I was a kid. I might even have grown up to be a newspaperman." Another commercial ended, "I think there's something for everyone in the newspaper. It's even got television listings—so you'll never miss the best shows—like Lou Grant." A set of print ads with Asner's picture was part of the package offered to newspapers. The accompanying promotional brochure said, "Here's a chance to have the services of one of today's top television personalities, Ed Asner, to help build your newspaper's readership."

Although the Asner campaign had the blessing of the Promotion Committee, it did not go though the laborious "prioritizing" and budget review that we otherwise generally had to follow in every aspect of the Readership Project. In fact, it represented a reversion to the Bureau's normal method of operation, which was to rise to opportunities as they presented themselves and to worry about budgets when we started to scrape the bottom of the barrel.

The campaign was popular,[10] but there were the inevitable

complaints. For instance, Pauloski pointed out[11] that "we have a problem, because Ed Asner does some promo ads for the CBS station that carries his show, and he endorses the news team on that CBS station. For us to turn around and use him in a similar way for the newspaper might be difficult."

This was, however, an uncommon situation. The commercials were widely aired by papers that added their own logotypes at the conclusion. All this came to an abrupt end when a viewer wrote to Asner:

> The *Tribune* [Lou Grant's fictional newspaper] represents the way a newspaper ought to deal with the news, and its credibility and good reputation remain intact as people know that it reports the truth. I am, however, in a great deal of turmoil as I see your endorsement in our local papers, which have the reputation for not reporting the truth in its news, controlling the city and county politically, endorsing candidates for office, one in one paper and the opposition in the other paper, even though they are owned by the same people. The papers are anti-feminist, pro-nuclear, pro big corporations, anti little people, and the list goes on . . . Your name lends credibility to them.

Robert Crutchfield of MTM, Asner's agent, sent this letter to Sohmer,[12] asking him "to bring an end to this campaign. . . . The ads seem to imply that Asner is supporting the individual publication rather than the newspaper industry—which was our original understanding. At any rate, he has asked for a 'cease and desist.' " We ceased and desisted.

The Idea of a National Promotion

As an old promotion executive, Silha was convinced that newspapers underpromoted themselves individually and failed to promote the medium at all with any collective effort. He sounded this note on every possible occasion. But the cost of any meaningful national promotion might easily have stripped the Project's entire six-year budget within a few months. The expense would not have been disproportionate to what was at stake for the newspaper business. It would, however, far exceed the kind of money that publishers were willing to commit to the common cause.

Promotion directors were, however, inclined to think big. Pauloski wrote[13] that although

> some people—and I have to include myself in this group—think that a basic purpose of the Newspaper Readership Project should be to promote newspapers on the national level . . . most of what has been done on the promotion side has been in the preparation of advertising material to be used locally. . . . What I am suggesting would require a massive amount of dollars . . . but shouldn't a national multi-media campaign on behalf of newspapers be considered—a campaign that would use media other than newspapers?

Pauloski suggested that such a campaign "can help both improve the image of newspapers as well as stimulate circulation and readership." A multimedia campaign, using television and outdoor advertising, would have cost tens of millions of dollars. But apart from the expense, the idea of a national campaign had other limitations. As Taylor put it:[14]

> It is difficult to tell the public that newspapers are independent, impartial, and disinterested parties in disseminating news when there are so many instances where this is obviously not so. It is difficult to talk about integrity and standards when we have some newspapers regarding themselves as daily entertainment magazines in which the news is sensationalized or played down in favor of opinionated (and frequently inaccurate) columns—and features.

"It's Your Newspaper"

Advertisements were a way to reach large masses of people with fleeting messages. The Project also gave newspapers films and slide presentations that could provide intensive exposure to small audiences in school or community settings or on plant tours.

Slide presentations were the Bureau's forte. For our members to show them to advertisers, they came with scripts (which local newspaper people rarely delivered themselves) and with audiotaped narrations that advanced the slides automatically through an audiovisual device.

Two presentations were designed to show the dedication and professionalism of newspaper people. They used short interviews with newspaper employees and executives in a variety of crafts. The first one, "We Care," dealt with a cross-section of employees. The second, "It's Your Newspaper," was directed at blacks and used interviews with blacks only. (Its subtitle was "Black Newspaper People, Black Readers.")

A strong argument was made in favor of broadening this presentation to include Hispanics and other minority-group members. As the ANPA Foundation's enthusiastic director, Judith Hines, put it:[15]

> I have a genuine, growing concern about the fact that only blacks are portrayed in the slide show . . . Spanish surnamed people are, as of this year, the biggest minority in the U.S.,[16] and I have a hard time imagining a school where the appropriate black audience would not also include Puerto Ricans, Chicanos, and/or probably some Orientals. I know this point would cause the most upheaval to the show, but I think at least two or three role models other than black are essential to the acceptance of the show.

I finally won my point that each ethnic group identified with its own and that the message would be weakened if we tried to cover all of them with the same vehicle.

The presentation introduced eight black newspaper people in reporting, advertising, editing, engineering, photography, circulation, and the Newspaper in Education. Our purpose was to show that newspapers actually did employ black professionals. In the back of my mind was the hope that the film would not only help improve the identification of this minority group with the medium but might also accelerate an awareness of the need for minority recruitment among newspaper executives and managements.

We offered the presentation to journalism and communications departments and schools and finally offered it free to black colleges and universities. A letter addressed to the deans, chairmen, instructors, and guidance counselors pointed out that "They describe their jobs, share their philosophies as professionals. They are shown working with white colleagues on major daily newspapers." And it seemed to work, even at the elementary school level, as we were told by a seventh grade English teacher in Wyandanch, Long Island:[17]

During a follow-up discussion, students remarked that they were surprised to discover that black people held high positions on newspaper staffs across the country. Students who have been writing for the *Olive Gazette* were more than ever before motivated to create a good school newspaper, and some students said they would like careers in the newspaper business. It is interesting to note that their goals were more specific because they had been exposed to information about specific job titles and responsibilities.

A girl wrote, "It's helped me have more confidence in my race," and a boy who signed himself "Private Poet" wrote, "I never knew so many black people were important to your newspaper." He added in a P.S., "Don't tell anyone that I'm the poet, because I'm supposed to be the 'Private Poet.' "

"It's Your Newspaper" had the lowest acceptance of any presentation produced by the Readership Project. (It was purchased by only about sixty papers.) It was simply ahead of its time.

The Newspaper in Education

Newspaper reading habits were formed at an early age. When a newspaper was not a daily presence in the home, we learned from our research, children were far less likely to become readers. Year after year, a smaller percentage of households subscribed to a daily paper. The children of the 1970s were already offspring of a generation that had grown up with television since infancy. The future existence of newspapers depended upon their acceptance, as an essential element of daily life, by children who were being raised without their presence. Only the schools could substitute for the missing family influence.

A Newspaper in Education (NIE) program had been under way through the ANPA Foundation for a number of years before the Readership Project began. Now it was possible to expand this work through the addition of a field coordinator, Linda Skover, who traveled the country showing newspapers how to set up school programs.

Much remained to be done. In 1979, newspapers were spending some $2 million a year on staff time, teacher training, and supplementary materials. Some 45 million copies of newspapers were distributed during the school year, mostly at half price, and the programs reached 3 million students, 90,000 teachers and 16,000 schools. These were substantial numbers; they still represented only a tiny fraction of the total school population.

On individual newspapers, "Newspaper in the Classroom" programs were sometimes run within the circulation department, sometimes within the promotion department, and in other instances as a separate activity reporting directly to top management. Programs were operated according to widely varying philosophies. There was an essential difference between those papers that saw the task as one of long-term enhancement of the reading habit among the next generation and those that were interested mainly in giving an immediate boost to the circulation figures.

In some cases, federal, state, or local funds could be used by schools to purchase papers; in other cases students were offered subscriptions directly by the paper at a reduced price. Some programs were maintained throughout the school year; others were of brief duration. There were also differences in the grade levels at which the newspaper was introduced into the classroom. It was used as a teaching aid in elementary school reading and arithmetic classes, but it was also used in high school courses in home economics, economics, civics and current events, English, and a variety of other subjects.

From the start of the Readership Project, there was a call for evaluation, from both the Promotion and Research Committees. Did these expensive programs accomplish anything, the publishers wanted to know. It seemed to me that the problem was one of comparing different approaches rather than of evaluating the aggregate effects of diverse activities.[18]

> Is there greater promise in a program that focuses on elementary grades or in one that focuses on the high schools? Do even short programs of two weeks' duration or less have a positive effect or should the programs be restricted to full year programs? What is the value of teacher training in the form of seminars and courses or in supplementary teaching aids in making the program effective? Is there anything to be gained by integrating other educational devices, such as the use of films or TV in the NIE programs?

The suggested design could provide a research model for newspapers to use in evaluating their own individual activities.

The original proposal was most ambitious. It was to study NIE programs, both large and small, within each of the four major geographic regions, and in each category to study pairs of programs that offered contrasts with regard to the intensity of the teaching assistance they provided, the grade levels they concentrated on, the duration of the newspaper orders they provided or required of the schools, and the subjects for which the newspapers were used. The idea was to study exposed and nonexposed students in each program, matching each group for grade level, standing in school, program track, family newspaper usage, and family demographics. The hope was to obtain identical performance data from each program and to try to control as far as possible for the quality of teacher training. Altogether, the plan called for 6,400 students in the experimental groups and 3,200 in the control groups.

Our national study of "Children, Mothers, and Newspapers" indicated that adults who had participated in such programs as children were more likely to become newspaper readers in later life. The effects were especially marked among those people who as children were not exposed regularly to a newspaper at home.

As always, the need to move ahead on substantive matters was inseparable from the task of overcoming the defensive reactions of individuals and organizations whose established activities gave them a claim to the territory into which we wanted to move.

The NRP Committees were not the only industry groups in the picture. ANPA's own Committee on the Newspaper in Education had a research subcommittee, which recommended a "longitudinal" five-year tracking study to be conducted by an "outside independent research group." [19] The committee had a $10,000 budget for this purpose—a sum that would barely scratch the surface. The Bureau's Thelma Anderson, arriving in their meeting as a newcomer and outsider, managed to win the committee's confidence. They agreed that she could be the "independent" researcher. Anderson wrote,

> What they really want is some action on this longitudinal measure, and if I proceed with it, they would want their $10,000 spent on my travels and an assistant they conjured up. Indeed, [the Atlanta newspapers' education coordinator] Tom Speed would like me to spend it all this year, because they see it being carried over to next year's budget without more money. They want that money

spent—the sooner the better—but they want it spent on the longi-tudinal instrument.[20]

Referring to another study done by the Bureau for the same committee, Anderson observed, "If we release the figures over their objections, they will feel that once again it's evidence that NAB is taking over and they have no voice."

Our elaborate testing plan to compare the effects of different approaches to newspapers in the classroom turned out to be less than successful. It was hard to overcome suspicion of our pur-poses and to get the necessary cooperation of school administra-tors and of newspaper educational specialists who felt that their ways of doing things—or even their very jobs, might be threat-ened.

The logistical problems involved in getting the NIE evaluation study implemented were reviewed at length by Tolley.[21]

> One of the first problems we encountered were the difficulties the NIE coordinators had in identifying the classes which would fit the study design—that is, to find grade levels in which there were at least 100 youngsters using the newspaper one way, another 100 who were using it another way, and a third non-using group—all in the same grade level and subject. Now in mid-January we are reviewing the same issues but we're three months delayed. Thelma contacted papers again and again throughout this period to try to keep things going.

Fortunately, the results of our study were highly favorable, showing that Newspaper in Education programs encouraged both newspaper readership and awareness of current events.

In 1976, more than 300 papers were conducting an NIE program (counting morning and evening combination papers separately).[22] Between that year and 1983, when the Readership Project ended, the number of newspapers offering such programs doubled to nearly 600. By 1989, it was nearly 700.

Miscellaneous Proposals

New editorial ideas that had the objective of attracting juvenile readers were among the more interesting proposals that came our way. Several of them were commercial ventures, crass in conception and crude in execution. One that was neither had been generated at the Bank Street College of Education.[23] It was a twelve page brightly colored Sunday supplement called "Two to Get Ready," which rose far above the level of the conventional children's features in its imaginative quality, visual appeal and informational content. We gave the sponsors every possible encouragement, and several papers ran it as a test, but the enterprise foundered on its economics. This venture, so much in the public interest and in newspapers' self-interest, never moved into a full-scale operation, because newspaper publishers were willing to carry it but not to pay a share of the cost. Advertisers argued that the rates would be excessive because a high proportion of the copies distributed would inevitably go to families without children. They preferred to address the "child market" in the tested environment of Saturday morning television, with its endless succession of mindless, violent, mechanically produced cartoons.

Proposals also came from a variety of independent suppliers who had found out about the Project. (For example, Gerontological Planning Associates proposed to increase newspaper circulation by attracting the older adult market—the last target on our list.)

Exchanging good ideas among newspapers was a high priority in the area of promotion, as it was with editors and circulation people. At the Promotion Committee's recommendation, the Project sponsored distribution of a new INPA "Idea Newsletter" to share local promotional ideas. (This was done and has continued with improvements in format.) A supplement called "Newsfun," produced by the Anderson, South Carolina *Independent/Daily Mail*, was sent out as an example of an "imaginative workbook . . . which you might want to adapt for your own newspapers." (John Ginn, the publisher, was a Newspaper Readership Project activist.)

A number of imaginative ideas were raised at meetings of the Committee but were never acted upon. One was for a presentation or ad entitled, "How To Read the Paper in One Minute." The weeklies' National Newspaper Association wrote to solicit a $200 sponsorship of a contest entry in their national Better Newspaper contest. Silha was eager to promote newspaper Action Line programs. He was also particularly enthusiastic about an idea submitted by a firm of reading specialists, McLagan & Associates, to create a full-page series that newspapers could run to help people improve their reading skills.

Silha also suggested that in the last three years of the Project, a fresh emphasis should be placed on the internal promotion that newspapers provide for their own features and writers. I discovered that "broadcasters buy more linage on newspaper entertainment pages to promote their audiences than newspapers devote to their own in-house circulation promotion ads." This led to the suggestion of a one-day seminar under the auspices of the Promotion Committee to review a sampling of the in-house promotions, compare them with those conducted by other media, and come up with guidelines.

Media General's John Mauro, one of INPA's designated committee chairmen, suggested a presentation showing newspapers how to organize public relations programs. I proposed that newspapers coordinate their sponsorship of organized community projects and lead up to a national event, like a newspaper-sponsored marathon. This led to a general discussion of special events. Hornby (who represented the editors on this committee, in addition to his research duties) believed that the day of the "event" seemed to have passed in favor of promoting news features and individual reporters. After his paper dropped these events, he said, there seemed to be less community involvement, and he was "intrigued by the return of this kind of thinking, moving back toward events." Taylor commented that events were the first to go in lean year budget cuts.

I also raised the subject of adding to the small display on newspapers in the National Museum of History and Technology in Washington, an important educational force with large numbers of visitors.

> The tiny Henry Luce Hall for Newspapers in no way reflects newspaper publishing today. To establish something better at the Museum might prove costly, since they accept funding only if it is enough for a curatorial appointment. But there ought to be something some place which portrays the newspaper business as an exciting 20th Century business, not just as something related to Peter Zenger and Gutenberg.

When I checked into it, this would have turned out to be an extremely costly enterprise. Budgets always seemed to inhibit our promotional efforts more than other aspects of the Project. If newspapers underspent in their own individual promotions, they were certainly not about to open their purse strings to promote the medium in the abstract.

"The Indispensable Newspaper"

The Readership Project's single most costly production was also its most controversial. From the outset, Silha pressed the argument for a showcase presentation that could serve as a promotional centerpiece for all our activities—a film that would dramatize the newspaper's importance and utility in daily life.

Silha saw practicality as the newspaper's most singular aspect and wanted to promote it as "the high utility medium." This contrasted with the editors' philosophy that placed the news and its meaning at the center of things. (Silha was not unmindful of the nature and importance of news; he was a director of the Associated Press.)

Our proposal was to produce a film of merit and integrity that would be used widely for public relations purposes by newspapers around the country. It was provisionally entitled "The Indispensable Newspaper." We wanted it to have special appeal both to young people and to minority groups, targets identified by our research as below average in newspaper readership. There were political considerations, too. The film had to be usable by both small and large newspapers. We had to be sensitive and even-handed in dealing with newspapers in competitive markets.

Planning began well before the Project's formal inaugural. My original description of "The Indispensable Newspaper"[24] said that

> the film's basic purpose is to show the value of the newspaper to the reader. It should say that the paper has something for everyone but that no one reader is expected to read everything in it. It should suggest that there might be fresh ways of looking at the paper in order to get the most out of it. A key point will be to demonstrate that reading is a highly individual matter. Everyone reads the paper in his own way and likes (or ignores) different features. We want to relieve any sense of anxiety or intimidation that arises from the newspaper's coverage of complex or unfamiliar material.

Although at this point there's no limitation on the film's content or style, it is likely that it will have a documentary feeling or character. The use of a professional actor or host should probably be avoided if he lacks authenticity. We should avoid any trace of the contrived hokum that characterizes a lot of industrial films.

The film should spotlight the newspaper's basic function as the vehicle that uniquely expresses and maintains the links that tie people to their home communities and to the wider world. But this fundamental civic function of the press should not be sentimentalized or idealized. The film viewer should be reminded that the news consists of much more than just the top headlines and the dramatic stories of the day; that it also includes all the innumerable minutiae that add up to the sum total of his changing interests.

The proposal quickly ran into opposition. The *Milwaukee Journal*'s circulation director, Harold Schwartz, was concerned that the film's main target was disaffected youth:

> I wonder if a movie designed to reach the non-newspaper reading youth and the turned-off young people will also be suitable for showing to civic organizations, tour groups, and so forth. . . . If the desire is to reach the young people—then a fresh message is needed that takes into account the "grooming" and dress modes, lifestyles, and the new "living together" phenomenon and the general lack of concern over the community and society in general. . . . You mention a professional actor should not be used. I believe that you need the finest professional actor you can have in the newspaper film.[25]

I had to assure him that if "a film is sufficiently well done, it could be interesting to young people."

Lee Canning, a former editor who was promotion director of the Minneapolis dailies, also questioned whether the film could serve both to attract new readers and maintain the loyalty of present readers. In his view,[26]

> The values of the two different groups are different and in many cases completely opposite. What present readers find appealing will be rejected by non-readers and vice versa. . . . Young people in their 20s have different value systems from their elders, and any presentation, whether it be a $150,000 film or a 15¢ newspaper, that aims its basic content at both will miss both targets.

In response to the argument that newspapers tie people to their home communities and to the wider world, Canning observed, "people in their 20s are not community oriented; they are 'self oriented.' " I wrote back that "when I referred to people in their 20s, it was with the expectation that we would try to keep in mind their special dispositions and the special problems they present as a target audience. But I don't think that this first film should be aimed at them. It should, however, be good enough to involve and interest them."

The real difficulty of the assignment lay in the fact that we wanted to dramatize what was essentially an abstraction, the principle of the newspaper's value to the reader. This did not seem especially amenable to dramatization, especially as we had to cover a rather large range of subjects. We had to limit ourselves to what happened after the newspaper reached readers' hands. This meant that we could not exploit the more interesting and dramatic process of producing the newspaper itself.

That process had been shown very well in a documentary film called "First Edition," which had been produced for the *Baltimore Sun* just before the start of the Project.

"First Edition"

"First Edition" showed the editorial meetings and conversations out of which the shape of one day's newspaper was evolved. It followed the adventures of reporters covering the stories and scenes of news in the making. The film ended with the papers rolling off the press. With the cooperation of the *Baltimore Sun* and the producers, we offered prints for sale to other papers.[27] and heavily promoted the fact that "First Edition" was nominated for an Academy Award. Our experience showed the difficulty of getting newspapers to use any promotional tool en masse and in concert. Of the seventy prints sold to newspapers, eleven were returned. Only eighteen papers completed evaluation questionnaires we sent out. Of these, nine out of ten had a positive reaction, but it turned out that the most widespread use of the film was not with outside groups or schools, as we had intended, but for showing to the newspaper's own staff.

The main criticism was that the film was too sophisticated for juvenile audiences and that it required a study guide or preliminary introduction for children to be able to follow it. A midwestern publisher commented,

We thought it was great . . . but . . . we questioned the profanity and the use of words such as "screw," "shack up," etc., if we were to show this in community high schools. . . . Although we know the kids use this language from the time they're in kindergarten and on the school bus, we question if we as family daily newspapers should be bringing it into the classroom . . . It's a shame, because the film is so good—and it doesn't need the questionable parts to enhance it. We're trying to find a way to delete the objectionable parts.

This voice from the grass roots should have warned us of what lay in store for our own venture into film production.

"I Saw It in the Paper"

Film making was not altogether a new enterprise for the Bureau's creative staff, but it was not part of their everyday routine. After reviewing the work of a number of documentary film makers, they selected the Maysles brothers, David and Albert, a team known for such notable productions as "Grey Gardens" and "Salesman." The Maysles made themselves so unobtrusive that the people they were filming became oblivious to the cameraman's presence and were portrayed candidly expressing their normal feelings, conversations, and interpersonal conflicts.

At an early stage of our planning, I told the Maysles about an experience I had had in the late 1940s at Standard Oil (New Jersey). The public relations department, where I was working, retained the great director Robert Flaherty to make a film called "Louisiana Story." The idea was to show that the oil business was humane and that its drilling rigs did not disrupt the fragile environment of the coastal bayous. Flaherty produced a masterpiece—at a huge cost overrun and with total defiance of the timetable. We also wanted a work of genius—within budget and on time. But "Louisiana Story" had a unitary theme of great eloquence and simplicity, while the essence of our requirements in 1977 was to show the variety of practical, mundane, utilitarian functions to which the newspaper is put every day—or at least to which it could be put if the people who weren't reading regularly would only shape up.

In their concept treatment for "The Indelible Ritual: A Celebration of American Life Through the Newspaper," the Maysles said that it would be a film

> which will show just how the newspaper records ritual, initiates ritual, and ultimately emerges as ritual itself in our American life. Here we are using the notion of ritual in its broadest and and yet most intimate or individually relevant sense: think of such personal rituals as birth, entering school, marriage, anniversaries, and community rituals like the Saturday football games, celebration of local historical pageants, elections, political campaigns. These are rituals which touch us all and for which we all consciously or unwittingly look beyond information—to our newspapers for confirmation or validation of their importance (and thus *our* importance).

Their outline of the film segments concluded by saying:

> it is important to reiterate that this is a working structure, a roadmap if you will, loosely guiding us from past to present, from the newspaper to the ritual and back. We have discovered through our experience, however, that the funniest, most original and meaningful situations have a way of happening when and where we least expect them and succeed far better and more succinctly than anything we can predict or imagine . . . we believe "The Indelible Ritual" will be at once humorous and intimate, kaleidoscopic yet pointed, a subtle portrait of how newspapers chart and dignify the passage of our lives and our history.

The Maysles' proposal aroused a reaction from Taylor, who was "disturbed" by the word "ritual." "It has connotations that might be misunderstood at the general audience level at which this film may be shown. I suggest the substitution of the word 'tradition,' which is more understandable and acceptable and which would work equally as well." Taylor pressed for a Canadian component, "perhaps even dealing with the conflicts between our countries, which were well recorded by the newspapers of the day." (This was ultimately included, in spite of restrictions on the American camera crews.)

The Maysles' proposed film "treatment" called for a number of episodes shot in a variety of locations. By pure coincidence, one was the site of an annual "Pioneer Festival" in Livingston, Montana, where Hornby owned the local newspaper, the *Livingston Enterprise*. The rest of the Committee did not consider this an obstacle and overrode his strenuous request that the sequence be eliminated or moved to an alternative site. "The South needs more emphasis," he argued.

The Promotion Committee recommended (to the Steering Committee) immediate approval for the production, but not before a protracted discussion that exemplified the perils of collective management.[28] Simons described the proposed film as

> a portrayal of the role of the newspaper in people's lives. It is connective tissue in all life's activities and links the past and the present in a unique way. It shows the continuity of the newspaper's role in people's lives and helps people to understand themselves.

In the discussion, advice was offered to stress the basic news content in the newspaper, to give "good play" to young people, to cover the breaking news, to stress the use of the news by individual citizens rather than by organized groups, and to treat the news with a "degree of generality" "in order to avoid producing a film that would quickly become dated." Friedheim recommended that the title be changed from "The Indispensable Newspaper" to "Your Indispensable Newspaper." He also wisely suggested that political leaders should be excluded to avoid dating the film and that athletes like Mohammed Ali be used in preference to someone like Joe Louis who might be unknown to the young. The minutes record further observations by Committee members:

> Consideration should be given to the use of humor within the film and to the desirability of a positive, upbeat ending. There should be strong emphasis and appeal for youth . . . On the question of how good the final film product will be, Mr. Bogart pointed out that no one knows. "At this point," he said, "there can be no guarantee that this or any film will be a success. Hollywood studios sometimes invest $10 million in a commercial film and end up with a dud."

Hornby again tried to eliminate the Livingston sequence and was overruled a second time.

As the production process got under way, the members of the committee were caught up in the glamor of show business. They went on a field visit to the Maysles' studios, viewed the first cut of the film on an editing monitor, and were enraptured. We were confronting the impossibility of predicting in advance the success of the creative process. At what point would we accept an awareness of failure?

The film, retitled "I Saw It In The Paper" opened with a nostalgic scene of dancers in nineteenth century costume waltzing at the Livingston Pioneer Festival. Other episodes included the Boston Marathon and an apartment hunt in San Francisco (in which the terrible word "gay" was uttered by a real estate agent). There was an antinuclear demonstration in New Hampshire, addressed by Dr. Spock. These arguments were countered by construction workers and a Long Island family busily conserving energy. Two sequences involved blacks. One showed a high school civics class in which the newspaper was being used in a discussion of current events. The other showed a job hunt by a despairing, chronically unemployed young woman in Detroit who was taught to use classified ads to get her leads. In another scene, an elderly piano teacher with the air of a great artist instructed a talented young pupil. There was a country music festival in West Virginia. Each short episode offered a vignette of newspaper usage in one form or another. None was funny, but some were quite touching and even memorable. The film's uneven artistic quality reflected the constraints that were placed upon its makers.

Since a showing of the film by itself could serve no serious purpose, I wanted to use it as a point of departure for discussion in the classroom or by community groups and for this purpose prepared a "Discussion Leader's Guide" with detailed instructions.

The marketing plan[29] called for primary distribution through individual newspapers. The film was to be promoted to them through a series of mailings and such events as a press premiere and invitational showing for officials of major educational organizations. I had ambitions to show it to the Public Relations Society of America, film festivals, on public broadcasting stations, to journalism educators, advertising clubs, the AAAA Convention, and eventually through theatrical distribution.

Efforts to get the film on public television were successful in a few instances, but New York's Channel 13 wrote, "The problem is not with the quality of the film, but with the general purpose for which it was produced. Its message is the importance of newspapers. This represents a conflict of interest for public broadcasting. It is our policy not to broadcast programs in which the producer/funder has a direct relationship or interest in the subject."

Premiere and Aftermath

The film was "premiered" at the annual meeting of the Southern Newspaper Publishers Association in Boca Raton, Florida, as part of a longer review of what the Readership Project was doing. The SNPA was a popular convention, and not merely among Southern publishers. The substantive side of the program was usually kept to a bare minimum to enable golf to have its rightful place. In fact, a not insignificant part of the morning business meeting on that occasion was taken up with announcements and discussions related to the golf tournament.

My introductory comments pointed out that:

> our Promotion Committee decided early in the game that we did not want a conventional industrial film with an actor sitting on the edge of a desk on a studio set office narrating sincerely into the camera . . . We might have made this point in the equivalent of a 27–minute long television commercial, but in this age of the hard sell, that wouldn't have been convincing or memorable to the people we want to reach, especially the key targets whose readership is below par: young people, blacks, blue collar workers. We wanted to make them think about newspapers, not just please ourselves. And because of that, some of you are going to think this movie is just too darn subtle. I don't think you're going to forget it.

I was right and wrong. They thought it was too subtle, they didn't forget it, and they didn't like it. But I did not recognize that at the time.

The film received applause, but it was not wildly enthusiastic. The comments afterward were all favorable, but they were apparently an incomplete sampling that reflected the triumph of traditional Southern courtesy over candor. I was sufficiently deceived to write the Maysles' producer, Charlotte Zwerin, and her associate, Tom Simon, after the showing to SNPA,

> There were about 300 of the most critical people in our business in the audience; the response was excellent. Quite apart from what our significant public seems to be telling us about your movie, I want to convey to you the admiration and enthusiasm that all of us feel for what you have done and our appreciation of your talents and dedicated efforts.

To my surprise and chagrin, McKnight's report, in one of the first issues of *The Editors' Exchange*, described the SNPA's reactions as mixed. How mixed they were, I found out later at a meeting of the Steering Committee. Neuharth insisted that we stop promoting the film because it was disliked by publishers and was hurting the Project. (He alternated rapidly between elfin charm and glowering menace.) I argued that the very images that were disturbing to small-town Southern publishers—the long-haired, unkempt student demonstrators, the despondent ghetto blacks, the passing reference to homosexuality—gave the film credibility with the target groups. The meeting became somewhat tense, with Neuharth cracking his knuckles angrily. This gesture was often remembered later by Silha, who went to work for him as a consultant after his retirement from Cowles Media.[30] In spite of my own irritation with him, Neuharth was merely demonstrating the sensitivity to popular taste that had made him a publishing phenomenon.

Other comments ranged from the quizzical to the irate. The ad columnist of the *New York Daily News*, Bob Donath, after a showing for the press, wrote, "Without any element of hard sell—the imperative to 'read today'—I wonder if the Parent Teachers Associations, Garden Clubs, and whoever else sees the movie will get the point. Maybe only newspaper lovers, regular readers all, will get the message."[31]

One publisher, who returned the print he had ordered, said,

My main criticism of the film would be an overabundance of "action footage" often bordering on boredom and a lack of specific references to newspapers. Where, for example, were references to and uses of letters to the editor, editorials, and analytical columns? Do you not agree that technological advances, which are increasingly important in being able to "read it in the paper" should have received some sort of treatment, if only brief?

An educational coordinator from the Ft. Wayne newspapers wrote to the ANPA Foundation's Hines:

Label this as a film review from the rubes in the Midwest . . . Our collective opinion is that the Emperor has just been sold another suit of clothes. It may be long on art, but woefully short on substance . . . the messages and information are too obscure to be readily grasped by our average Rotarians, let alone a group of high school students. . . . Can't we get the next effort previewed out here in the boonies?

The publisher of the *Los Angeles Times*, Tom Johnson, soon to be the chairman of the Bureau Board, wrote, "'I Saw It In The Paper' is a very weak presentation. . . . Ugh!"

Rhea T. Eskew, the head of Multi-Media, a major newspaper and TV chain, wrote Silha,[32]

> If the film, "I Saw It In The Paper," cost as much as I hear it cost, then I have to challenge our decision to make a contribution to the Readership Project. Our management committee reviewed the film and was unanimous in using the stage vernacular to say that it laid an egg. I really am disappointed. Incidentally, one of our people made the observation that every time one of our trade groups steps outside of print to promote newspapers, we get into trouble. I guess I have to agree.

He signed his letter, "Somewhat ruefully yours." Naturally, such a reaction called for a painstaking response. I pointed out that the film's $140,000 budget represented only about 8 percent of the total pledged by the newspaper industry for the initial three-year period of the Project.

Pauloski objected to the fact that the members of the Promotion Committee were listed on the brochure entitled "Getting the Most Out of 'I Saw It In The Paper.' "[33] He had received calls from people who wanted to get a refund and asked why he had endorsed the film. He asked that his name and the names of his newspapers and INPA not be used "in a promotional effort on behalf of something that we individually and/or collectively have not endorsed." Citing both his own reaction and those of others seated near him when the film was shown, he had not heard one positive comment, and

> those who said anything at all said something negative. . . . My suggestion would be that the Newspaper Readership Project admit that it is a failure and abandon efforts to promote and sell it . . . I wonder really how useful is a product that requires an explanation as to how it's going to be used and requires an admonishment to those who are going to see it that they shouldn't be critical of the film itself but should think rather about the things the film covers. A good film that is designed to tell a story does so without any preliminary or follow-up explanation. If it requires everything that

is being suggested for this one, then it can't do the job for which it is intended. . . . If film producers want to do creative work, and they're investing their own money, that's their business. But when they're given an assignment to prepare a product which in effect is to be a sales piece—even if a very subtle one—they shouldn't go so overboard on creativity that they turn off the very customers for whom they are working and create such negative response among the audience they are trying to reach.

I assured Pauloski that the brochure with his name on it had been sent out only to papers who had already ordered the film and not in any general mailings. I promised to avoid any identification of individual committee members in any future mailings. "It seemed in order to credit the Promotion Committee, even though with the normal turnover not everyone now on the Committee had gone through the full process of reviewing the film proposal in its various stages, the treatment, and the final film itself." I noted that the 9 percent return rate on sales of 121 prints of the film was lower than the return rate for "First Edition" and was well within the normal range for our member versions of advertising presentations. I added, somewhat petulantly, "We have never yet found it possible to satisfy everyone in the newspaper business with everything we do, so we just try to do the best we can and learn from our mistakes."

Taylor made some of the same points to Pauloski.

I can appreciate your concern at being the brunt of the complaints of two dissatisfied customers—but that is likely to be the fate of any member of a committee that has a changing membership—and which is involved in as many ongoing projects as we are. . . . Frankly, I have, in turn, had a number of comments from people who like the film. They prefer the understatement and agree that the factual but gentle way the influence of the newspaper is shown and the many lives and events portrayed is more effective than it would be if a more strident approach had been used . . . I think it boils down to the fact that with a medium such as a movie, it is impossible to be all things to all people. It happens commercially every day when the public disagrees with the film critics, and the critics themselves disagree with each other. And I think in the assessment of films, one's reactions are much more likely to be stronger than they are in judging other media . . . one either enjoys them immensely—or dislikes them intensely—with little in-between ground. . . . To sum up, the best way to do a job by committee is to decide on objectives and then brief experts who have a track record of producing the required results . . . That is what has occurred.

Even our good friend Mauro reported that virtually every reaction he got was negative when he showed the film to his advertising staff, the department heads of his newspapers, and a varied group of Richmond citizens.

> I came away with the conclusion that the message is so subtle that no one picked it up, and if no one picks up the message, then you really haven't communicated . . . As you know, I was chairman of the Promotion Committee, which was responsible for its development, and so I gave it as fair a test as I possibly could.

In returning this letter to me, Burke wrote, "The reactions are all so uniformly negative. Perhaps the king really doesn't have any clothes on after all."

At the winter ANPA Board meeting, reactions were so strong that Smith felt the film was endangering the whole Project. He wrote Neuharth,[34]

> My main point with Otto was my concern, resounded even stronger by you and other ANPA officers, about the movie. I told him that we unanimously feared the damage which may be done to the entire project and our organizations if we persist in heavily promoting and identifying ourselves with the movie. He shares our concern. At the same time, he believes that non-newspaper people are the audience we want to reach, and that the movie may have merit for that purpose.
>
> We agreed that we should re-examine how, when, where the movie is promoted or shown, and that this is and should be an appropriate subject for discussion at the Steering Committee meeting.

The Bureau's new chairman, William H. Cowles 3rd, reacted to Neuharth's comment with a more balanced opinion:[35]

> My first impression of the Project's movie was not favorable, and I find myself unable to change my mind. I am uneasy about the movie's impact on newspaper publishers. Non-newspaper readers, however, might be impressed favorably in a subtle way. If the movie has value, I doubt it would be to persuade NAB directors that the Bureau should undertake its share of the Project's activities.

Not all reactions were negative. Terry McDonald of Young & Rubicam's Media Department sent Silha her "honest opinion": "In one word—TERRIFIC." Jud Kinberg, a professor at California State University at Northridge, said that the film gave his students "expanded insight into the functions and value of the daily newspaper."

> The class's reactions to the film were very good. They wanted to know more as a result, generally more about the whole operation that creates the news and the newspaper.

A survey among students in New York, Richmond, and Los Angeless found varying reactions to the different elements of the film. Few said that any section had left them cold, and large proportions had found them memorable. But by the time this research was done, the reactions of the target audience were almost irrelevant.

For some reason, the Maysles never entered the film in any contests, though it may have been of award-winning quality. In spite of its artistic merit and integrity, it fell short of the objectives we had set ourselves. Probably the basic problem lay in our definition of what we wanted it to accomplish. In retrospect, it seems unlikely that an essentially didactic film of this kind could ever succeed in influencing the audiences for which it was intended.

"I Saw It in the Paper" may have been a perfect example of the kind of promotion that advertising agencies design to serve the client's needs for self-gratification rather than to sell the product. It is surely beyond the power of any film with a limited distribution and audience to affect the changing reading habits of an entire nation, and all concerned understood this from the start. Yet it still seemed essential to provide newspapers with instruments of persuasion that might have some kind of cumulative impact, used many times in many places.

While films represent a particularly powerful form of communication, the Bureau's preferred medium for presentations had for many years been slides coupled with an audio cassette narration. Most newspapers already had slide projectors and cassette players that were being used for sales presentations to advertisers and that could be put to work with the general public.

At the next Promotion Committee meeting[36] I announced that we would prepare a slide presentation to accomplish the same purpose as "I Saw It in the Paper," but with "a more direct message than the film."

And so it did. "Read All About It" was fifteen minutes long, punctuated, in the words of our promotional leaflet, with "music, colorful slides and humor."

It describes the newspaper as a daily almanac, filled with lists —stock market closings; sports scores; TV and movie schedules; public records. More than twenty different kinds of lists are mentioned. The newspaper is pictured as a shopping tool that helps save time, footsteps and money . . . a watchdog over the people we vote into government office . . . a source of news and opinion . . . a literary trip into adventure . . . and more. There were no angry people with beards. And best of all, You may even want to create a totally personal presentation by adapting the script format of "Read All About It" to your own newspaper story. In other words, this presentation allows you the opportunity to make the final determination on what your audiences will see and hear.

This was an offer publishers could not refuse.

Froth and "First Freedom"

If "I Saw It in the Paper" was too highbrow, the next film we distributed, ". . . . But You Can't Take It For Granted," was a frothy piece of nonsense prepared for the Crown Zellerbach Corporation and initially used as a public relations vehicle with the newspapers in the Western States who were that company's customers for newsprint.[37] The film portrayed a fantasy in which newspapers have disappeared and the public is forced to depend on alternative sources of information. The highlight was an episode in which a small retailer dresses up in a rooster costume and dances up and down in the street on a pogo stick to attract customers to his store. There was no adverse commentary on this innocent and simple-minded entertainment.

A very different theme was sounded in the Project's last movie, "First Freedom" (actually a videotape produced by Richard Dorne of the Bureau's creative department).[38] It consisted of interviews with four newspaper men who had dealt with controversial stories that invoked First Amendment issues. John Seigenthaler, publisher of the *Nashville Tennessean*, and Max Frankel, then editorial page editor of *The New York Times*, were among the eloquent participants. The introductions and conclusion were delivered convincingly by Smith, who looked every inch the newspaper publisher out of Hollywood's central casting.

"First Freedom" was intended for classroom use in the Newspaper in Education program, but it also responded to a larger and growing concern among editors and publishers. This centered on indications that a good part of the public lacked a fundamental awareness of the constitutional guarantees of free expression, the reasons for them, and their value and importance for a democratic society.

To a large extent, editors' concern on this score was prompted by national opinion polls that showed many people disagreeing with the First Amendment when faced with a series of hypothetical issues. Other polls showed what was interpreted as low credibility for the news media and particularly for newspapers compared with TV. It was unclear how these indications of ignorance, apathy, or disesteem related to the diminished frequency of reading or to the decline in dependence on the press as the major news source. But it seemed apparent that attitudes and habits were related in some way and that the industry's sales and public relations problems were intimately intertwined.

Freedom of the press might appear to be a noncontroversial subject among newspaper publishers, but "First Freedom" had its critics, too. It used a clip from an ABC news program showing newscaster Frank Reynolds reacting angrily to a confused report he was getting on his earphone and expressing his concern for getting the facts right. According to Smith,[39] "Alvah Chapman [chairman of Knight-Ridder] believes that the total effect might have been improved if we could have dramatized newspaper efforts to avoid and correct mistakes rather than using the Frank Reynolds episode." I replied that "it was an extraordinarily vivid presentation of a newsman's professional concern that condensed into a brief dramatic moment what would otherwise have taken rather lengthy and complicated explanation if it had been done in the form of a retrospective account by a newspaper journalist." In a venture like the Readership Project, I said to some of my associates, the only sure way to stay out of trouble was to do nothing at all.

CHAPTER 8

Calling to Action While Closing Down

The Readership Project was conceived as a device to focus the attention of the newspaper business on the subject of circulation, to mobilize its energies and resources, and to get it to act in its own best interest. No one held the illusion that the studies, reports, presentations, and conferences generated at the national level could in themselves have any effect on the public's reading habits. Our hope was to initiate changes at the 1700 individually managed dailies that made up the business. Not only their managements but their entire workforce had to be stirred to action. Was this something that could be done effectively in a few years' burst of activity, or did it demand a long-term continuing program? Debate over this question carried through the brief life of the Readership Project.

Start Your Own Readership Project

One of our first and most critical tasks was to communicate to the 250,000 people in the newspaper business some awareness of what the Project was all about. We concentrated on preparing presentations, replete with case histories and success stories, for the Project's co-chairmen and the chairmen of the Bureau and ANPA to deliver at industry conventions.

The kind of contact taking place among newspaper specialties at the national level had to be reinforced by comparable activity at the grass roots. This meant encouraging every newspaper to develop a counterpart of the Readership Project within its own management and staff. The underlying argument for this was put in a booklet, "Start Your Own Readership Project," which I wrote at an early stage. (A slightly revised version, prepared for our final report, is included in the Appendix.)

Half a year after the Project started, at the January 1978 INAE convention, we brought on stage representatives of four papers that had already launched readership committees and projects of their own.

Robert Giles, executive editor of the Rochester newspapers, reported on research that "has stressed the importance of establishing a separate identity for each of the two daily newspapers, keeping urban and suburban interests satisfied in the process." Fourteen task forces had met weekly for six weeks and produced a variety of new editorial features. He commented that

> Every process involved in production and delivery of these newspapers is involved in these content changes, and this required meetings with the production department, circulation department, advertising department, and promotion department to work out changes involving each of these operations. "Upfront," for example, required us to absorb typesetting for 40 additional columns of type a week. We did this by switching more editorial copy to a scanner. This approach has provided many guarantees: that the survey findings would be put to work; that the staff would have full participation; that the editors and publisher would have full communication; that other departments would get into the act, and that results would come from a proper mix of research findings and professional judgment.

Lionel Mohr, marketing vice president of the *Toronto Star*, announced the launch of a new Sunday edition, a switch to morning publication on Saturday, new sections, the inauguration of a computer-based circulation system (still very much a novelty at that time), and an expanded NIE program.

John Ginn, publisher of the Anderson, South Carolina, *Independent and Mail*, had set up a readership committee with no fewer than nine subcommittees. Long- and short-term goals had "been set in the areas of product, distribution, promotion and pricing, and separate responsibilities . . . assigned for planning and implementation." Among other things, his paper had experimented with employee carriers, was examining and overhauling all its distribution functions—including the handling of complaints—and was reevaluating press times.

Edward Murray, publisher of the *Boulder Daily Camera*, said, "We've established close links between our advertising and circulation departments to make sure they develop maximum penetration where advertisers want it most."

> We've surveyed readers' and non-readers' reactions to our publication. But beyond that, I personally, and eleven of our top people, have been knocking on doors to get reader reactions firsthand. We got praise, flak, ideas, and a strong impression of how important it is to get the paper to the right spot on the front porch every day at the right time. Each of us had a goal of ten new subscriptions and each of us succeeded. That's one reason we've been growing daily and Sunday at a 5 1/2 percent rate.

When Silha addressed the Canadian Daily Newspaper Publishers Association in the spring of 1978, we substituted reports on the readership committees of the *Ottawa Citizen* and the Sault Ste. Marie, Ontario, *Star* for the U.S. examples, in addition to the report on the *Toronto Star*. And with Smith as the moderator, the session was repeated in July 1978 before the ANPA production conference in St. Louis.

At that meeting, John Hager, president and editor of the Owensboro, Kentucky, *Messenger and Inquirer*, said that the formation of his readership committee "simply focused attention on our commitment for improvement." After discussing innovations in promotion and in his editorial product, he concluded,

> Two occurrences relating to Readership Council work have been particularly thrilling to me. The first was the heart-warming reaction of schoolteachers to the NIE seminar which we sponsored last summer. The other occurred only a few weeks ago when Jean Clarke, our in-charge day-shift compositor, modestly tendered to me well-written, perceptive proposals for content improvement. Her interest and initiative alone prompted this report. The only thing any of us could take credit for is the atmosphere which convinced her that her views would be appreciated as indeed they are. That's the real human reward in this Readership Project.

Over the six years of the Project, the same format was used in a variety of other convention presentations. There was no question that those whom I solicited to give testimony were real enthusiasts. Would their newspapers have embarked on similar enterprises without the presence of the Project? Without question many of them would have, but there also seemed little doubt that the Project had provided a catalytic spark, a format, materials to use, and a sense of sharing in a larger effort. This was precisely what we were trying to achieve.

By the end of 1978, we had compiled a directory of 335 newspapers with readership committees, in some cases evolved from existing staff committees. Celeste Huenergard, a reporter for *Editor & Publisher*, investigated eighteen of them[1] and found that reader research was a recurrent element.

Joe Soldwedel, general manager of the Yuma, Arizona, *Daily Sun*, cited a house ad with the headline, "How Do We Bug Thee?" (to elicit complaints) "as just another example of what can come out of a good readership committee." The executive editor of the San Angelo, Texas, *Standard-Times* had added *The New York Times* wire because "it gives us even more credibility even though the AP may have a better story." The Muscatine, Iowa, *Journal* had changed its weekly farm page to "a free-standing giveaway farm and rural section." The Joplin, Missouri, *Globe* had beefed up its radio promotion and was offering two college courses in the newspaper. ("Subjects include taxation and death.") At the Hudson, New York *Register Star*, "engagement and wedding announcement forms now ask the applicant to indicate the number of copies he wants of the paper that carries his item." With such small steps, the newspaper business was inching toward its future survival.

More ambitious activities were under way at larger papers. At the Spokane newspapers, where the Bureau's new chairman, Bill Cowles, was the publisher, the formation of a "Marketing Committee"

> marked the first time that both newspapers' managing editors, plus circulation, advertising, the general manager and myself, the publisher, gathered around one table to discuss common problems. It has been a most rewarding experience for our operation and for those who participated.[2]

A major effort to attract nonreaders, particularly eighteen- to thirty-four-year-olds, was launched with a multimedia advertising campaign, a sweeping reorganization of the circulation department with a new level of supervision called zone managers, a new post of distribution director, and an incentive bonus plan for district managers. A new managing editor made numerous editorial and makeup changes.

Our efforts to stimulate the formation of Readership Committees were periodically renewed. A survey of publishers in December 1980 received 258 replies. Of these, 142 reported that they now had an interdepartmental committee to deal with circulation and readership; 35 were called readership committees, 26 marketing committees, and the others went by a variety of different names; 38 of them dealt with circulation and readership only, while 103 also dealt with other subjects.

One publisher who did not have such a committee explained, "Too many other irons in the fire." Another said, "Probably in the distant future we will be interested." There were other comments: "Right now we're more concerned with staying in business." "At this point not staffed to undertake such a project." "A Readership Committee tends to unravel from the daily demands of putting your product on the street to a philosophical meandering considering the role of a newspaper."

In a memorandum sent out to the publishers in October 1980, I acknowledged that many of the committees "have not been functioning actively." A message from Silha and Smith said, "We want to urge you and all other publishers to consider these local Readership Committees as your personal responsibility. . . . As you know, the project will come to an official end as an independently funded entity in June 1983. That makes it all the more important to get a local committee structure in place to carry on what should be a continuing response to the challenges we will still face in building readership and circulation."

At the end of the Project, when we repeated the survey, we found it difficult to track exactly what had happened. We had urged that meetings be held monthly, but many newspapers apparently found it hard to sustain that frequency. Committees often degenerated into routine meetings of department heads. While the model was accepted as a novel and desirable idea in some places, it clearly did not result in the kind of massive grass roots participation that we had hoped for. Readership was evidently not a subject for sustained discussion. But contacts across department lines were becoming more common.

Getting Publishers To Act

The idea that the Project should have a roving ambassador in the field came up in its second year. It was recommended by the Promotion Committee and approved and budgeted by the Steering Committee. The field advisor's assignment would have been to energize the local readership committees by showing presentations, reporting on research findings, consulting on local problems, and cross-fertilizing ideas from one newspaper to another. We wanted someone who would be able to speak with expert knowledge and authority, gain the acceptance of publishers, editors, and circulation managers alike, be willing to travel most of the time, yet work for an extremely modest salary on a job of only a few years' duration. To complicate matters, anyone who came from one professional specialty might have been rejected by the others.

The names proposed included that of Lee Hills, a distinguished journalist who was the retired chairman of Knight-Ridder Newspapers. But it was difficult to visualize an elder statesman of the newspaper business leaving his well-heeled retirement to put on one-day road shows at newspaper plants across the continent in the style of an old-fashioned evangelist. The job was never filled, perhaps because I was never able to dedicate enough time to the search. This represented an error in managerial judgment, because putting the Project's materials to work was critical to its success.

The Michigan State newsroom study made in 1983[3] showed that less than a third of the rank and file had heard of the Project, and only 8 percent had read any of its reports. The *Saratogian*'s Wolferman commented, "It would appear the NRP was so busy blazing trails in the crusade to better understand the reader that the scouts forgot to look back to see if the troops were marching close behind. They weren't." At least, not all of them.[4]

What accounts for the failure of so many newspaper managements to take the time necessary to learn what the Project produced and to think about ways to apply it? The answer has to be found in two conditions, one pandemic and one peculiar to the newspaper business.

The more general explanation relates to the disorienting effects of the information explosion on all organizational activity. There has been a vast increase in internal corporate communications and in the number of specialized publications of all kinds. The consequent proliferation of "essential" reading matter has been multiplied by the universal access to photocopying equipment, launching a flood of paper that jams the in box of every executive and professional. The result is that little if any of it receives careful attention. Documents are commonly dealt with, not according to their absolute importance, but in terms of a priority defined by the immediate pressures of the day and the negative consequences of ignoring them.

In the newspaper business, this universal problem was exacerbated because of the pace set by the need to churn out a new product each day. Newspaper executives spent much of their time reading, but they were reading ephemera.

The device of the "executive summary" assumes that all information can be condensed into a single point or two on the basis of which some critical decision can be made. But in fact, much information is not of the kind that can be boiled down to essentials. Its value lies in the insights that arise from the detail.

Much of the material produced by the Readership Project was intended to be thought about and discussed rather than to be acted upon immediately. Moreover, it was to be discussed in the context of the individual newspaper's own distinctive problems. The conception behind the local Readership Committees was that they would provide a mechanism through which discussion about local application of specific reports or presentations produced by the Project would generate fresh ideas, which in turn could be passed along. As it was, a great deal of the material, undiscussed, was easily ignored or forgotten.

What Happens Next?

The Project was originally supposed to be jointly chaired by the heads of ANPA and the Bureau. Both Silha and Smith were prevailed upon to stay on when their terms expired in the Spring of 1978. They served for the remainder of the Project, providing both continuity and their extraordinary talents.

Neuharth, who succeeded Smith as chairman of ANPA, was

inclined from the outset to believe that circulation drops occurred by the publishers' choice. With the value of Gannett stock showing a continual appreciation, he argued that the numbers were retreating because papers were voluntarily relinquishing costly delivery to subscribers in outlying areas, whom advertisers did not want. A survey among circulation managers showed that this occurred in only a small minority of the cases where newspapers had shown losses. I reported these findings to the Bureau Board, without comment. Neuharth was silent.

Both in temperament and background, Silha was in sharp contrast to his successor as Bureau chairman, Bill Cowles, just as he was to Cowles' namesake John in Minneapolis. Silha was bluff, enthusiastic, and in a steady charge through life in a career whose achievements were entirely his own. Cowles was the third-generation heir to one of the country's great publishing fortunes, based not only in the Spokane papers he published but also in a very substantial ownership share of the (Chicago) Tribune Company. Youthful looking, fair haired, and delicately featured, he looked and acted like a scion of ancient European royalty—courteous, almost diffident in manner, slightly hesitant and soft spoken, and generally wearing an earnest expression. When he first appeared on the Bureau Board, he was lampooned at one of the directors' dinner parties as one who had "clawed his way to the top." But wealth cannot always guarantee popularity; Cowles achieved that himself.[5]

The Project was announced as a three-year program. After little more than a year of operation, the Readership Council[6] was already clearly affirming its wish to see it continue beyond that time, if this had the support of the sixteen constituent organizations. I presented some options to Silha, Smith, and Friedheim.[7] The first was:

> 1. . . . ending the program on schedule in June, 1980. In that event, we would still want to keep the Readership Council. . . . the Readership Report. . . . and a) The News Research Bulletin; b) The ANPA Foundation's NIE Program; c) The Research Institute's development work on circulation equipment; d) The collateral work of ICMA, INPA, and ASNE.
>
> 2. . . . a renewed fundraising appeal for another two or three-year period. . . . However, it is unlikely that the problems that we are addressing will be solved over the span of another couple of

years. . . . In effect, we would simply be postponing a decision that might better be made now. . . .

3. . . . set up a new organization, a Newspaper Readership Institute, and perhaps try for foundation status. . . . it would resolve ambiguities as to work priorities, permit a small, tightly run staff to confine its attention and energies to the subject of readership, and provide for a higher degree of accountability. The disadvantages of this arrangement are that it would mean an inefficient duplication of certain administrative services and limit the ability of the staff to use freely the occasional services of specialized personnel. . . . Also, creating yet another permanent organization with its own governance and politics may be the last thing in the world the newspaper business needs.

4. A continuing Readership Project could be housed within either NAB or the ANPA, and the dues of that organization raised to cover the additional expense. . . .

5. Finally, we can continue the organizational handling of the Project much as it has been going, with a division of assignments between NAB and ANPA, and raise NAB dues to cover the budget requirements currently being met through the special contribution.

From the standpoint of the Bureau's management, the idea of a dues hike at this time is undesirable, coming so soon after the dues equalization plan went into effect.[8] Inevitably, however, the inequities and the uncertainties in any voluntary contribution plan make it less preferable than a system which assures a routine flow of income.

Silha, Smith, Friedheim, and I met in Detroit to discuss these differing possibilities. By now, the cocktail time buzzing among the publishers had become intense, and there was considerable discussion, within both the Steering Committee and the Bureau's Executive Committee, about whether the Project should be extended. Silha and Smith argued persuasively that three years was much too short a time to produce tangible effects. Since the Project had taken off from a dead start, its growing momentum would be lost if it were forced to decelerate so soon after it went under way.

While we at the Bureau shuddered at the improbability of accomplishing the Project's objectives within the allotted three-year period, ANPA's leadership seemed eager to get it over and done with, so that the most necessary activities could be folded into their ongoing operations. Their proposed "wind-down" plan, as drafted by Friedheim,[9] was comprehensive and tidy:

1. The Readership Project per se should be completed in June 1980 at the end of the three-year term for which special funds were raised. No additional fund-raising drive should be undertaken.

2. *The Newspaper Readership Council* should continue in existence as a coordinating and information-sharing body with the same organizations in membership. It should meet for one day each year at the Newspaper Center with ANPA hosting the meeting and Council members covering their own travel and hotel costs. . . .

3. The Council should offer no permanent or long-term *programs or projects.* It would, however, serve as a clearing house through which special projects could be proposed, considered and, if approved, jointly initiated with joint ad hoc funding *informally* coordinated. . . .

4. All responsibility for *newspaper marketing research* in its broadest sense should be reassumed by the Bureau and funded in its budget. . . .

5. All responsibility for production and distribution of suggested *newspaper promotion ads and campaigns* should be reassumed by the Bureau and by INPA and funded in their budgets. . . .

6. All Readership Project *circulation training programs* which are underway in 1980 and for which a continuing need is then evident should be assumed by ANPA's training department. . . .

7. ICMA should continue to administer the program for disbution of circulation training materials developed by Knight-Ridder. . . .

8. All *Readership Project equipment and systems development programs* underway in 1980 and for which a continuing need is then evident should be assumed by ANPA/RI.

9. All Readership Project NIE work underway in 1980 and for which a continuing need is then evident should be assumed by ANPA Foundation. . . .

10. ASNE should continue as primary sponsor for *The Editors' Exchange* which should be published monthly. . . .

11. ANPA should establish a *Readership and Circulation department* with two professional staff and one secretary. This department would assume responsibility for the ANPA News Research Report and. . . . *The Readership Report* . . .

12. ANPA should combine the current News Research and Circulation committees into a new *Readership and Circulation committee* providing oversight of the above work of the Readership and Circulation staff department and making program recommendations to the ANPA Board and officers. . . .

Although this attempt to call an early halt to the Project ran into opposition from the other newspaper associations, it ultimately prevailed in the firm decision to cease activities after a second three-year period.

The Decision To Terminate

It may appear extraordinary that the elected officers of ANPA and the Bureau should have pulled, for a while at least, in opposite directions. Both organizations served the same constituency. The same publishers served on both boards, some at the same time, others sequentially. There were, as I have noted, some differences in the composition of the two groups, with the smaller, independently owned papers more heavily represented on the ANPA Board. The real explanation must be sought less in the character of the particular individuals in the elected leaderships at any one moment than in the inherent structures and operating styles of the two organizations and in the way their respective managements defined their institutional self-interest.

From the perspective of the Bureau, the decline of readership posed a vital threat to its advertising sales mission and required an activist response with minimal regard for protocol or personal sensitivities. From the viewpoint of ANPA, as the senior organization of the newspaper business, it had the unique responsibility of brokering and coordinating among the various professional groups. Circulation lay squarely within its sphere, and the Readership Project represented an unnecessary intrusion into the orderly processes through which the industry deliberated upon its problems and majestically arose to handle them. If the managements of the two organizations merely fulfilled their requisite roles, those publishers with whom they worked most closely were more subtly coopted to assume the appropriate institutional posture.

Cowles expressed his opinion on the future of the Project with characteristic caution:[10]

> It seems to me that the Project has demonstrated its great value to the newspaper industry. Its momentum, therefore, should be continued. Perhaps the best way of accomplishing this would be to merge into ANPA and the NAB those activities which should be continued. I believe this would be preferable to a proliferation of organizations serving newspapers. Much has been accomplished by the Project, and I believe it holds great promise for the future. At

this point I would encourage the Readership Project's Steering Committee to assess the Project's effectiveness, to suggest activities which should be continued, to identify more which might be phased out and to define new directions, if any, which might be desirable based on experiences of the first two years.

Both Graham (who became chairman of ANPA in 1980) and Knight-Ridder's Chapman felt strongly that the Project should be terminated by a definite date and not be permitted to continue on indefinitely as a permanent fixture of the newspaper business. This seemed to be the prevailing opinion, and I shared it. A permanent industry-wide organization would require its own funding mechanism, its own board of directors, and its own superstructure of advisory committees, which would, in part, duplicate those already in place at the Bureau and ANPA.

I referred to Friedheim's twelve points as "a valuable point of departure."[11]

I would hope that you consider it a final fallback position rather than the optimum plan for continuing the momentum that has been set going in our business in the last twenty-one months.

The first question we must consider is whether your proposal is an adequate response to the tremendous challenge our business faces in restoring circulation and readership to their proper levels. Your own membership survey last year showed unmistakably that this is regarded by publishers as the most important subject on the industry's agenda. . . . There is just too much at stake to give this anything but our best shot and our most energetic efforts.

Such efforts, in my opinion, require budget, leadership, and effective coordination. I miss these elements in your proposal. Could a Newspaper Readership Council which meets only once a year and has no committee structure or funds at its disposal be anything more than a pro forma organization? It is certainly better than nothing at all, but I think this route simply means marking time and confronting the same questions more urgently at another bend of the road.

The work of the individual newspaper readership committees at the local level is the key to our success. To sustain their enthusiasm and activity requires: (1) a continued output of useful material to stimulate them and (2) an active coordination and liaison function. We badly need a full-time road man who can visit newspapers, talk about the tools available, and find out what is working and what is not, as input for the Readership Report.

You suggest that there might be "joint, ad hoc funding informally coordinated" for special projects. Can an ad hoc approach which has to be fought through and funded in every individual instance ever be remotely as efficient as a sustained program with an established plan and priorities?

I felt when we started the Project that there was no way that organizations like INPA and ICMA and ASNE, with their very limited staff resources, could substitute for a full-time professional staff dedicated to the Readership Project. My opinion on this point hasn't changed. With the best will in the world and the utmost cooperation from the dedicated people who run these organizations, there is just no way that they can be expected to take on the burden as volunteers. . . .

I can assure you that the management of the Bureau has no interest in aggrandizement. We do not want to disturb our Board or our membership with new financial demands. . . . We should try to renew the Project for another three years at the same level for which it has been funded in the current period, retaining our present structure and division of labor. The rate of contributions might go down by 25%, or even by a third, but a viable program could still be sustained at this reduced level.[12]

At an ANPA Board discussion,[13] Vice Chairman Small, who detested the film, expressed concern that the programs be controlled by the Council and the Steering Committee, and not by staff decisions. "I hope the Board won't give the NAB staff a blank check," he said. Smith defended me, saying that our mistakes resulted from good intentions. Neuharth said that except for the film, publishers generally seemed pleased by what the Project was doing. Raleigh's Daniels pointed out that at the outset we had promised to absorb the Project after three years. If we were to extend it and break the faith, we needed to strengthen the plan on how eventually to fold the activities back into the ANPA and the Bureau. Graham said it was essential to insure that "the big mistake" (the film) was not repeated and also that there were not a lot of smaller ones. She wanted to know exactly how the Project was to be terminated.

The Board's decision to go for a three-year renewal, like that of the Bureau Board soon afterward, was coupled with insistence on a gradual wind-down which was to leave all of the money spent and the Project terminated by June 1, 1983.

To my mind, the arguments over funding were nickel and dime

stuff in a multibillion dollar business. In a summer 1979 address to the Inland Daily Press Association in Chicago, I cited a new study by Booz Allen & Hamilton. It showed that

> for every thousand dollars of gross revenues that local television stations take in, they spend $9 just for audience ratings alone . . . By way of comparison, the $600 thousand that has been contributed for each of the three years of the NRP represents less than a nickel for every $1 thousand of our business's gross advertising revenues. Some people may very well feel that it is too much, some might feel that it's not enough. After all, it's your nickel.

Winding Down

While debates proceeded at high levels over the future of the Readership Project, its ongoing activities had to be sustained, and plans for possible future work had to be funneled through the committee structure. In the first three years, 4 percent of the budget had been spent for projects of the Equipment and Systems Committee, 20 percent for Circulation Training, 20 percent for Promotion, Public Relations and NIE, 33 percent for Research, and 23 percent for administration and communication. By July of 1979, the four operating committees had reviewed and proposed individual projects that would have required a budget of some $3,800,000—far more than could be reasonably anticipated from any fund-raising effort.

At a meeting of the Bureau's Executive Committee, Chapman insisted that we define the Project's objectives in precise terms.[14] I proposed the following "realistic" goals:

1. To arrest the decline in the circulation-household ratio [which had fallen from 1.32 in 1946 to .8 in 1979, and which stood at .68 in 1990].
2. To restore the ratio to a .9 level and maintain it there for at least three years.
3. To restore average weekday readership to a level of 75% or better for at least three years.
4. To provide a mechanism for continuing communication and contact among the leaders and memberships of the various newspaper associations.
5. To break down interdepartmental barriers to communication

within individual newspapers and to encourage an interdepartmental approach to the solution of readership problems.

Since the decision to raise funds for another three years was coupled with a firm decision to cease operations at the end of that period, both ANPA and the Bureau faced the immediate necessity of preparing a final "wind-down" plan. ANPA's statement went right to the point:

1. Insure that available Project funds are used for the most important and valuable readership and circulation programs.
2. Prevent cost over-run.
3. Continue the interdisciplinary cooperation of all segments of the newspaper industry in dealing with readership and circulation opportunities and issues.
4. Facilitate the personnel reduction/reassignment plans of organizations with staff members whose salaries are paid for with Project funds.
5. Insure that full accountability for the execution of Project activities is retained by the Newspaper Readership Council.

By contrast, my own response[15] was irresolute, laying out alternatives for higher powers to consider. When the money ran out, I said, the Bureau would be unable to continue with any of its present activities except "(a) by volunteer efforts, at the expense of its primary mission; (b) by conducting individual projects on a self-liquidating basis or through special funding individually obtained in each case [or] (c) by a special surcharge on Bureau dues." Under "volunteer" efforts, I mentioned our "continuing analyses of industry circulation and audience data, competitive media activities, and social and economic trend," which were "by-products of our normal advertising sales activities."

I promised that our staff "would continue to counsel with member newspapers on readership matters" and that "our Insert Division would continue to work closely with newspapers developing computerized subscriber lists that might have applications for advertising purposes." I pointed out that the prices newspapers paid for promotion and training materials covered only the actual costs of physically reproducing them, and not the vastly larger developmental costs. As for the possibility of a surcharge on Bureau dues:

> The 1980–83 budget proposal . . . calls for an expenditure of approximately $700,000 a year on projects assigned to the Bureau. If we were to continue at this level after 1983, without special funding, it would require an increase of approximately 10% (at current levels) in the Bureau's dues income. This surcharge on dues would come on top of increases already mandated by inflation and by our recently adopted dues equalization plan. At this point, the Bureau management could hardly recommend it to our Directors. . . . The area of circulation marketing deserves continuing, industry-wide effort just like advertising sales, even when a satisfactory growth rate is resumed.

I went on to make what was by now an obligatory declaration of faith:

> The Bureau's mission is to sell and promote the sale of newspaper advertising. No one has proposed, or would seriously propose, that present programs on behalf of this mission should be cut back to make way for readership activities. . . . The Bureau's dues income has been growing at about half the rate of the increase in newspaper advertising investments, and at substantially less than the general rate of inflation. . . . In the final analysis, our discussion centers on the willingness of the publishers to ante up the additional funds required to cope with the marketing of circulation as a sustained part of the Bureau's regular program of activities. . . . The Bureau can continue to maintain a strong contribution to the research, promotion, and training functions of the Readership Project at 1/3, 1/2, or 2/3 of the proposed $700,000 a year level. In my judgment, an activity funded at a level of under $250,000 a year (in current dollars) would not be viable.

The Future of Advertising Committee

The arguments over the fate of the Readership Project overlapped with another discussion. While the Project originated in the problem of newspapers' declining share of advertising, there was never any illusion that falling readership was the only cause of that problem. Publishers and advertising directors still worried about the gains made by direct mail, free weeklies and local broadcasting, and about newspapers' ability to sustain their competitive position. What was needed, some thought, was a comprehensive long-range plan.

For the April 1979 Bureau Board meeting, the senior staff gave a more than usually detailed review of the principal marketing and advertising trends to which the industry would have to respond. In concluding this report I asked,

> How much should current profits be sacrificed to instituting long-range improvements in our product and in our sales methods? . . . Is our research and development investment appropriately balanced between the technological and production aspects of the business and the editorial and marketing functions? . . . As we face inflation in newsprint, energy, and labor costs, how much of these increases can we pass on to advertisers without pricing ourselves out of the market? How much can we pass on to readers without losing more of them and thus raising our cost-per-thousand to advertisers? . . . Much of [selling and promotion] is still used unproductively in competitive selling against other newspapers. How could or should this be changed?

Further questions related to zoning, the growth of inserts, format standardization, the satellite transmission of advertising, improvement in reproduction quality, and the prospect of the customized newspaper. ("To develop it requires progress in computerizing subscriber information. . . . Can the packaging of unused information become a significant source of added revenue?") Other questions dealt with advertising systems and procedures; the idea of a one-bill, one-order system for advertising; the rationalization of advertising rates; and the creation of a centralized newspaper data base. Finally, there were the recurrent questions about readership and the prospect of electronic home communications systems. "And in talking about all these issues, we must consider . . . how should the function of the . . . Bureau change?"

To confront these questions, Chairman Cowles appointed a Committee on "The Future of Advertising," with Robert G. Marbut as its chairman.[16] Marbut was President and Chief Executive Officer of Harte-Hanks Communications, which he had transformed from a small Texas family-run newspaper chain into a publicly held multimedia company with national ambitions. A Georgia-born engineer, Marbut moved from Exxon into the management consulting business; Harte-Hanks had been one of his clients at McKinsey and Company before its owners invited him to run it and take it public. (Eventually the company went private again in a leveraged buyout on the grounds that the stock market undervalued its holdings and thus made it vulnerable to an unfriendly takeover.)

Marbut's smiling, mild, quiet demeanor disguised a driving sense of purpose and an incredible capacity for work, which seemed to fill all of his long waking hours. He spent much of his time in the air, attending to his correspondence while he commuted to the sites of distant ventures and international conferences. (His notes on one important discussion "were lost once when my briefcase was stolen in Russia, and then carefully put back in Russia in a location where I knew they wouldn't be stolen or lost again." [17] It is doubtful that the KGB was able to get much use out of this information.) Good natured but sensitive, intense, and intellectually incisive, driven by forces of demonic energy, Marbut was the very model of an unprepossessing million-dollar-a-year executive.

His managerial style embodied the most advanced business school philosophy; he delighted in the orderly charting of opinions. At three meetings lasting a total of eight hours, Marbut skillfully guided the new committee to agreement on a planning procedure. The focus was to be on the fall Board meeting, at which the fate of the Readership Project was also to be decided. The meeting was to be held at Jasper Park Lodge in the Canadian Rockies, an idyllic venue for high-level cerebration. The primary objectives[18] were "to raise the consciousness of the Board [as] to what is happening [in] the marketing aspects of our business" and "to set the stage for action by the NAB (including at least a rough definition of what NAB's strategic goals should be, what NAB's specific long-term objectives should be and other things that should be done in the industry. . . ."

To accomplish this "consciousness-raising," the members of the Board were asked to complete a questionnaire on their expectations of significant future trends. They were also sent a substantial stack of briefing material. The questionnaire was based on one developed for Cox Newspapers by Robinson Associates, a research organization whom we had previously employed in several studies using the Delphi forecasting method. This procedure began with an extended group discussion among experts, in which they identified possible developments or events that might significantly affect a given field of activity within a definable period of time. With the events listed, the participants were ballotted on their likelihood and potential impact; they discussed the results and were ballotted again. In studies we made among general merchandise retailing and grocery executives, questionnaires were also returned by hundreds of experts across the country, and the findings were transformed into Bureau sales presentations. While I participated in the Cox study, which focused on the future of the newspaper business, the research had been kept confidential to this point.

The questionnaire I sent to the Directors asked for judgments on ninety-five "events." As I reported to the Board at Jasper Park,

> Most of you see the world of the year 2000 as not dramatically different from the world of 1979. . . . You see profits as more likely to be affected by those possible developments that relate directly to the newspaper business and least likely to be affected by those events that deal with the broad economic or social environment.

If the publishers foresaw no dramatic changes in the economic or social environment, they were also cautious about the prospect of big changes caused by the impact of new communications technology.

> Hardly any of you think that the conventional printed newspaper of today will be largely replaced through home communications systems. . . . But a majority of you do believe that by the year 2000 homes on the cable will have a two-way communications potential, including the possibility of ordering merchandise.

As to newspaper economics, the publishers foresaw no significant change in the balance of circulation and advertising revenues or any great increase in the proportion of single-copy sales. They did not think a customized newspaper produced by inkjet technology would be feasible by the year 2000. They correctly forecast that by the mid-1980s most papers would have subscriber names on the computer ("a very optimistic assessment, considering how small a percentage of newspapers have them there now"). Nearly half believed that special interest sections would be offered to readers at an extra price.

On the advertising side, the publishers' view of the major trends were identical to those of the retailers we had surveyed earlier. They saw further concentration of ownership but geographic decentralization in the planning process. And in spite of all the alarms we were currently raising on readership, the consensus was that circulation-to-household ratios would stay within their present range.

I suggested that the findings might be considered from three aspects:

(1) Of the events that you think are unlikely to happen by the year 2000, are there any (like the spread of telecommunications) that will be coming soon enough in the 21st century so that steps ought to be taken now by your own organizations, by the industry, or by the Bureau to invest, investigate, educate or plan for their coming?

(2) On some potentially significant developments, there are substantial differences of opinion. . . . These points are worth taking up one by one. . . . What more do we need to know? What do we need to do?

(3) Consider the events that most of you think are about to happen. Some of them may require that we take defensive action now. Others may require that we gear up to implement what we believe to be inevitable. How should we do this? And specifically, how, if at all, should we follow up on the results of this discussion so that we're not merely guessing about the future but working to shape it?

The directors split up into four discussion groups[19] and independently reviewed the issues that had been posed. In summarizing what was said, I pointed out that "there was a large degree of consensus and convergence in their opinions."[20] There was agreement that newspapers had to prepare for important changes in electronic communications, that their great strength was in their editorial franchise, and that much of the information they developed and processed could be disseminated electronically. Newspapers had to "meet the growing need of advertisers for targeted marketing" and had to maintain circulation. "There is still a lack of coordination and a certain duplication of effort in the work of the industry's various associations and organizations. . . . The industry needs a continuing task force assigned to planning for the future. . . . There is a particular need for the early-warning spotting of significant social, marketing and advertising trends and technological developments."

The implication of all this was that "The Bureau must assume leadership as the industry's marketing arm," expand into new "marketing-oriented programs" and "move rapidly to correct the major problems that the industry faces with its customers: (1) Standardized or centralized ordering and billing; (2) Standardized and simplified rate cards; (3) Format standardization; (4) Further reduction of national/retail (advertising) rate differentials." Other specific proposals were for more research and promotion, a "program for satellite transmission of advertising and insertion orders," and the establishment of a "newspaper marketing institute to train, retread and upgrade the professional quality of the industry's personnel." In the subsequent decade substantial progress was made in most of these areas.

An Endorsement from ASNE

The immediate needs of the Project's second three-year term had to be faced before the long term questions of the Bureau's future. The ANPA Board of Directors had already adopted a five-point resolution endorsing a special $3 million fund-raising campaign for the period of 1980 to 1983.[21]

In the new spirit of ecumenism, the presidents of ASNE and ICMA had been invited to the Bureau Board's Jasper Park meeting. Since the ASNE Board was meeting at the same time, Hornby could not come. In a letter of August 30, he asked his publisher, a suave corporate lawyer named Donald Seawell, who was a director of the Bureau, to present the views of ASNE.

> From the editors' viewpoint, the project has had a very successful beginning, but only a beginning. Perhaps most important, for the first time in our history, the various newspaper organizations are working together effectively at the national level on a common problem. . . . This experience and national machinery-for-communication would alone justify the effort and vision NAB put into starting this project.

After reviewing the "project accomplishments to date," Hornby mentioned "certain unsurprising kinds of problems:"

> Organizational jealousies are always lurking in the wings—individual groups would like to recapture the various segments of the franchise which NAB and ANPA bestowed on this overall project.

Inflation reduces the real effectiveness of expenditures and saps the strength of project supporters.

So it would be easy to let the NRP go down the tube at this point, or let it slink off stage by inadequate funding. That has been our industry's response at some times in the past—a crisis program, turned off too early at the first blushes of success.

We editors are often accused of providing a great deal of rhetoric and some energy on these occasions, but no dough. Risking this reaction from those of you who have to foot the bills, let us just say this: We editors believe that if the NRP is allowed to wither, not only will we have lost a real chance to keep our industry working together to solve the readership problem, but we may have lost the last real chance to do so. . . .

NRP's results so far must be driven home to all levels of the industry. Much more continuing readership research is needed. In the distribution and promotion area we have not yet really impacted the individual newspaper level. The inter-departmental structures at the various papers will soon wither if there isn't a vigorous field program conducted from the project center.

ASNE recommended that individual papers increase their support by 60 percent, to raise funds of $1 million per year. Hornby's statement concluded,

NAB took the lead in establishing the project, and we editors hope NAB will continue to lead in seeing it through. The editors will continue to give the program their wholehearted support; we only wish we had money to add to energy and rhetoric!

This statement, which Seawell read dramatically to the Board, represented a stunning transformation of ASNE's original attitude. It helped to solidify support for the second three-year phase, which the Board approved without dissent, implicitly committing its members to come up with the bulk of the additional money. The question still remained whether the leaders of the newspaper business considered readership worthy of a serious collective program over the long-term.

The Bureau Sticks to Its Knitting

The Future of Advertising Committee met again in New York[22] some weeks later to review what had been said in Jasper Park. It now formally recommended to the Board that "the Bureau's functions should be expanded to make it a total marketing organization for the newspaper industry, "working more closely with the ANPA and other industry organizations, and perhaps changing its name" (to the Newspaper Marketing Bureau, of course). The committee looked beyond the proposed 1983 cutoff date for the Readership Project. It proposed that "The Bureau should take on its assignments for the Readership Project as a continuing part of its job description. . . . The Newspaper Readership Council should be renamed the Newspaper Industry Council to serve as an overall advisory group on policies and projects not related specifically to advertising sales.

But this was not the view of a somewhat different (and more powerful) set of players who met a few days later to tidy up the last details. These were the members of the Project's Steering Committee and the Executive Committees of the two boards, who were brought to Dearborn, Michigan for the Bureau's automotive meetings.[23] I reminded the participants[24] that "Agreement on the post-1983 phase is desirable both to facilitate the 1980–83 fund raising and also to provide for an orderly termination of 1980–83 programs." There was, however, to be no post-1983 phase. The signals sent out by the Future of Advertising group turned out to be wrong. On May 31, 1983, the Project would come to an end, period.

The Future of Advertising Committee's recommendations for the Bureau's expansion were reviewed several months later at a joint meeting with the Executive Committee.[25] The reception was cool. According to Cowles, there were still questions among some members of the Executive Committee about the wisdom of broadening the Bureau's marketing responsibilities. The Tribune Company's Stanton Cook argued that the Bureau should continue to concentrate on advertising sales. "Be prepared for the steely-eyed bastards!" he warned. And Lloyd Schermer of Lee Enterprises, later to be the Bureau's chairman,[26] introduced a new complication into the argument. Changing the Bureau's mission would change the job description for Kauffman's successor as president of the Bureau, for whom a search committee had been named.

Editor & Publisher,[27] in a by-lined article by John Consoli, had already reported that "Ad Bureau's Kauffman looks for a successor" and observed that "Bogart, executive vice president and general manager, is the second highest ranking Bureau exec, but insiders feel he is too research oriented and does not have a solid enough sales background. He is, however, well liked among the Ad Bureau board members, sources said." (Craig C. Standen, Manager of Marketing Services for R. J. Reynolds, was named an executive vice president of the Bureau in 1980 and became president when Kauffman retired in 1982.[28])

An Orderly Withdrawal

Fund raising goals for the second three-year period of the Project were rapidly reached,[29] amid renewed expressions of support from the newspaper associations.

Hornby's successor as president of ASNE was John Hughes, the editor of the *Christian Science Monitor*.[30] In his cultivated British accent, Hughes narrated a tape for the Project's report to the 1980 ANPA convention, saying that "ASNE is much enthused by what has taken place to date" and "sees much that is still to be accomplished."

There is a slanderous myth abroad that newspaper editors are negative and skeptical curmudgeons. Well, insofar as the Newspaper Readership Project is concerned, I can assure you that ASNE, and the editors it represents, are positive and supportive.

As a matter of fact, this project has caused many editors to become born again. Firstly, it has caused many of us to start talking for the first time to our advertising departments and circulation departments and promotion departments. This has been a traumatic experience for many of us, because we've discovered there are a lot of people in those fields much smarter than us, and who have a lot of good ideas about how to make our newspapers better.

Secondly, it's caused many of us, for the first time, to start talking to our readers. This, too, has been traumatic, for some of the surveys we've conducted under the Readership Project's auspices indicate that our readers consider us distant, arrogant and unresponsive.

Finally, our involvement with the project has brought us closer to the experts in both NAB and ANPA who've shared a tremendous amount of expertise with us.

We at ASNE realize we have an organization that is often very talkative, has a lot of vigor, but sadly, doesn't have much money.

. . . So, from the editors, a hearty vote of appreciation, and a strong endorsement to continue.

It was highly unusual for the Executive Committees of ANPA and the Bureau to meet jointly, but they did so again at the 1981 ANPA convention in Chicago, and adopted a formal resolution that "The Newspaper Readership Project has made a positive and significant contribution to our industry." They also called for a "wind-down and transition" plan to be prepared under the direction of former NAB Chairman Cowles.

It was time to offer a timetable for the Project's final dissolution. I drew up a schedule for the major projects still outstanding. But still refusing to give up on the post-1983 phase, I suggested[31] continuing a number of activities, none of which would require significant new funding, although they would involve some expense or manpower for the organizations involved.[32] I went on to argue

> that the current problems of maintaining circulation were inseparable from the future questions that newspapers face as we move into the new era of telecommunications. That proposition seems more self-evident than it did four and a half years ago. The Bureau has no budget to study or initiate programs in either area. A modest start would require approximately $250,000 a year for staffing and program spending. This would permit us to turn out several advertising campaigns each year, produce two presentations either for circulation training or NIE and promotional use, and conduct one or two modest research projects. It would also provide some staff support to encourage the work of local Readership Committees.

The Bureau's new chairman, Edward Estlow, the president of Scripps-Howard Newspapers, visited me to review the steps under way. He commented two days later,[33] "This exercise reminds me of an anarchistic orchestra to have all members finish at the same time."

Cowles had a new suggestion of his own.[34] "Budget discipline" had suddenly become the principal concern:

> In the Readership Project's final fiscal year (1982–83) budget management might be most effective if all funds were to be allocated on a net basis to those organizations undertaking specific programs. The NRP, in effect, would become a grant-making organization in its final year. NRP would need little, if any, budget for its own

direct expenses. Such a procedure would accomplish the following purposes: a) assure no cost overruns for NRP, b) reduce or eliminate NRP bookkeeping, c) encourage budget discipline . . . .

Smith wrote back in his customary statesmanlike tone:[35]

All of this exercise, of course, raises the real challenge of closer cooperation and coordination between ANPA and the Bureau, particularly. In a sense I think the two major industry organizations must resolve any questions about charter, purpose, the sphere and extent of operations, and reach a mutually satisfactory agreement of who will do what. Personally, I believe that this must extend to a decision by the responsible Boards of which of the other organizations they should accommodate and include in a sponsoring way for those activities which are worthwhile for our business.

I am not proposing in any sense an umbrella or newspaper organization federation. On the contrary, we must be very sensitive to the respective feelings and turf that each claims. But a healthy relationship between the two senior organizations, and between them and the others, might help us to see that dollars and energies are wisely spent.

A memorandum from Burke[36] asked for guidance on behalf of the ANPA staff:

Should there be a significant reduction in expenditures during the last two years in order to provide funds for a stretchout of readership and circulation activities after May 31, 1983? Or should the Project attempt to fund these activities at the previous level, as originally planned?

Burke went on to suggest that "it might be desirable to allocate *final year* funds on a net basis to those organizations undertaking specific programs." His list of activities to be continued was virtually identical with mine.[37]

Chapman now offered prudent financial advice:[38]

If indeed some activities are appropriate to be continued then, in my view, it would be unrealistic to continue to fund NRP at the $800,000 per-year level for the final two years ending May '82 and May '83, followed by $0 funding thereafter.

Every effort should be made to determine which activities may be continued beyond 1983 and some dollars set aside in reserve to "cushion" the absorption of those functions by the organization with which they will eventually reside.

Our proposed revised budget for the last two years eliminated the position of field advisor to the local Readership Committees and also cut several projects of comparatively low priority. The resulting savings ($262,000) would make it possible to continue the *Editors' Exchange* and the post of NIE field advisor for three years after the Project ended.

Meanwhile, the other newspaper associations were being heard from. Their verdict was unanimous. They wanted the Council to continue, and some saw it as a mechanism through which further funding of pet projects might become possible in the future.

On behalf of the circulation executives,[39] James Robinson of the *Toronto Star* said that the

> ICMA Executive Committee and Board strongly supports the continuation of the Newspaper Readership Council after '83, as (1) a forum for the exchange of information, (2) a clearing house for the development of new programs and projects, (3) a vehicle for furthering the ecumenical spirit the industry has enjoyed for the past five years, (4) a group within the industry which would be in the best position to coordinate North American public relations programs designed to increase the public's awareness of the value of the daily newspapers.

Even the classified advertising managers spoke up: Lawrence Healy of the *Boston Globe,* president-elect of ANCAM, wrote,[40]

> I think this should be an ongoing committee, but it does not need massive funding—meetings may be held with open discussions on what each group is doing to maintain the reader and attract new ones—future research by the Bureau, if done in module style, can be adapted by all members . . . to their specific needs.

For INPA,[41] Towles said that "the NRP should continue after funding ends to serve as a forum for the exchange of information and ideas . . . I feel strongly that it would be a waste to lose the input and talent of Council members as to overall direction of projects initiated and funded by the Council, provided, of course, that the ANPA and NAB desire and would be attentive to such advice and counsel." (Towles was keeping his distance.)

Dilthey, of the Newspaper Personnel Relations Association,[42] also agreed that the advisory body of the Newspaper Readership Project should continue. "There is no way each newspaper can develop individual circulation training programs the likes of what has come out of NAB in the past four years."

On behalf of the Newspaper Research Council, the *Chicago Tribune*'s Timberlake said[43] that

> One of the great values of the Newspaper Readership Project has been the development of base line research which can serve as a standard for the industry. A prime example is the study, "How The Public Gets Its News" [which, it will be recalled, was actually not funded by the Project]. . . . Perhaps the most important benefit of the Newspaper Readership Project has been in bringing the various operating components of the newspaper industry together to wrestle with common problems. . . . The industry's involvement in grappling with the issues of readership and circulation problems as reflected in the Readership Project should not be abandoned . . . It is clear . . . that the involvement of the NAB as the industry's sole professional research staff group should be maintained.

Most gratifying to me, however, was an endorsement from the editors. O'Neill wrote[44] to Cowles, Silha, and Smith,

> On behalf of ASNE, I would like to recommend in the strongest possible terms that the newspaper industry continue to support a national research program to track readers and indeed information users of all kinds on a long-term basis. . . . Research is a vital tool in our business for editors and circulators as well as ad directors. It should become a regular function of the industry rather than a short-term project designed to deal with a special problem. . . . The national research program [should] be continued on a reduced but permanent basis to provide social trend tracking, longitudinal readership studies, special analyses, communication of findings, and research on new issues being raised by developments in telecommunications.
>
> The NAB [should] continue to be the principal manager and coordinator of the national research effort with broadly defined goals and general industry support. In research, the NAB is the industry's principal resource, but to serve the total needs of newspapers, it must range well beyond the marketing priorities of the Bureau.
>
> The National [sic] Readership Council [should] be continued as the basic administrative mechanism. This will help preserve the new pattern of inter-disciplinary cooperation that has been one of the most important achievements of the NRP. However, the Coun-

cil must be reorganized in a way to give members a more meaningful role so that their interest and participation will be sustained.

Soon afterward, O"Neill left the newspaper business in splendid style, as the management of the Tribune Company toyed with the fate of its troubled *Daily News*. In his farewell address to the ASNE,[45] O'Neill began by saying that "standing on the gallows for the last five months, waiting for the trapdoor to fall, has been a stimulating experience." He went on to tell the editors:

> We should cure ourselves of our adversarial mindset . . . in the final analysis, what we need most of all in our profession is a generous spirit, infused with human warmth, as ready to see good as to suspect wrong, to find hope as well as cynicism, to have a clear but uncrabbed view of the world.

The Last Act

Responding to the strong show of support from the newspaper organizations, Silha and Smith[46] wrote to all of the committee chairmen recommending that the *Editors' Exchange,* the NIE Field Advisor Service, and the Readership Council itself be maintained for an additional three years beyond May 1983. "Continuation of the Council as an industry-wide interdisciplinary body will contribute a great deal to the newspaper business, not only with regard to readership issues but for other newspaper issues that need and deserve our attention."

The last meeting of the Readership Council was held over a year[47] before the Project's termination date. At that time, Friedheim "noted that ANPA officers favored the synergism of the Readership Council and are likely to want the Council continued as a forum for discussing industry-wide issues." However, when push came to shove, ANPA regarded the Council as redundant with its own reconstituted Circulation and Readership Committee. The Readership Council never met again after the Project ended.

In making our final reports on what the Project had accomplished, we declared a victory in the manner of the Nixon administration after its withdrawal from Vietnam.

The struggle would continue without end, but we had arrived at a reasonable point to call a halt.

In the Project's last year, we offered to lend papers four of our presentations ("How the Public Gets Its News," "Children, Mothers, and Newspapers," "Report on Sunday," and "A New Look at Old Age"), just for the cost of shipment. Not many took us up on the offer. The sense of urgency was no longer there as circulation figures stabilized.

Still, a survey made among the Bureau's member publishers in 1982, shortly before the Project came to an end, found that readership and circulation were rated as the number one problem facing the newspaper business. Nine of every ten publishers wanted the Newspaper Advertising Bureau to remain active in this area. But we could not and did not. Before the final date of May 31, 1983, the Bureau began to absorb several of the Project's able employees onto its own regular payroll. Others were dismissed on a schedule that allowed their termination pay to be covered by the Project. The dual bookkeeping nightmare came to an end.

Within the Bureau, the Project quickly became a dead letter. The final volume of our last major research effort—a 1982 repetition of the earlier national survey of reading habits—was not coaxed out of the Research Department until late in 1984. The Project's publications and presentations were still occasionally being sold to newspapers a half dozen years later.

Unbeknownst to me or the Steering Committee, the ASNE had quietly invested the funds allocated for *The Editors' Exchange* and proceeded to finance the publication from the revenue, thus giving it an extended and useful life.

In the United Kingdom, a Readership Project modeled on the American precedent was set up in 1982 and continued until 1986, with extremely limited resources. It conducted several studies of readers and produced a number of promotional and training presentations. This project was entirely the creation of the provincial press, which was never able to get the national and Sunday newspapers to join with it in a single common organization.

Appraisal and Aftermath

At the outset of this memoir I described it as an institutional case history. Institutions are human relationships embodied in forms that persist beyond the comings and goings of particular individuals. Different institutions can overlap in their human com-position and in their functions. Their components may be called institutions too. In the period I have described, the American press fit the definition of an institution, but apart from its collec-tive aspects, it was made up of many individual newspaper orga-nizations, each of which was an institution in itself. A given com-pany often owned a number of media properties, each of which had its own identity and generated its own loyalties and styles of behavior. Every newspaper craft and profession, as I have tried to show, had its own sense of direction. The voluntary associations that defined these crafts had conflicting priorities and may even have had contrary short-run goals. Institutional conflicts arose from a clash of personalities and private motives rather than from a disparity of fundamental interests reflected in clashing systems of belief.

All of the organizations within the newspaper business had the common objective of advancing its financial success. All served the same masters. Jockeying for position and power was not al-ways an expression of the self-interests of their various member-ships. It sometimes arose from the need of hired functionaries (like myself) to preserve or expand authority, to hang on to an established pattern of performance with a minimum of change or interference, or to gain whatever they could in the way of material or psychic rewards.

Was the Newspaper Readership Project an institution? In its short life it was well on the way to becoming one, insofar as those of us most closely associated with it felt that it had a command on our energies that transcended the demands of the organizations we worked for. It was never permitted to achieve permanent institutional status because the newspaper publishing elite wanted no ongoing claim on their time and treasure.

The financial well-being of the press depended on how it was perceived by advertisers, but this perception was largely indepen-dent of what any given newspaper did on its own. A paper that succeeded in bucking the circulation trend might move its position up on an advertiser's newspaper schedule, but it could not affect that advertiser's judgment of how newspapers as a medium stacked up in vitality or cost efficiency compared with the other media available.

Individually, in private conversations at industry functions, publishers often expressed agreement with my much repeated admonition that long-term investment in newspapers' collective future would pay off better than pursuit of their own papers' immediate short-run goals. But back in their counting houses, manipulating the abacus, confronted with the pressures of their staffs and the workaday realities of their businesses, they inevitably gravitated toward pragmatic decisions that favored the short run and the immediate. The institutional needs of the newspaper industry were remote and abstract compared with those of their own organizations. And in publicly owned companies, the exigent demands of the quarterly financial statement easily outweighed any reasoned understanding of what was really in the long-range interest.

Does the experience of the Readership Project shed any light on Professor Ogburn's dictum that "you can't bend a trend"? It may be too early to answer that question, though in 1990 it seems unlikely that the habit of daily newspaper reading will soon regain the near-universality that it had in the 1960s.

During the years of the Project, daily circulation began to inch up slowly from the recent low point of 60.7 million daily, to which it had fallen in 1975 from a level of 63.1 in 1973. (In 1990, it was 62.8 million.) Sunday, which had never declined at all, kept growing. The rate of decline in audience levels, which had dropped precipitously from the 80 percent point in 1970, fell only slightly from 69 percent in 1977 to 67 at the Project's conclusion in 1983. (In 1990 it was 62 percent.)

By the end of the Project's first three years, I was able to say that

> the slide in circulation and audience has been arrested, and hopefully turned around. It would be nice to credit this to the Readership Project, but realistically we must assume that it takes considerable time to see the effects of a 3/4 of a million-dollar-a-year program on a 20 billion dollar a year industry.[48] [Combined advertiser and consumer spending in newspapers doubled in dollar volume by 1990.]

The Project did demonstrate, however, that the direction and pace of a social trend can be modified. In the case of newspaper circulation, this was being done on a microlevel every day, as newspaper managements made judgments about what they considered an acceptable rate of profit on the trade-off in revenue between advertising and circulation, on the cost/benefit ratio of buying additional circulation or cutting some off deliberately. These decisions of individual publishers were discussed and commented upon so that they influenced other decisions of the same nature in other places. They ended up as what might be termed industry policy, even though that policy merely represented the aggregate of individual decisions independently arrived at.

The activities that the Project undertook in the newspaper industry's collective interests seem to have had long-term effects, if not directly on the readership trend, then at least on newspapers' individual strategies for coping with the trend. The modest investment in the Project does appear to have had a major effect on the willingness of the industry's leaders to tackle common problems even when this required significant and sometimes costly changes in established ways of doing things. If only by promulgating the ideology of cooperation, it made newspaper organizations more accustomed to cooperation and to the exchange of ideas.

For better or for worse, and I believe overwhelmingly for the better, the Project greatly stimulated research on newspaper readers and newspaper operations, making managements both better informed and also more information conscious. The years of the Project saw more editorial experimentation, more applications of new technology to distribution, greater emphasis on personnel training and more management attention to readership and circulation. They were years of great soul-searching, much of it conducted in public, about the long-term future of the newspaper business. All of these developments continued for years afterward and created a permanent impression on the character and practices of the press. Would these changes have taken place in any case? No doubt they would have but perhaps not at quite the same pace or in the same way.

The Project brought together the (in some cases antagonistic) newspaper organizations in a degree of harmony that all recognized as desirable and unusual and that persisted to a surprising degree. It served as a catalyst for discussion and action on individual papers. It provided newspapers with a large quantity of information, stimulation, and material for promotion and training.

The critical question remains the following: How much leverage could $4 million spent over a six-year period be expected to exert on a huge industry, when success depended essentially on the efforts of each individual newspaper's management and staff?

As I mentioned at the outset, many other important developments were occurring in the newspaper business while the Readership Project was in progress. Newspaper plants were being revolutionized by new technology. Preprinted inserts became a more important component of the total newspaper, changing the physical characteristics of the paper in the reader's hands and thus changing the reading habit itself.

Large newspaper chains were swallowing up smaller ones. More and more afternoon papers in morning/evening combinations were merged or dropped by their owners. A growing number of small- and middle-sized papers were changing their publication time from evening to morning.

Partly in response to these changes and partly in the struggle to restore lost circulation, there was a tremendous ferment of innovation in newspaper content and production methods. Papers established regular sections, changing the emphasis from day to day. They increased their coverage of business and sports news. They offered news summaries and introduced modular layouts. The revolution in newspaper technology facilitated changes in makeup and appearance. These were further assisted by the development of standard advertising units and the standardization of newspaper page widths and column formats. There was greatly increased use of color, and the color improved in quality. Graphics and charts became more prominent.

Fearful of further circulation losses, newspapers restrained their price increases to readers but continued to ratchet up their advertising rates to meet profit goals. Their share of the advertising market continued to drop. But competitors were having their problems too, and newspapers generally remained strong and prosperous.

In 1985 the Bureau Board set up a new Future of Advertising Committee. Its purpose was to examine all aspects of the newspaper business to see what could be done to restore newspapers' share of the advertising market.[49] No reference was made to the earlier committee of the same name. Six years and new worries had blurred the memories even of those publishers who had been present at the earlier round. Following the example set in the Readership Project, ten task forces were set up, with representatives of all the principal newspaper associations.[50] There was no fund-raising effort this time; the Bureau provided funding and diverted manpower from its normal activities, and again I had the assignment of pulling everything together.

The task force on readership and circulation was assigned a top priority, under the chairmanship of Reg Murphy, publisher of the *Baltimore Sun*.[51] When it met, the questions that were raised were exactly the ones that had prompted the Readership Project in the first place, and with which the earlier committees had wrestled intrepidly. However, few of the current leaders among the publishers, editors, and circulation managers were familiar with the details of the Readership Project, knew that it had already provided answers to the questions they were asking, or knew the extent of the materials that had been produced. One of the first questions on the agenda was whether the Readership Project should be revived. The unanimous answer was no.

In 1989, the Bureau and the ANPA announced a new joint effort to build readership and circulation, to be financed out of a reallocation of their existing resources. A Gallup survey of ANPA members found that publishers still overwhelmingly considered readership to be the industry's principal concern. To deal with the situation, a committee was formed.

Afterword

Individual newspapers come and go, yet the newspaper seems destined to survive, both as a means of conveying information and as an important social institution. There is certainly no assurance that newspapers will continue in their present form or at their present level of readership, but it seems reasonable to conclude that they remain unique in their functions and destined to continue in one form or another for the foreseeable future. The notion that they are bound to go the way of the dinosaur does not sustain serious inspection.

To understand the unique function of newspapers, we must be aware of the difference between how communication works in space and in time. Print media communicate in space, through symbols that must be interpreted and processed with some mental effort. Print permits extended narration or exposition and also diversity in the number of elements it places simultaneously within the reader's reach. For this reason, newspapers cover many more subjects than can possibly be compressed into the news on television or radio. They maintain substantial staffs of reporters and writers to provide this material; this makes them the repositories of the basic information that holds their communities together. They support wire news and syndicated feature services that offer far more copy than even a very substantial newspaper can print on any given day.

Permanence is no longer a unique characteristic of print, since the VCR has made old television programs as easily retrievable as newspaper clippings have always been. But electronics—at least to this point—offer no match for the convenience, tactility, and speed of printed messages that can be captured at the reader's own pace. The complex expanse of a newspaper spread of pages can be rapidly skimmed by the reader's searching eye, whose attention moves automatically toward those items that speak to the individual's interests. Because the reader can return again and again to these items of interest, the process permits reflection—and absorption of its meaning.

In two-way conversation, we can also return to a subject over and over with our interlocutor to clarify and expand what we have already heard. But in the one-way, oral, communication of broadcasting this is not possible as the sounds fly by. Reading is a demanding mental activity, in which we are constantly translating the symbols of print characters into meaning. Obviously, human beings thought before they invented writing, but thoughts that are embedded in writing and that must be deciphered attain greater richness and complexity.

Suppose we agree that the ability to read is now an integral part of the civilized human heritage and is destined to remain so. Does that mean that the daily press must inevitably be part of what we read? Why can't we do our reading from computer terminals or use books and periodicals instead of the daily newspaper to supplement the top-line information we get from the broadcast news?

The answer must be that our world is increasingly complex and specialized and human affairs are more interdependent. The constantly changing information on which people depend is simply too voluminous to be replenished at less than daily intervals. The record requires a continual update, which radio and television provide for only a handful of stories at a time. There was a time when newspapers in most large American cities provided timely editions continually from dawn to bedtime. With the decline in the number of newspapers and in overall street sales, people in most places can now get a fresh newspaper only once a day. Yet each day's paper is a distinctive and irreplaceable record of that place and date. It embodies the collective memory without which no society can exist. This makes the story of the Readership Project not just a bit of ancient history but an expression of dilemmas and debates that will continue to enliven the American media scene for many years to come.

Excerpts from the Final Report to Contributors, 1983

More than 870 different newspapers, individually or through their groups, contributed to the funding of the Project. As of May 31, 1983, the Project's estimate revenues from contributions totalled $4,316,300; revenues from the sale of materials and programs totalled $474,700; and earnings from investments $192,500, for an approximate total of $4,983,500.

Of the available funds, an estimated $2,016,800 has been disbursed to outside suppliers of materials and services, $532,000 was assigned to the American Society of Newspaper Editors for The *Editors' Exchange*, $6,500 to the American Press Institute, $207,000 to the ANPA Foundation for an NIE Field Adviser, $260,000 to ANPA, and $1,961,200 to NAB to cover staffing and overhead.

Start Your Own Readership Project!

Your paper already has an investment in the Readership Project, and you should make sure you are getting as much as you can out of it. This requires more than just ordering materials from the catalog that follows. It means that you ought to have a plan, and a continuing program.

Hundreds of papers have started their own Readership Committees, but it requires active interest and support from top management to make them work effectively. Here are some of the questions asked by papers starting from scratch.

Do we have to call it a Readership Committee?

Call it whatever you like. The main thing is to have an active interdepartmental committee that deals with circulation and readership. Some papers prefer to call them Marketing Committees.

Who should be on it?

No more people than can meet around a table informally without the need to funnel every comment through a chairman. Most of your departments should be represented: editorial, circulation and promotion (plus research and marketing, if you have anyone with those titles). Remember that advertising, financial, personnel, and production all have something important to contribute. Your public relations and educational specialists will add a new ingredient. But don't limit yourself to department heads; get the brightest people you have and those who might contribute the perspective of women, minority groups, young people, the diverse elements in your community. In practice, the typical committee has half a dozen members, though they range in size from three to thirteen. Three out of five are made up exclusively of department heads or members of management, but the remainder also include rank and file staffers. In five out of six cases, the membership is fixed, while one in six has a rotating membership. Most commonly, the publisher heads up the committee, or it may be the general manager or the editor.

How often should the Committee meet?

Often enough so that its members accept it as an important regular part of their work assignment. Monthly meetings may not be too often, at least in the early stages. Many of the active committees are meeting weekly.

Where should the Committee begin?

It should start with a status report of your own readership situation. You may already have the necessary information compiled and charted, but in many cases it probably isn't. If you don't have a research department, someone should be given this job well before the Committee's first meeting. Consider: (1) the circulation trends, area by area, for your own newspapers and for the print competition (including weeklies, shoppers, and city magazines); (2) the effects of pricing changes, zoning, and editorial innovations; (3) the social, population, and economic trends in your market; (4) the radio and TV audience situation; and (5) the results of any audience and readership studies you may have made. Try to get everybody to look at and think about this information before you meet so that you will come to the first meeting with some specific ideas, questions, or problems you want to talk about.

How can we compare the trends for our own newspaper against those that are generally true, to see whether we're like other papers our size or different?

If you don't have a file on readership and circulation, set one up through your researcher (or the individual you designate as such). This should include census reports, ANPA News Research Center reports, research memos and reports from the Newspaper Advertising Bureau, and clippings from the trade press and from newspaper association newsletters. Keep current on the innovations and experiments in the business.

What about the work we're already doing to build readership?

Your committee can review this along the functional lines of the NRP. Take up every relevant subject one meeting at a time: editorial product, promotion and public relations program, school activities, circulator selection and training, distribution systems and equipment, subscription and street sales, subscriber service, research. Bring everyone up to date. Then ask for suggestions, questions, and a constructive critique. Keep a record of points that require action and of who's responsible for follow-up.

Do we have to do new research to make this thing work?

Not necessarily. But chances are you'll be asking yourselves some questions you may not be able to answer without it. Chances are also that someone else has asked similar questions, and there may be an answer for you someplace—or at least a partial answer. Find out before you start a survey of your own, and if you do one make sure it's done by professionals.

How do we make our activities mesh with those of the Newspaper Readership Project?

By keeping track of all the individual activities, reports, and materials the Project has produced to see how you can use them. Every single thing that's been done is intended to be applicable by newspapers at the local level, and you'll be missing a good bet if you don't seriously consider how to adapt them to your own special needs.

Just because we set up a Readership Committee does that mean we have a Readership Project going?

Hardly, but you'll have taken the first step. Assess your present situation, your growth potential, and your key target groups. Define your long-term readership objectives and then set up some realistic short-term goals.

Lay out a series of tasks in every department that, if accomplished, will bring you closer to your goals. Figure out what these tasks require in time, in organization, and maybe in extra budget. Evaluate the probable range of dollars and cents return on that investment. Set up a plan with specific assignments and a timetable. Hold it down to what can be done. Keep reporting back to the Committee on what's happening and keep generating new ideas. If you do research, take the time to talk through its implications. Get your entire staff aware of what's going on and involve them if you can. Now you have a Readership Project going!

What kinds of things have local Readership Committees accomplished?

1. Changed the daily time of publication.
2. Started a Sunday newspaper.
3. Changed the format of the Saturday paper.
4. Started new zoned editions.
5. Added special interest sections on different days of the week.
6. Changed the page format and the number of columns.
7. Changed typography.
8. Added new graphics.
9. Expanded the weather report.
10. Beefed up coverage of local sports.
11. Set up a news summary.
12. Brought in a second wire service.
13. Introduced an op-ed page.
14. Realigned the comics.
15. Started an action-line column.
16. Set up suburban news bureaus.
17. Revised the subscription rate structure.
18. Instituted a training program for district managers.
19. Retained an advertising agency.
20. Set up a computerized subscriber information system.
21. Set up a new procedure to handle subscriber complaints.
22. Started a Newspaper-in-Education program.
23. Began a plant-tours program.
24. Realigned circulation districts.
25. Set up a marketing department.

What makes for a successful Readership Committee?

The experience of the past half-dozen years shows:

1. It is interdepartmental. It brings together specialists whose normal business contacts are brief and focused on specifics and gives them a forum for discussion of the big, challenging questions that confront the whole newspaper.

2. There is some means set up to provide staff participation or involvement. Whether or not rank and file staff members are represented on the committee, they can be involved through in-house communications, contests, or the organization of task forces dealing with particular aspects of building readership.

3. The Committee meets on a regular schedule, and the meetings take precedence over each week's predictable crises.

4. The Committee has top management support and involvement.

5. It sets specific goals and faces each meeting with a firm agenda.

6. It develops individual assignments to tackle each problem area it deals with.

7. It starts with facts rather than conjectures and develops relevant information either from available national or other studies or from original research among readers in its own area.

8. It allows enough time for discussion to be thorough and reflective, at a different pace than meetings on the workaday routine.

9. The Committee's members strive for firsthand exposure to readers. They may participate in group interview or discussion sessions, go out to interview readers with a survey questionnaire, sell subscriptions door to door.

10. The Committee is willing to experiment. They recognize that some of the innovations they try will flop, but they feel the risk is justified.

11. They study other newspapers, both their products and their operations, and they do this systematically.

12. They actively use the materials from the Newspaper Readership Project and invest the necessary time and effort to adapt those materials to their own situation.

13. They never think their job is done, because in today's competitive media environment it never will be.

Agenda Suggestions for Newspaper Readership Committees

1. NRP presentations and materials. Review each available item. Discuss possible adaptations to your local needs, including possible production of new presentation segments, if necessary. Develop a marketing plan for showing and a timetable with assigned responsibilities.

2. NRP research reports. Take each major report as a topic for discussion. It should be read by everyone before the committee's meeting, and everyone should be asked to come armed with a list of proposals or suggestions for specific applications to your own newspaper. A different meeting date could be set aside for each significant target group, e.g. children, adolescents, young people, older adults, blacks, working women.

Where possible, relate the data from national studies to available survey information in your own market. For each target group, consider implications of the research for editorial content and style, promotion and distribution.

3. Critical comparisons. Get hold of a variety of papers that you would consider roughly comparable to your own in circulation size, market type, publication time of day, competitive situation, etc. Assign individual members to these papers and present a running analysis comparing their treatment and style to your own. How do you assess the way they handle weather, editorials, local sports, comics, international news, "people" stories? How do you think your paper stacks up against its contemporaries and why? Are there any good ideas that could be borrowed? Are there any worth discussion?

4. 1980 Census. Assign someone to prepare a detailed analysis of the new census data for your market, tract by tract, neighborhood by neighborhood. Examine the trends since 1970, 1960, 1950. What are the principal changes in population, in type of housing, in occupational distribution? What could it mean in terms of distribution practices or in terms of editorial content?

5. National print competition. How does it differ in your market from the overall national pattern? Advance analysis can show how the circulation-to-household radio for individual magazines in your market compares with that for the country as a whole and for other markets of comparable size. Discuss the implications of such variations. (For example, a comparatively low penetration for *TV Guide* in your market might mean that your paper is doing an exceptionally effective job with its TV section. But a comparatively low penetration for the news magazines may simply mean that there is less interest in national and international news relative to other markets.)

6. Local print competition. Examine all the shoppers and community weeklies and city magazines (if any) in your market. Estimate their circulation and readership. Do they cover news or subjects that your own paper does not? Are there any ideas or subjects that you might want to pick up from them?

7. Newspaper in Education. Review the materials available from the ANPA Foundation and from major newspapers with outstanding NIE programs. Review what you are doing. What are the principal questions you face with respect to the scale, timing, and resources of your own program? To what extent can these questions be answered? From what you've learned, are you covering enough schools? Covering children in the right grades? Aiming at the right parts of the curriculum? How can your present activity in this area be improved?

8. Pricing. Track the pricing history of your weekday and Sunday products, both for single copies and for subscriptions. Track your circula-

tion figures against that record. Compare your changes in circulation rates against changes in your advertising rates. Compare both with the record for newspapers in similar markets. Use all these charts as the agenda for a discussion of pricing. What questions or lessons come out of the comparisons?

9. Distribution. What are the opportunities for growth in circulation or for improvements in your operational methods? How does your growth in subscriptions compare with single-copy sales? What is your turnover rate among subscribers? How many cancellations are salvageable? What is your turnover rate among district managers? Among carriers? Consider possible innovations under each heading that you perceive as a problem area.

10. Original research. If you have had a recent study of your readers (and nonreaders), you have probably taken the time to review the results at length and to consider their action implications. But if you do not have a recent study, it is worth taking the time to consider what kinds of information you'd like to have and how you could use it. The exercise will be valuable even if there is no possibility of getting the necessary funding for new research.

Catalog of Materials

Ad Campaigns

Don't You Hate Not Knowing?

A series of nine, 1,000 line promotion ads designed to build new—and steady—readership among all age groups, particularly young people. Theme: Newspapers keep you on top of issues that affect your life.

"Foxy" Campaign

Ten ads targeted on special readership groups: the "foxy" fashionables, the "earthy" plant lovers, etc. Also included, 5 storyboards for 30–sec TV commercials and a "How To" promotion campaign book.

Take Our Word

Six ads illustrated by cartoonist Bill Bramhall. Readers discover what puzzling one-word headlines mean and get pointed reasons why they should subscribe to the daily newspaper.

Buzz Off

Eight 250–line ads with two-word stopper headlines. Focuses on particular parts of the paper—classified, news, food, etc. Shows how the newspaper is not only interesting, but useful.

For the Good Life, Read Every Day

This series of ads highlights the many ways that the daily newspaper adds to the reader's quality of life day to day. Each ad focuses on a newspaper section with a headline that underscores the reader benefit. For example, "Sports: Newspaper readers know the score."

Newspapers Give You More

Seven ads designed to demonstrate the vitality and value of the daily newspaper for its readers and advertisers. Theme: Newspapers give you more of what you want to know.

What's in It for Me?

Twelve full-page, camera-ready ads designed to attract and increase readership among key demographic groups: executives, homemakers, teenagers, elderly, professionals, owner-operators, technicians, farmers, young adults, working women, blue-collar workers, and consumers. Accompanying brochure offers suggestions for compatible radio and/or TV tie-ins.

Films

First Edition

A behind-the-scenes look at the news-gathering, writing, editing, and decision-making that go into one day's issue of a modern newspaper— the *Baltimore Sun*. Mentions of the *Sun* are incidental to the main story of how a newspaper works.

. . . But You Can't Take It for Granted

Suppose the daily newspaper suddenly disappeared. That's the premise for this hilarious film of how one town tries to cope with the daily departed. It's ultimately a serious statement on the importance of the newspaper in our day-to-day lives.

I Saw It in the Paper

Award-winning filmmakers David and Albert Maysles took their cameras from Long Island to San Francisco, celebrating the special place of the newspaper in our lives. The film makes its point subtly to those readers who might be turned off by conventional promotion. Comes with 6 copies of handbook for discussion, for leaders and teachers.

The First Freedom

A 21–minute film or videocassette presentation addressed to senior high school, college, and general audiences. It is intended to get people thinking about something they may ordinarily take for granted: their free press

—what it is, how it works, and why it matters. It brings together the unique, first-hand perspectives of five distinguished American journalists to discuss some of the vital issues affecting press freedom today.

Slide and Cassette Presentations

Read All About It

A promotional presentation that's all about newspapers. Designed for use whenever and wherever you want to tell a positive newspaper story—to community groups, plant tours, "Career Day" school programs, etc. Can be customized to your newspaper.

We Care: Newspaper People and Their Readers

Designed to acquaint people with the professionalism and concern for the public that newspaper people bring to their work. Includes directions for localizing presentation.

It's Your Newspaper

Shows newspaper industry's commitment to covering the black population and its concerns—and how newspapers involve blacks in the entire process of producing the paper.

Good News About Newspapers

Advertisers, general audiences, and especially your own newspaper people will benefit from this upbeat presentation. It sets the record straight on the newspaper's unique and enduring position as an advertising vehicle and a community catalyst, its assimilation of new technology, its fresh editorial approaches to readers' new information and entertainment needs.

The Newspaper in Education

ANPA Foundation Field Services

On-site visits to newspapers for NIE, assisting and advising on the following: starting an NIE program; circulation, promotion, editorial, budgetary, and administrative concerns with NIE; critiquing existing programs; expansion of existing programs; contacts with local school superintendents; in-service workshops for teachers; creation of in-paper youth-oriented pages; developing in-service workshops, curriculum guides, and promotion.

Newspaper in Education Ads

Five camera-ready case history ads that reveal how NIE works in five different schools.

Newspaper in Education Audio-Visual Presentation

Shows the program in action in 5 school districts around the country. Effective tool for use with parents, educators, community groups.

Spacekid Learns To Read the Newspaper Like an Earthling

Cartoon format slide and cassette presentation. A valuable tool for classroom use. Children in grades 3–5 learn to take their individual paths through the newspaper, gaining skills for learning from news stories.

Circulation Management
Slide and Cassette Presentations

What Circulation Does

Designed to provide a clear picture of the role the circulation department plays in the newspaper organization. The presentation explains how the department fulfills each of its major areas of responsibility: distribution, sales, management, and planning.

Circulation: The Key to Successful Marketing

Reports on fifteen case histories taken from newspapers large and small, chain-owned and independent, that illustrate different approaches to maintaining and building circulation.

Booklets

Screening Form for District Manager Selection: Instructional Manual

A simple personality test designed to help newspapers evaluate candidates for district circulation manager positions. Fourteen questions answered on a 5–point agree-disagree scale measure the candidates' attitudes in areas that research has shown are characteristic of successful district managers. Can be administered in a few minutes.

Your Career in Newspaper Circulation

Aimed at young people, this booklet offers a brief, stimulating introduction to career opportunities in newspaper circulation. It describes how a modern circulation department works, how to get started, the challenges, and career potential.

Sales and the Single Copy—How To Get the Most From Your Single Copy Sales

A comprehensive overview of the business of selling single copies of the daily newspaper, based on the experiences of 17 experts. This 16–page booklet is a valuable how-to for everyone involved in single-copy selling at newspapers of every size.

The Circulation Spouse's Survival Manual

This booklet is designed for the mates of newspaper circulation personnel. It gives spouses a better understanding of what the circulation department does and why doing the job well requires so much of circulation people. It also suggests some of the ways to cope with occasionally troublesome situations.

How To Set up a Circulation Information System

Outlines the basic steps in setting up a circulation information system.

Developing a Computerized Circulation Information System

Details ways to set up computerized files and to purchase hardware and software from vendors, as well as information about computer storage and retrieval.

Building a Subscriber/Non-Subscriber File

Describes the steps to be undertaken to create and maintain information on subscribers and non-subscribers.

Training for the Circulation Phone Room Staff
Slide and Cassette Presentations

Making Connections: The Art of Cold Call Subscription Selling

This sales training program reveals a new, flexible approach to cold call subscription selling. Teaches phone room sales reps control of all kinds of call situations.

Stop the Stops: Handling Customer Complaints

Telephone training program for customer service departments, for selling new subscribers and keeping old ones. There are lessons on how to open a call, close a call, and everything in between.

District Manager Training
Workshop Program

This is a workshop for district managers and/or carrier leaders who work directly with newspaper carriers. The workshop covers all aspects of circulation as it pertains to the carriers and the routes. These include: recruiting and motivating new carriers; obtaining parental approval and support; retaining good carriers; training carriers to sell, deliver and collect; handling day-to-day management problems such as down routes, apartment collection, high carrier turnover, motor routes. The workshops are structured around interactive problem-solving sessions that involve role-playing and audience participation. By discussing problems and potential solutions, and sharing ideas, programs, methods and procedures that other newspapers have used successfully, workshop participants will gain valuable job skills that they could not learn in isolation.

Slide and Cassette Presentations

The Worst of Jobs, the Best of Jobs

A colorful presentation that will give your DMs a thorough training in the fundamentals of successful district management.

The Roquefort Files

Cartoon format. A district manager shares his on-the-job experiences, the problems he's faced in his district, and the solutions he's come up with. Many good training techniques, practical information, sound advice—and lots of fun.

Motivating Carriers: You Make the Difference

Explains how to train juvenile carriers. Designed to motivate carriers, supervisors, and circulation managers.

Managing Adult Carriers

For district managers and advisors who supervise (or plan to supervise) adult carriers. Actually two shows in one—covering recruitment and also training and motivation.

Carrier and Recruitment Training
Slide and Cassette Presentations

Three Times Three

Informative, entertaining sales training program that gives newspaper carriers a pleasant, positive approach to door-to-door sales. It teaches a three-part sales strategy that even the shyest carrier can master. (With flash cards).

Carrier Recruitment Campaign

To be used with school or juvenile groups in carrier recruitment. Features two young carriers who talk to kids in their own language. Upgrades image of the carrier's job by showing real rewards it can bring him/her. (With review booklet).

Newspaper Design

A summary and illustration of a seminar held by the American Press Institute. The booklet evaluates the effectiveness of various newspaper designs, exploring the way newspapers can make themselves more attractive and more convenient for readers.

Research Presentations (Slides and Cassette)

How the Public Gets Its News

Report on a 1977 national survey about the newspaper audience, its reading habits, and the comparative reading interests of regular and occasional readers and nonreaders. This study also highlights the differences between newspaper reading and TV viewing and provides suggestions on how to build readership.

Children, Mothers and Newspapers

A 1978 study of American youth, ages 6–17. Their newspaper reading at home and in the classroom, their interest, exposure to TV and other media. The presentation suggests a strategy for winning the next generation of adult readers. Also features interviews with mothers.

Report on Sunday

A multimarket study that examines the attractions of Sunday newspapers, particularly to young readers. It describes the special character of the

Sunday reading experience and the readership of different sections by different kinds of people. This presentation suggests that lessons learned from Sunday papers can be applied to strengthen daily readership.

A New Look at Old Age

A variety of surveys supplied the data for this study of the interests and activities of people over 65, who head one in five newspaper-reading households. This presentation highlights the growing importance of this age group and points to opportunities for newspaper readership among older people.

Research Reports

A National Study of News Audiences (1977)

How the Public Gets Its News (Summary booklet).
Technical Report

News Sources and Interests of Blacks and Whites

The Personal Newspaper

Young Adults and the Newspaper
Supplemental analysis of data from the National Opinion Research Center

The Influence of Childhood Exposure to Newspapers on Adult Newspaper Habits

Seven Days in March
Stories appearing in the press are compared with the stories covered by TV network news programs

Two Dimensions of News: Interest and Importance Ratings of the Editorial Content of the American Press

Adult Readership of Weekly Newspapers and Shoppers

Readership and Coverage of Science and Technology in Newspapers

The Home Delivery Population: Characteristics and Readership Patterns

It's News to Me: Personal Reactions to the News
People's definitions of the biggest news story of the day, and of news that personally upset them or made them feel good

The Audience for Newspaper Advertising

The Daily Diet of News: Patterns of Exposure to News in the Mass Media

Identifying Prospects for the Daily Newspaper: Frequent Readers, Infrequent Readers and Nonreaders

The Desirability of Newspapers for Political Advertising

The Audience for Smaller Newspapers with Under 25,000 Circulation

A National Study of the Daily Newspaper and Its Audiences (1982)

Newspaper Pages, Ads and Readers
Analysis of reading and interest patterns

Readers Rate Their Daily Newspapers

Newspapers in American News Diets: A Comparative Assessment

Circulation and Home Delivery Patterns

Meeting Readers' Multiple Needs: Content and Readership of News and Features in the Daily Press

Circulation Studies

Circulation Coverage in Single-Ownership Markets with Separate Morning and Evening Editorial Managements
The study suggests that total circulation-per-household is greater when the papers use different staffs.

District Manager Job Satisfaction
An estimate of the seriousness of the problems of district managers; some comments about the sources of those problems, some inferences about the personal qualities of district managers, and some suggestions for the future.

The Front Page and Single-Copy Sales
Relates sales in four cities to weather, day of week, and significant news events.

Circulation Department Practices

How circulation departments in more than 500 papers are organized, how supervisors and carriers are paid, turnover rates, routes of youth and adult carriers, billing practices, and other facets of this part of the business.

Reaching Readers in Apartments and Other Dwelling Units

Daily Newspaper Audiences: An Analysis of Four Circulation Size Groups

Single-Copy Buying: A Three-City Study

Interviews at single-copy sales locations, followed by telephone interviews, with single-copy buyers, subscribers, and readers who buy their newspapers both ways. Reading habits and attitudes toward home delivery and single-copy purchasing of the three groups.

New Screening Form for District Manager Selection

Circulation: Key to Successful Newspaper Marketing

How circulation departments are organized and how they are changing.

Fifteen Case Histories in Circulation Management

Keeping in Touch With Your Carriers: Some Useful Tools

Model survey questionnaires.

Changing Role of Women

Women and Newspapers in the 1970s

Women in the Eighties

Changes in Newspaper Content

Inventory of Editorial Content: Weekday Editions (1979)

Inventory of Editorial Content: Sunday/Weekend Editions (1979)

Section Readership: A Summary of Individual Market Studies

Inventory of Editorial Content: Weekday Editions (1983)

Inventory of Editorial Content: Sunday/Weekend Editions (1983)

Assessment of New Technology

Who Will Pay? Consumers and Advertisers in the Electronic Marketplace
Opportunities and pitfalls posed by home information systems.

National Studies of Children and Adolescents

Children, Mothers and Newspapers

Children, Movie-going and the Newspaper

Mass Media in the Family Setting

Children and Newspapers
Traces the development of reading from ages 6 to 17.

Daily Newspapers in American Classrooms

Technical Report on Nationwide study of Children and Adolescents

Other Studies of Readers and Journalists

Older Adults, Older Readers: What We Know and Need to Find Out

Senior Citizens and Newspapers
Four-city survey

One of Our Media Is Missing: Readers' Reactions to the 1978 New York City Newspaper Strike

Changes in the Number of Papers Read, From 1970 to 1977

Trade-Offs in Readers' Editorial Content Preferences: A Computer Simulation

The Frequency of Newspaper Reading: Who Changes and Why?

The Sunday Newspaper: A Five Market Study

The Newspaper in Readers' Minds: An Analysis of Readers' Content Perceptions.
An in-depth assessment of content perceptions and newspaper uses of readers in four major markets.

Weekday Reading Patterns: A Two-Market Study
Factors affecting "today's" reading.

Changing Lifestyles and Newspaper Reading
Impact of significant changes in the lives of a national sample of people.

Newspaper in Education

A Survey of Newspaper in Education Programs (1976 and 1981)

Assessing the Impact of Newspaper in Education Programs
Shows positive changes in student attitudes toward newspapers and increased reading frequency; also gains in interest and knowledge of current events.

The Newspaper in Education: What It Does to Children's Civic Awareness and Attitudes Toward Newspapers

Guidelines for Conducting Newspaper in Education Research

Research Notes

(1) Watch Your Ps and Qs and CPMs. (2) Changes in Saturday Editions Among 100 Morning and Evening Combinations. (3) Daily and Sunday Newspaper Readership: 1977–1981. (4) Daily Newspaper Circulation: State-by-State Patterns and Trends. (5) Circulation and Audience: What's the Difference? (6) Movie Advertisements and Reviews in Newspapers. (7) Readers of the *National Enquirer* and *Star* are Daily Newspaper Readers Too! (8) Eyesight Problems and Newspaper Readership. (9) Teenage Newspaper Readership.

ANPA News Research Center Reports

(1) The 21– to 34–Year Old Market and the Daily Newspaper. (2) Content, Appearance and Circulation—An Analysis of Individual Newspaper Characteristics. (3) Newspaper Readership and Circulation. (4) Patterns of Newspaper Readership: What to Drop and What to Keep. (5) What Determines the News? A Review of the Scientific Research on News Values. (6) Newspaper Use Among New Residents. (7) The Frequency of Newspaper Readership. (8) Life Style and Readership—A Review of the Research Literature. (9) Nonreaders: Why They Don't Read. (10) An Analysis of Five Factors Affecting Newspaper Circulation. (11) A Comparison of Newspaper Use by Lower Income and Middle and Upper Income Blacks. (12) Newspaper Reading in Small Towns. (13) A Summary of Recent

Research. Where We Should Go Next. (14) Using Community Character-istics to Predict Newspaper Reading Habits. (15) Daily News Habits of the American Public. (16) Putting Research Findings to Work Is Not Always Easy, But It Is Always Rewarding. (17) The Influence of Community Attachment on Newspaper Reading Habits. (18) Newspaper Readership and Community Ties; Precision Journalism: Coming of Age. (19) News-papers and Television: A Review of Research on Uses and Effects. (20) Tracking the Attitudes of the Public Toward the Newspaper Business. (21) Personal Needs and Media Use; Locating and Identifying Stable New Subscribers. (22) Newspaper Readership and Circulation—An Update; Rate of Adoption of Modern Format by Daily Newspapers. (23) Newspa-per Readership Among Public School Children Grades 7–12. (24) The Comic-Strip Problem; Effects of a Year-Long Series of Energy Articles. (25) Accuracy in News Reporting. (26) The Influence of Local Information on Daily Newspaper Household Penetration in Canada; Personal Motiva-tions and Newspaper Readership. (28) Reader Interest in Business, Sports and Foreign News. (29) Minneapolis Meets New Information Needs. (30) Using Census Data; College Students' Use of Newspapers for Political Commentary. (31) Putting Research Findings to Work. (32) Subscribers' Reaction to Redesign of the St. Cloud Daily Times; Understanding the Research Process. (33) Community Ties and Newspaper Use. (34) Psycho-graphics Made Simple; Newspaper Readership and Proximity to Metro-politan Markets. (35) Reader Response to Front Pages with Modular For-mat and Color; Newspaper Errors: Source Perception, Reporter Response and Some Causes. (36) Metropolitan Dominance and Media Use. (37) The Public and Local News; Why Some Editorial Endorsements Are More Persuasive Than Others. (38) Morning and Evening Daily Newspaper Readers. (39) A Comparison of Subscribers and Nonsubscribers.

ASNE Reports

What Is News? Who Decides? And How?

A report based on a study of newsroom communications. Among the questions raised are: How do newsroom people communicate among themselves? How do they perceive the reader? Who determines what gets in the paper? How is 'news' defined? (Michigan State University research team.)

Changing Needs of Changing Readers

A 1979 study of newspaper readers based on focus group interviews. (Ruth Clark).

Pretesting Readers' Reactions to Format and Content Changes in Newspapers: The Ad Hoc Lab Study.

With the testing program outlined in this report, newspapers can try out changes before they are incorporated in the paper. (Ruth Clark and Greg Martire).

The World of the Working Journalist (Michigan State University).

Note: The original catalog also listed a number of publications and presentations not funded by the Readership Project, distributed by ICMA and INPA.

Notes

Preface

1. Ogburn's long jaw and lanky figure made him look like an over-sized Daniel Boone. As befitted the holder of an endowed chair at the University of Chicago, he was authoritative and earnest in manner, although he secretly spent spare evenings attending wrestling matches, long before these were made popular by television. Governor Eugene Talmadge of Georgia, known for snapping his red galluses more than for his erudition, kept Ogburn's book *Social Change* on the otherwise empty bookshelf behind his desk. When a visitor once queried him about it, he explained, "See that book? That there book was writ by a Georgia boy. That book and the Bible have all there is to know in 'em."

2. *Press and Public* (2d ed., Hillsdale, NJ: Lawrence Erlbaum Associates, 1989).

1 · The Newspaper Business

1. The *Herald-Tribune, Journal-American,* and *World-Telegram and Sun* (briefly combined and resuscitated as the *World Journal Tribune*) had suffered from notorious featherbedding practices. Their aggregate circulation was 1,227,779 before they went down on April 24, 1966 for a devastating strike that lasted more than four months.

2. ANPA's membership was limited to daily newspapers, while the National Newspaper Association, founded in 1885, served the interests of nondaily community newspapers.

3. Edwin Emery, *History of the American Newspaper Publishers Association* (Minneapolis: The University of Minnesota Press, 1950.)

4. Edwin Emery, *History* p. 12.

5. Quoted in George Seldes, *Lords of the Press* (New York: Messner, 1938), p. 7.

6. One bulletin, October 3, 1900, listed prospective new advertising clients. These included, "Hy-Jen breath purifier," "Poudre de Fatigue," "Kennedy's Medical Discovery," "Koch's Lymph Cure," "Omega Oil," and "Pink Pills for Pale People." There was also a notice that, "Some time ago we had a request for the address of Dr. Perin, the palmist. We understand that for the next few days he will be located at the Latonia Hotel, Covington, Kentucky." At the 1894 convention, a paper pointed out "that newspapers were losing general advertising to magazines because newspaper advertising rates were too high, compared to the rates offered by the magazines, which were rapidly expanding their circulation. . . . The answer suggested by members in the discussion included harder work on advertising solicitations, lower rates for general advertisers, and better promotion of newspapers as an advertising medium." (Emery, *History*, p. 41).

7. This was begun by the International Circulation Managers Association in 1952 and taken over exclusively by ANPA in 1965.

8. Its start-up in 1979 was widely interpreted to express dissatisfaction over the way that the newspaper business's affairs were covered by its principal trade publication, *Editor & Publisher*. This weekly had a venerable history and an attitude of protective small-town boosterism toward the newspaper business. Its managing editor, Jerry Walker, Jr. (the son of a former editor), saw himself as a fearless investigative reporter and seemed to delight in sniping at the Bureau and other industry organizations.

9. The American Society of Newspaper Editors, the International Newspaper Marketing Association, the International Circulation Managers Association, the Newspaper Personnel Relations Association, and the International Newspaper Advertising and Marketing Executives. A few steps away is the American Press Institute, which runs training workshops and seminars for the full array of newspaper professions.

10. A number of these organizations had long histories. ICMA was founded in 1898, NAEA in 1900, ANCAM in 1919, ASNE in 1922, NNPA in 1930.

11. Renamed the Society of Professional Journalists in 1988.

12. As I describe below, retail and classified sales departments were added to the original national sales function, as well as a division that handled the placement of advertising inserts and a department that dealt with cooperative advertising.

13. In the mid-1980s, film was largely replaced by video.

14. Much of this has been summarized in two books: *Strategy in Adver-*

tising (2d ed., Lincolnwood, Ill: National Textbook Company, 1985), and *Press and Public.*

15. On the national level, organizations like the Advertising Research Foundation, the Audit Bureau of Circulations, and the Advertising Council (which created and disseminated public interest advertising *à la* Smokey the Bear) had a special importance because of their tripartite character. They provided an opportunity for social and professional contacts that cut across the demarcation lines of medium, agency, and client. Directors of these organizations enjoyed a feeling of common involvement in a worthy professional cause that transcended their immediate business interests. Directorships were highly prized because of their prestige, but in addition, they involved periodic meetings (with spouses in attendance) at sunny watering places in Florida and the West.

2 · Perceiving the Problem

1. The research was directed by John B. Stewart, an assistant professor at Harvard, who published the results in his book, *Repetitive Advertising in Newspapers* (Boston: Harvard Business School, 1964).

2. After considerable resistance from the military, this was eventually published. Leo Bogart, ed., *Social Research and the Desegregation of the U.S. Army* (Chicago: Markham, 1969; New Brunswick, N.J. Transaction, 1991).

3. Memorandum of August 6, 1964.

4. Letter of August 24, 1964.

5. Letter of August 24, 1964.

6. They were to be divided equally among publishers, advertisers, and urban affairs specialists. The subjects to be covered included the growth and population changes in metropolitan areas, economic trends in retailing and manufacturing in central cities and suburbs, the social problems of urbanism, and urban fiscal and administrative problems.

7. Memorandum to Lipscomb, April 12, 1967.

8. Letter of May 3, 1967.

9. Letter of May 26, 1967.

10. Undated memorandum to Lipscomb.

11. According to the generally accepted industry estimates prepared by McCann-Erickson, Inc. To put this trend in longer range perspective, newspapers' share was 36. 3% in 1950, before the emergence of television as a mass medium. It was 26. 1% in 1990.

12. Roanoke, Va., El Cajon, Cal., Inverness, Fla., Elizabethtown, Ky., Westminster, Md., Los Alamos, N.M., and Greensboro, N.C.

13. The Ralph Ingersolls (Junior and Senior) of Ingersoll Newspapers, and the Millers of Allentown, Pa.

14. E. W. Scripps Co. went public in 1987.

15. The task was handled by Frank Stanczak and William Rinehart, the Research Institute's director.

16. This was done through a committee chaired by the president of the New York Times Company, Walter Mattson, with staff support from Bureau vice president Charles M. Kinsolving, Jr.

17. January 31, 1979.

18. Letter of July 23, 1976 to Robert Smith, publisher of the *Minneapolis Star* and *Tribune*.

19. October 2, 1973.

20. October 9, 1973.

21. Memorandum of April [no date], 1974.

3 · Organizing the Project

1. Address to the ANPA, May 5, 1976.

2. June 20, 1976.

3. Letter to me of June 15, 1976.

4. Letter of June 25, 1976.

5. July 21, 1976.

6. Address to the ICMA convention, July 26, 1976.

7. August 3, 1976.

8. These studies and those listed under the next heading were described in detail in an attachment.

9. These would include the ANPA Foundation's Newspaper in Education program, the ANPA's News Research Center, the public relations activities of both ANPA and the Bureau, and the ANPA Research Institute's developmental work on equipment design.

10. August 11 and 12, 1976.

11. September 1, 1976.

12. July 1, 1977.

13. November 19, 1976.

14. November 26, 1976.

15. On January 24, 1977.

16. January 24, 1977.

17. Held on March 31, 1977 in Detroit in connection with the Bureau's automotive meetings.

18. On April 6 in Washington.

19. ANPA, the Bureau, and the professional newspaper associations have welcomed Canadian members since their founding. The Canadian Daily Newspaper Publishers Association was founded in 1919.

20. Later Senior Vice President.

21. "Significant considerations in developing a communications plan," June, 1977.

22. On September 7, 1976.

23. September 10, 1976.
24. The first one went out in September, 1976.
25. February 15, 1977.
26. February 2, 1977.
27. January 25, 1977.
28. November 19, 1976.
29. January 15, 1979.
30. Salpy Hancock.
31. Nabscan was the creation of Richard Neale, the Bureau's specialist on the retail grocery business. In the mid-1970s he became aware of the important implications of the Universal Product Code, which was beginning to appear on the packages of grocery products. Decipherable by laser scanners at supermarket checkout counters, the Code provided an up to the minute record of all sales transactions by product and by brand. Neale examined the results for grocery stores that had turned their records over to him for a small fee. He was able to produce many case histories documenting the effects of newspaper advertising by comparing sales of a product before an ad ran with sales in the following week. Neale convinced Kauffman and me that this was a development of great promise, not merely as an advertising sales tool but as a replacement for the existing methods of measuring changes in the market. A small staff was hired in an effort to put the collection and sale of the information on a commercial basis, and additional chains of supermarkets were induced to add stores to the sample. However, all funding had to be squeezed out of the Bureau's regular budget. Nabscan never received the kind of substantial investment required to launch it as a successful enterprise. The project was plagued from the outset by problems in processing the massive amounts of data that were generated from a diversity of retailer sources, each with a different system of programming and presentation. Even when the data were produced in an acceptable format, no serious attempt was made to interpret and analyze them. The costs of generating the information escalated, and sales were slow. Competitors (including the mighty A. C. Nielsen Company and Time, Inc.'s SAMI) entered the field.
   Scanners did, indeed, become the new frontier of marketing research. A new competitor, Behavior/Scan, devised a system by which scanner-generated purchase records for individual households could be linked to their television viewing in selected all-cable markets. But this happened long after Nabscan had become a considerable strain on the Bureau's budget, on its normal sales activities, and on staff morale. Nabscan was finally sold by Kauffman to the research company that had been responsible for its data processing, and it later ended up in the hands of Mills and Allen, an international conglomerate, which folded it in 1987.
32. October 19, 1977.

4 · A Struggle Over Research

1. This misuse of surveys was criticized in my book *Silent Politics,* in 1972. (This has been republished as *Polls and the Awareness of Public Opinion* (New Brunswick, N.J.: Transaction Books, 1985).

2. Later renamed the Newspaper Advertising Sales Association.

3. In 1976, the ABC began to issue reports that included audience data but later abandoned the practice in the face of opposition from newspapers in competitive markets.

4. Memorandum of August 3, 1976.

5. These would investigate the status of training programs, the employment of adult carriers, direct billing and advance payment systems, subscriber lists, distributors, carrier systems and compensation and incentive programs.

6. These would include the ratio of editorial costs to total manpower costs and operating expenses; distribution costs involved in rack, newsstand, and subscription sales in different types of residential areas; and an editorial salary survey.

7. Memorandum of September 28, 1976.

8. Memorandum of September 28, 1976.

9. Leo Bogart, *Premises for Propaganda* (New York: The Free Press, 1976).

11. March 17, 1977.

12. Draft manuscript received September 8, 1976.

13. Letter of September 16, 1976.

14. Letter of September 22, 1976.

15. Letter of January 24, 1977.

16. Letter of February 2, 1977.

17. Letter of May 11, 1977 to Smith.

18. October 28, 1977.

19. William H. Hornby, "Beware the Market Thinkers," *The Quill,* January 1976, pp. 14–17.

20. Letter of March 1, 1977.

21. January 31, 1979.

22. He told an ASNE convention that editors should draw a distinction between good and bad researchers, I being one of the good ones.

23. Letter of November 2, 1978.

24. He fired David A. Rood, editor of the *Escanaba Daily Press* and forced the resignation of Robert Skuggen, editor of the *Marquette Mining Journal.*

25. And in 1989 when the editors of the *New York Daily News* wanted to endorse one mayoral candidate for the Democratic nomination and the publisher wanted another, they compromised on a third.

26. June 7, 1977.

27. Letter of April 18, 1977 to Smith from Eugene Patterson, the outgoing president.

28. *ASNE Bulletin*, October 7, 1977.

29. Memorandum of June 24, 1977.

30. Zarwell's memo actually arrived too late to be applicable to the first year's research plans.

31. Burke's minutes of the June 7, 1977 meeting show that a low priority went to a proposed experimental study of video information services, which arose from my concerns about the potential impact of videotex and teletext on newspapers. A proposed study of reading by blacks was deferred. O'Neill proposed the use of research methods other than surveys and stressed the need to involve "knowledgeable" research companies. (We agreed to do this in a seminar discussion on the problem of youth readership.) The editors did like an idea we advanced for a series of seminars that would bring some of them together with newspaper researchers.

32. On August 10, 1977.

33. Minutes of the August 10, 1977 meeting.

34. Held in Chicago, September 12, 1977.

35. Memorandum to me, October 11, 1977.

36. Ibid.

37. Memorandum of September 19, 1977.

38. Ibid..

39. October 5, 1977.

40. In addition, McKnight had asked, "What is the relationship between the reader and news about government and public affairs, the newspaper's historically obligatory content? Are readers turned off by this category of news per se, or just by the form of its presentation?" (I argued that "it had high priority as the first major topic of our pretesting project.")

"What is the interaction of newspaper readership and TV watching?" "What is the modern reader's reaction to the daily episodic delivery of news? Would he be more attracted to the summary of a whole situation than to the daily delivery of incremental news? Is summary and interpretation and 'content' more attractive than thin layers of 'hard' news, the latest happening? What does a reader understand by 'news'?" (I replied that "the evidence in hand suggests that people don't really draw the line between straight news and the recaps and explanation of the situation to date. The readers of the news magazines, who like their news packaged, are also the people who are most oriented to the straight reporting that newspapers provide.")

41. October 16, 1977.

42. Letter received in October 1977. Ottaway was the head of a chain of middle-sized dailies that he had sold to the Dow Jones Company.

43. Letter of October 29, 1977.
44. Letter of November 3, 1977.
45. Minutes of the Readership Committee, February 9, 1978.
46. Memorandum of November 3, 1977.
47. January 16, 1978.
48. February 1, 1978.
49. On February 9, 1978. For Year 2 of the Project, the research proposals under consideration included studies of (1) changes in the frequency of reading "in a changing world," (2) newspaper purchase decisions, (3) "sharp focus studies" on public attitudes toward special types of news coverage and features, (4) college students and the paper, (5) blacks and the press, (6) the new woman and the newspaper, (7) restricted apartment house dwellers, (8) newspaper content in the public's mind, (9) audience response to video information systems, and (10) editorial content, newspaper innovation, and circulation change.
50. Minutes of the February 9, 1978 Readership Committee meeting.
51. Robert K. Merton, Marjorie Fiske and Patricia Kendall, *The Focused Interview*, (1956; Second Edition, New York: Free Press, 1990).
52. Memorandum of March 14, 1977 to Jack Vernon, then the research director for the *St. Petersburg Times.*
53. April 24, 1978.
54. Clark's interviews had been conducted in good-sized markets. She next approached Edwin Heminger, publisher of the Findlay, Ohio *Courier* and chairman of an Inland Daily Press Association task force on "the image" of newspapers, proposing that the study be repeated in smaller markets. Heminger asked Silha for Readership Project funding, but the suggestion was tabled for lack of a budget.
55. April 20, 1981.
56. *New York Times,* May 2, 1979.
57. October 15, 1979.
58. Letter to Lee Stinnett, July 8, 1982.
59. Clark's business activities were encumbered by a personal tragedy. In 1981, her daughter Judith, a radical terrorist, was arrested (and subsequently convicted) for the murder of a Brink's armored truck guard, in the course of a robbery attempt in Rockland County, NY.
60. Memorandum of November 9, 1977.
61. We reviewed these efforts a few months later, at a Research Committee meeting (February 9, 1978).
62. Its editor, Max McCrohon, was by this time a prime mover in ASNE and on the Committee. He later became editor of the doomed *Los Angeles Herald-Examiner.*
63. Five participating newspapers made up pages in two different versions, and 75 people (readers and nonreaders) were questioned in each city.

5 · From Research to Action

1. At a conference held at Syracuse University's Newhouse School of Journalism in 1985, editors' disdain of *Journalism Quarterly* was uninhibitedly expressed. See Nancy Wearthly Sharp, editor, *Communications Research: The Challenge of the Information Age* (Syracuse: Syracuse University Press, 1988).

2. Letter to Friedheim, June 25, 1976.

3. Memorandum of April, 1977.

4. June 29, 1979.

5. Elsa Mohn, *Morning and Evening Daily Newspaper Readers* (ANPA News Research Center, 1982).

6. Erna Einsiedel, *Comparison of Subscribers and Non-Subscribers* (ANPA News Research Center, 1983).

7. Robert Clark, "What 28 Newspapers Are Doing to Gain and Retain Readers," ANPA/Future of Advertising Project, 1988.

8. Letter of March 13, 1984 to the Chairman of ANPA's Readership Committee, Robert Achorn of the Worcester newspapers.

9. On July 9, 1979.

10. These were submitted on February 23, 1979 by Tolley, and included proposed studies of (1) the influence of Sunday papers on daily readership, (2) single copy sales from the buyer's perspective, (3) newspaper sections and their influence, (4) newspaper readership in suburbs, (5) how newsroom staffs saw readers, (6) reader response to the use of color, (7) innovation by newspapers, (8) using eye-camera records to learn why readers read what they do, (9) the attraction of the metropolitan center and its papers, (10) carriers and potential carriers, (11) science, technology and media, and (12) older readers. We also proposed (13) a new editors' bulletin summarizing significant social research, and (14) a conference on reading habits and skills. We again submitted (15) our proposal for a two part study of video information systems.

On March 24, 1981. the Bureau's research department submitted seven new proposals to the Research Committee: (1) a national sample survey of newspaper readers, (2) a synthesis of NRP research findings, (3) a project to track social changes, trends, and indicators, (4) a study on the "pull" of news, (5) research on leisure time and newspaper reading, (6) a study of "why don't subscribers read?" and (7) a study of the physical attributes of dailies as compared by readers. In addition, four proposals unsuccessfully made the previous year were repeated: minorities in the press, obtaining "a complete picture" of newspaper reading, a qualitative study of teenage reading, and a study of suburban newspaper readership.

11. The former research director of the Detroit Free Press.

12. As Murdoch expanded his television interests, he was forced by

Congressional action to divest himself of the Post, which he sold in 1988 to real estate magnate Peter Kalikow.

13. Memorandum of June 1, 1977.

14. On September 24, 1980.

15. A subsidiary of H. and R. Block, the tax specialists.

16. Memorandum of March 4, 1980, on behalf of ASNE.

17. Letter of March 31, 1980.

18. Letter of December 21, 1979.

19. The idea of starting such a newsletter aimed at editors was raised early in the Project and carried forward in a letter addressed by Richmond editor John Leard to Joe D. Smith. Such a newsletter "would capture the attention of busy editors readily and could become essential reading for all of them . . . it would make some research now sublimated better known and more accessible. It would make news research more meaningful and vital to more editors who still tend to handle some of it with disdain. It would assure cooperative activities among editors and research groups."

20. This was held in Chicago on November 28 and 29, 1978.

21. These were held in St. Petersburg in May, 1980, in Seattle in November 1981, Los Angeles in December 1981, and Minneapolis in January 1982.

22. APME News, July 6, 1982.

23. Memorandum of July 13, 1982.

24. St. Petersburg, April 11, 1983.

25. In a letter of February 14, 1983 to Gannett's John Quinn, I proposed yet another workshop before the Readership Project came to an end. "It could be centered on the subject of newspapers' treatment of cultural affairs and reviews . . . the chief value of the discussion to be in the opportunity of an interchange with leaders in some of the fields who, for one reason or another, have felt that newspapers have been neglecting them." This proposal was never activated.

26. August 10, 1977.

27. This was the research mentioned on p. 137.

28. These included: "A national monitor of informational needs and changing trends. A three-year study of attitudes toward a significant change in newspapers' style or format. A four-level market-size study to test 10 basic hypotheses the editors feel will make marginal readers into more involved readership." Other studies were proposed to segment the youth market, to determine the value of attracting young readers and the tradeoff of losing established readers; to find out the major type of news and information young people say they would be willing to buy a newspaper regularly to get.

29. November 10 and 11, 1979. The participants included, besides Bogart, Nunn and Thelma Anderson for the Bureau, Janet Chusmir of the

Miami Herald, Eleanor Holtzman, director of research of the DKG advertising agency, Suzanne Keller, Professor of Sociology at Princeton University, Carolyn Kent, research director of the Louisville Courier-Journal, Eleanor McConnell, research director of the Chicago Tribune, and the following editors: McCrohon, McKnight, O'Neill, Marjorie Paxton, publisher of the Chambersburg, PA, *Public Opinion,* Rosenfeld, Jean Sharley Taylor of the *Los Angeles Times,* Thomas Winship of the *Boston Globe,* and Lois Willie of the *Chicago Sun Times.*

30. In June, 1979.

31. The participants, on March 9, 1973, were: John Mack Carter, Editor of *Good Houskeeping;* John Dessauer, Managing Agent of the Book Industry Study Group; David Goslin, Executive Director of Behavioral and Social Sciences for the National Academy of Sciences; Arnold Grisman, Executive Vice President, J. Walter Thompson Co.; Judith Hines, Manager of Educational Services, ANPA Foundation; Francis Keppel, Aspen Institute (formerly U.S. Commissioner of Education); Girvan Kirk, Children's Television Workshop; Herbert Krugman, Manager of Public Opinion Research, General Electric Co.; Carol Nemeyer, Assistant Librarian of Congress; David Pearl, Chief of Behaviorial Science Research, National Institute of Mental Health; Ralph Staiger, Executive Director, National Reading Association; Thomas Sticht, National Institute of Education; plus Robert Ellis of Time, Inc. and myself. I chaired the meeting.

32. Summarized in a June 9, 1978 letter to McKnight and William Schabacker of ANPA.

33. Memorandum of December 31, 1974 to Arthur O. Sulzberger of *The New York Times,* then chairman of the Bureau.

34. August 11, 1986.

35. The black participants were Lionel C. Barrow, Jr., Dean of the Howard University School of Journalism, and a former Bureau researcher, Albert Fitzpatrick, Assistant Editor of the Springfield, Ohio *Sun* and *Daily News,* Jay Harris, Managing Editor of the *Philadelphia Daily News,* Nancy Hicks, Director of the Institute for Journalism Education, Robert Hill, a sociologist who was shortly to be named research director of the National Urban League, Pam Johnson, Publisher of the *Ithaca Journal,* Robert C. Maynard, Editor and Publisher of the Oakland Tribune, Dr. Chester Pierce, a Harvard Medical School psychiatrist and Charles Pittman, Promotion Director of the *Erie Morning News* and *Daily Times.* The white participants included Edward Bennett, Circulation Director of the *Baltimore Sun,* and Robert Clark, Editor of the Jacksonville newspapers.

36. ASNE *Bulletin,* March, 1982.

37. December 7, 1981. Bennett commented that "home delivery systems in areas of low newspaper penetration are difficult to maintain and frequently must be subsidized." He said "a book" could be written on the subject of collections among people at low economic levels.

38. Letter to Jay Harris, March 29, 1982.

39. Memorandum of June 18, 1980.

40. I proposed that "one or two observer-investigators should stay with each organization for a long enough period of time to be able to do the necessary field work unobstrusively and with the cooperation of all concerned. This approach almost dictates that ideas and hypotheses must be generated while the field work is in progress and then explored and tested as the study is extended to other locations. (This contrasts with the alternative procedure of going into the various locations simultaneously.)"

41. December 24, 1980.

42. March 4, 1982.

43. March 18, 1982.

44. My own comment on the Burgoon-Atkin report was that "this analysis would have been much more valuable if the study had been taken as a series of eight case histories and emphasis had been placed on the differences among the individual papers and how these were reflected in the attitudes of editors and staffs." (Letter of April 16, 1982).

45. Held at Crystal City, near the Washington, D.C. National Airport, October 25 and 26, 1982.

46. October 29, 1982.

47. Letter of December 7, 1982 to John Quinn, then president of ASNE.

6 · Circulation

1. June 1, 1977.

2. Letter of January 11, 1980.

3. Memorandum of July 2, 1979.

4. Letter of December 11, 1979. Of Novaseda's later presentation, "Three by Three," which taught the rudiments of salesmanship for ten-year-olds, Jardine wrote in a letter of December 12, 1980, "It is the best carrier training film that has ever been produced." He presented Novaseda with a plaque of appreciation at the organization's Las Vegas convention.

5. The textbook vacuum was finally filled, but only after a long and tedious odyssey. In 1978, at the urging of Harold Schwartz, the scholarly circulation director of the *Milwaukee Journal*, ICMA commissioned a text on circulation from Joseph Forsee of the University of Missouri Journalism School. (Forsee was the former circulation director of the *St. Louis Post-Dispatch*, and he later moved to ICMA as executive director.) The ICMA Executive Committee turned the assignment over to William Thorn and Mary Pat Pfeil, whose text, *Newspaper Circulation: Marketing the News* (New York: Longman), appeared in 1988.

6. Letter of November 20, 1978, to Albert Dilthey. I described the program as follows: "Each student is handled on an individualized basis, following a curriculum worked out personally by phone or by mail under

the guidance of a mentor who helps define his objectives and steers him in the direction of the proper readings and instruction. There is a set of core course requirements." The Readership Project provided publicity, public support, and a supply of reports and presentations for student use. The circulation marketing and management program was launched on May 18, 1983 and had its first graduate in 1984. But he was a small drop in a very large bucket.

7. Memorandum of September 9, 1977.

8. Prerequisites: introductory business economics, sociology and/or psychology, an introductory course in journalism or in mass media or mass communications.

Required Courses: (1) Introduction to Marketing, (2) Newspaper Circulation Management, (3) Principles of Accounting, (4) Personnel Administration and Management, (5) Organization Theory.

Elective courses might be drawn from this assortment: (1) Introduction to Computer Systems and Technology, (2) Urban Geography and Sociology, (3) Mass Media Organization and Management, (4) Introduction to Marketing Research, (5) Sales Analysis, (6) Principles of Distribution, (7) Industrial Relations, (8) Sales Promotion and Advertising, (9) Statistics, (10) Operations and Systems Research, (11) Business Communications, (12) Production Management. . . .

A course in newspaper circulation management could be organized in a number of ways: A sponsoring newspaper could supply, at its expense, a staff executive from its circulation department. The course could be planned and taught jointly by a circulation executive and a journalism professor with an interest or specialization in newspaper management. Or it could be given by the latter individual after appropriate briefing and study. . . .

9. September 29, 1977.

10. Letter of June 13, 1977.

11. Letter from Otto Silha, May 7, 1979.

12. I pointed out that "ninety-four percent of all households in the U.S. now have telephones, and four-fifths have checking accounts. This means that it is possible for us to communicate directly and outside of normal newspaper delivery hours, with virtually everyone who is a potential newspaper subscriber and also to complete the financial transaction with that individual directly and conveniently. By the end of this century, we may well be in the era of checkless banking. If utility bills are to be automatically debited from most customers' accounts, why not newspaper subscriptions, too?"

13. Here I referred to the editors' survey, which showed "that they believe that superior newspapers are financially successful. They also

believe that professionally, excellent papers originate a high share of their own copy, which is to say that their newsroom budgets are high. As we think about the problem of building readership, we have to acknowledge that it will require an investment to strengthen the quality and value of what we give our readers."

14. Its first meeting was held at the Disneyland Hotel in Anaheim, California.on June 13, 1977, timed to coincide with the annual conference of the ANPA Research Institute.

15. Letter of October 6, 1978.

16. For example, *The New York Times* had used a portable vending rack in supermarkets. In Denver, a number of different competing newspapers were sold from stack racks, placed on pedestals.

17. September 1, 1977.

18. An off-the-shelf Radio Shack unit was eventually found to serve this purpose.

19. In July 1978.

20. On April 11, 1978.

21. Memorandum of December 2, 1980.

22. Another unpublished booklet was drafted by Jaffe in March 1979. It described "hardware and software considerations to develop a computerized circulation system." The Committee felt this to be too technical.

23. The idea was first broached in October 1978.

24. On October 2 and 3, 1979. The program covered such subjects as newspaper circulation systems, circulation marketing strategy, the development of subscriber/nonsubscriber lists, circulation marketing management, and the broad questions of distribution and subscriber service, circulation accounting and control. A number of the Committee's members were featured speakers. The case histories presented ranged from the use of microcomputers by the Roswell, New Mexico *Daily Record* (circulation 13,000) to the highly sophisticated operations in Atlanta, which used two mainframe systems with more than 300 terminals.

25. When the Readership Council held its final meeting, Todd identified the three remaining top priority needs in the areas of circulation and distribution: (1) to provide assistance to newspapers wishing to build a subscriber/nonsubscriber file system, (2) developing a satisfactory on-line inserting machine, and (3) a single-copy vending machine.

26. On October 8–10, 1980. This program included separate workshops for beginners and advanced newspapers on a variety of subjects: circulation systems, draw control [over copies shipped into the field] and billings, advance payment systems, the selection of hardware and software, mailroom and distribution procedures, manifests, truck routing, and bundle labels.

7 · Promoting the Medium

1. Memorandum of June 6, 1977.
2. Letter of April 15, 1980.
3. Letter of August 20, 1979, to Smith and Silha.
4. March 5, 1982.
5. Letter of March 17, 1982.
6. Letter of March 25, 1982.
7. Minutes of Promotion Committee meeting, December 16, 1977.
8. Quoted in a letter of January 28, 1980, from James Pauloski.
9. He had left the Bureau under Silha's auspices to start a promotion firm, later moved from CBS to NBC to a brief tenure as president of Columbia Pictures, before becoming an independent TV film producer and novelist. In short, a typical career for a Bureau alumnus.
10. One hundred forty-seven papers ordered the ads and the commercials; one hundred seventy seven the ads only, and eight the commercials only.
11. February 12, 1979.
12. February 29, 1980.
13. Letter to John Taylor, February 12, 1979.
14. Letter of February 28, 1979.
15. Letter of August 15, 1980.
16. This was not really so.
17. Letter to the educational services consultant of *Newsday*, Patricia Houk, from Jocyln W. Krug.
18. "Proposal for Evaluating Critical Elements in the Effectiveness of NIE Programs," 1977.
19. October 1977.
20. Memorandum of October 26, 1977.
21. January 26, 1979.
22. This was found by an ANPA Foundation survey that was turned over to the Bureau's Thelma Anderson for analysis.
23. Associated with Teachers College at Columbia University.
24. March 29, 1977.
25. Letter of April 19, 1977.
26. Memorandum of April 20, 1977.
27. "First Edition" was shown to members of INPA at four regional meetings in the fall of 1977, preceded by a five-minute videotaped introduction linking the film's purpose to the aims of the Readership Project. According to John Mauro's report to the Readership Council, reactions were "overwhelmingly positive . . . the film received an ovation with each showing."
28. Burke's minutes of December 16, 1977.
29. November 8, 1978.

30. Silha's work as a go-between in Gannett's later purchase of the Des Moines papers was described sardonically in Neuharth's memoirs, *Confessions of an S.O.B.* (New York: Doubleday, 1989), p. 201.

31. However, after reading *The New York Times*'s report on the film, Ann Pasanella of the Columbia University Center for the Social Sciences suggested that we might have been subliminally influenced by [the sociologist] Paul Lazarsfeld, who "so many times wanted to write something about or teaching a unit on reading the newspaper."

32. March 29, 1979.

33. Letter of February 15, 1979.

34. February 8, 1979.

35. Letter of February 16, 1979.

36. January 30, 1979.

37. Crown, through the cooperation of John Tyler, the company's advertising director, allowed us to make prints generally available, and it was sold to eighty newspapers with a total circulation of 14,000,000.

38. Dorne succeeded Simons as creative director in 1988.

39. Letter of January 18, 1982.

8 · Calling to Action While Closing Down

1. *Editor & Publisher,* January 6, 1979.

2. Cowles made his report as part of our presentation to the ANPA/RI conference in Las Vegas in August 1979.

3. This is the Burgoon/Atkins study described in chapter 6.

4. Earlier, at the fall 1980 APME convention, Robert Cochnar and Joseph Harper reported on a mail survey of fifty editors. Virtually all of them said they were familiar with the *Editors' Exchange,* with the ANPA News Research Report, and with the Readership Report. But only 20 percent had seen the report on the "Brave New World of Information Technology." Thirty-five percent had seen "Children, Moviegoing, and the Newspaper," 60 percent had seen "Women in Newspapers in the 1970s," and 50 percent had seen "The Newspaper in the Education of Children." Seventy percent said that the *Editors' Exchange* was put to practical use, and 80% said that they had applied some of the findings of the Clark report. Thirty-six percent said that the ANPA News Research Report was of practical use in the newsroom.

5. He became chairman of ANPA in 1989.

6. At its meeting of October 18.

7. Memorandum of October 27, 1978.

8. The dues equalization plan was a three-year program that eliminated disparities created by past changes in the Bureau's dues formula. For many members it resulted in hefty increases in their payments.

9. January 19, 1979.

10. Letter of February 16, 1979, to Smith.

11. Letter of March 6, 1979.

12. I also commented on another point, that perhaps overstepped permissible bounds, because it dealt with ANPA's own operations:

"I am puzzled by your proposal of a merger between ANPA's News Research and Circulation Committees. The former has always been oriented toward the kind of scholarly research that journalism professors find attractive and manageable at their customary scale and pace. Circulation people are totally empirical and activist. I just don't see how the two orientations can be merged in a single committee. Is it realistic to expect that the Bureau should continue to do readership research and develop promotion campaigns and fund these projects within its regular budget? Our budget is extremely tight. There is simply no way that these additional projects could be accommodated except at the sacrifice of our central task: promoting newspaper advertising. If you'll recall, it was precisely the difficulty of doing this from a corner of the desk that led us to the Readership Project in the first place. While I greatly appreciate your willingness on behalf of ANPA to assume additional financial burdens connected with the Project after June 1, 1980, I think the Steering Committee still faces some tough questions."

13. April 21, 1979.

14. Memorandum of July 12, 1979.

15. Memorandum of August 6, 1979.

16. Marbut became chairman of the Bureau in 1988.

17. Letter of October 15, 1979.

18. Defined by Marbut with his usual speed in a letter to me on June 28, 1979, two days after the last meeting of the group.

19. These were chaired by Marbut, Dolph Simons of the Lawrence, Kansas, *Journal-World*, Daniel Burke of Capital Cities, and William Ott of Knight-Ridder.

20. Memorandum of November 5, 1979.

21. Meeting in Zurich, September 25–26. 1979.

22. November 5, 1979.

23. November 8, 1979.

24. November 1, 1979.

25. January 13, 1980.

26. 1982–84.

27. October 6, 1979.

28. Standen resigned in 1990 to become Marketing and Advertising Vice President of Scripps-Howard Newspapers.

29. Minutes of the Steering Committee, April 14, 1981.

30. Hughes, a former foreign correspondent, later became director of the Voice of America in the first Reagan administration.

31. Memorandum of May 13, 1981 (prepared for the Readership Council meeting on May 15.).

32. These were the Newspaper Readership Council, the Newspaper in

Education program, The *Editors' Exchange*, the circulation district managers' workshops, the Bureau's analyses of media and marketing trends, the ANPA News Research Center, ICMA's circulation training presentations, and promotional ad campaigns to be developed with volunteer help from INPA.

33. May 28, 1981 letter to Neuharth.

34. Letter of June 4, 1981.

35. June 9, 1981.

36. June 16, 1981.

37. He asked for "continuation of the Readership Council as a cooperative, industry-wide advisory body," the News Research Center reports and other communications to be handled by ANPA, NIE programs, the *Editors' Exchange*, circulation training materials to be produced by ICMA, promotional ad campaigns from ICMA, and circulation training and media trend analyses to be done by the Bureau.

38. Letter of June 16, 1980 to Cowles.

39. June 22, 1981.

40. June 9, 1981.

41. June 16, 1981.

42. June 24, 1981.

43. June 24, 1981.

44. June 3, 1981.

45. May 5, 1982.

46. September 8, 1981.

47. April 6, 1982.

48. Address to the Newspaper in Education conference, March 28, 1980.

49. Harold W. Andersen, publisher of the Omaha *World-Herald*, was chairman of the Steering Committee.

50. The task forces covered readership and circulation, standardization, reproduction quality, promotion and public relations, marketing data, ad pricing, national ad sales organization, sales personnel, alternate distribution, and classified advertising.

51. This committee sponsored a number of noteworthy projects, including another national survey of reading habits, several examinations of pricing practices and economics, and a valuable manual, "Readers: How to Gain and Retain Them," of which the principal author was Burl Osborne of the *Dallas Morning News*. The Bureau stretched its budget to cover all the costs of the Future of Advertising task forces. To coordinate with this project, the ASNE established a Future of Newspapers committee.

Index